Children and Childhood in Western Society Since 1500

STUDIES IN MODERN HISTORY

General editors: John Morrill and David Cannadine

This series, intended primarily for students, will tackle significant historical issues in concise volumes which are both stimulating and scholarly. The authors combine a broad approach, explaining the current state of our knowledge in the area, with their own research and judgements. The topics chosen range widely in subject, period and place.

Children and Childhood in Western Society Since 1500

SECOND EDITION

Hugh Cunningham

Harlow, England • London • New York • Boston • San Francisco • Toronto
Sydney • Tokyo • Singapore • Hong Kong • Seoul • Taipei • New Delhi
Cape Town • Madrid • Mexico City • Amsterdam • Munich • Paris • Milan

PEARSON EDUCATION LIMITED

Edinburgh Gate
Harlow CM20 2JE
United Kingdom
Tel: +44 (0)1279 623623
Fax: +44 (0)1279 431059
Website: www.pearsoned.co.uk

Second edition published in Great Britain in 2005

© Pearson Education Limited 1995, 2005

The right of Hugh Cunningham to be identified as author of this work has been
asserted by him in accordance with the Copyright, Designs and Patents Act 1988.

ISBN 0 582 78453 0

British Library Cataloguing in Publication Data
A CIP catalogue record for this book can be obtained from the British Library

Library of Congress Cataloging in Publication Data
Cunningham, Hugh.
    Children and childhood in western society since 1500 / Hugh Cunningham. — 2nd ed.
        p. cm. — (Studies in modern history)
    Includes bibliographical references and index.
    ISBN 0–582–78453–0
    1. Children—History.   2. Parent and child—History.   I. Title.   II. Studies in modern
history (Longman (Firm))
    HQ767.87.C86 2005
    305.23′09182′1—dc22

                                                                    2004051487

10   9   8   7   6   5   4   3   2   1
09   08   07   06   05

Set by 35 in 10/13.5pt Sabon
Printed in Malaysia

The Publishers' policy is to use paper manufactured from sustainable forests.

Contents

Plates

[*In central plate section*]

1 *Child Holding An Apple* by Caesar van Everingden
2 *The Age of Innocence* by Joshua Reynolds
3 *The Child Enthroned*, c.1894, by Thomas Cooper Gotch
4 Illustration from 'The Royal Commission on the Condition and Treatment of Children Employed in the Mines of the United Kingdom' (1842)
5 Interdepartmental Committee on Physical Deterioration, British Parliamentary Papers, 1904, Vol. XXXII
6 From *The Twentieth-Century Child* by Edward H. Cooper, 1905 (frontispiece)

Acknowledgements

We are grateful to the following for permission to reproduce copyright material:

Plate 1 courtesy of Canon Hall Museum (Barnsley Metropolitan Borough Council); Plate 2 courtesy of Plymouth City Museum and Art Gallery; Plate 3 courtesy of The Bridgeman Art Library/www.bridgeman.co.uk; Plate 4 courtesy of Mary Evans Picture Library; Plates 5 and 6 courtesy of The British Library.

In some instances we have been unable to trace the owners of copyright material, and we would appreciate any information that would enable us to do so.

Preface

In the ten years since this book was first published anxieties about childhood in the western world have risen from what was an already high level. The worries range widely, encompassing children in poverty, the abuse of children at home and in institutions, the impact of new media, and the dangers which confront children when outside the (no longer safe) territory of home and school. Governments have responded to these worries: in England, for example, there is for the first time, a Minister for Children. More broadly, reflecting the thrust of the 1989 United Nations Convention on the Rights of the Child, there is a growing realisation that what children have to say may be as, if not more, important than what adults say.

The agenda of historians has in many ways reflected these worries and innovations: the aim has been to give historical context to contemporary concerns and developments. Have children always loomed large among the poverty statistics? Is the sexual abuse of children something new, or has it always existed? How did the adult public respond to earlier media innovations and their impact on children? How has the idea of children's rights developed over time? In preparing this second edition I have tried to take account of this new writing. Much of it is concerned with children and their families at the interface between their own privacy and the public realms of the state or voluntary institutions. The focus is on children who were abandoned, or fostered, or had brushes with the forces of law and order. The initiatives of authorities of one kind or another are one theme, but so also is the attempt to recapture what it was like to be a child in a specific situation at a specific time. This emphasis on the experience of being a child has been taken further with attempts, using autobiographical and other evidence, to identify when and how childhood began to be seen as a formative influence in the construction of a self-identity, rather than a period of life marked in many ways by its deficiencies.

These new emphases in the study of children and childhood in western society raise an issue only touched on in the text: what are the bounds of 'western society', and how far are the ideas and practices of the west unique to that society? It is certainly possible to identify other societies with ideas about childhood which seem very similar to those in the west. The uniqueness of the west lay in the fact that the time when key ideas about childhood were developing in the eighteenth century coincided with the growing influence of the west over other parts of the globe. If the world is in some degree (but by no means wholly) a legatee of western ideas of childhood, it is because the west exported childhood, and sometimes children, as part and parcel of an age of imperialism.

CHAPTER 1

Introduction

Shouldn't childhood be defined by the child?

In June 1992 an eleven-year-old, caught up in the siege of Sarajevo, wrote in her diary,

BOREDOM!!! SHOOTING!!! SHELLING!!! PEOPLE BEING KILLED!!! DESPAIR!!! HUNGER!!! MISERY!!! FEAR!!! That's my life! The life of an innocent eleven-year-old schoolgirl!! A schoolgirl without a school, without the fun and excitement of school. A child without games, without friends, without the sun, without birds, without nature, without fruit, without chocolate or sweets, with just a little powdered milk. In short a child without a childhood.

Zlata had a clear sense of the ingredients of a childhood: innocence, school, fun, games, friends, nature, sweets. Deprived of them, she and her friends 'can't be children'.[1] For Zlata a child was not simply someone aged between, say, birth and fourteen; a child could be a real child only if he or she had a 'childhood'.

My aim in this book is in part to trace the development of this late-twentieth-century belief that children are real children only if their life experiences accord with a particular set of ideas about childhood. Will we find Zlatas in 1800 or in 1500, distraught that what they have been taught to expect of childhood is so at odds with the reality? Has 'childhood' in the past conveyed a set of ideas different to those which Zlata articulated?

I want also to explore the lives of children. Both 'children' and 'childhood' appear in my title because we need to distinguish between children as human beings and childhood as a shifting set of ideas. Have there been, in the five hundred years since 1500, significant changes in the experience of childhood, and, if so, when did they occur? To put the question thus bluntly is to invite the riposte: it depends on country, on social class, on gender. That, certainly, is true; it will nevertheless be my argument that there were patterns of change in the experience of childhood in Europe and North America which were broadly similar, and which eventually encompassed all social classes and both genders.

It is in many ways much easier to write a history of childhood than of children. There is an accessible body of literature and of images, such as advice books, fiction and portraiture, which make it possible to piece together the ideas about childhood prevalent amongst particular social groups at particular points in time. It is possible to go further to look at the role played by childhood as an idea in a society's explanation of the world as a whole. It has, for instance, been common to imagine the history of humankind as equivalent to the life cycle of a human being; some societies have seen this as an ascent from savagery/childhood to civilisation/adulthood, others as a descent from primeval innocence/childhood to corruption/adulthood. A view of the world incorporates a view of the nature of childhood.[2]

Ideas about childhood in the past exist in plenitude; it is not so easy to find out about the lives of children. There are sources which can tell us about their numbers in relation to adults, their life expectancy, the ages at which they were likely to start work and leave home, and so on, but those seeking to recapture the emotional quality of the lives of children in the past encounter formidable hurdles. The letters and diaries of parents seem to be one way of surmounting the hurdles, but they tend to be written only by the articulate and well-to-do, and in them our view of the child is mediated through the perceptions of the adult. Children themselves have sometimes left behind written materials, but too often what they write in their diaries tells us more about the genre of diary writing and the desires and expectations of adult readers than about the experience of being a child.[3]

The issue which has underlain much recent historical writing about children has actually been more to do with parents than with children. Did parents in the past, it is asked, love their children? Whether or not children loved their parents is apparently not an issue. The question as posed is impossible to answer, partly because we simply do not know, and can never know, very much about the intimacies of relationships between parents and children, and partly because it assumes that we would recognise love if we saw it, and record its absence if it was not there, as though it were a material object like a table; in fact, of course, it may have expressed itself in very different ways in different societies.[4]

There is, then, a problem for the historian of childhood and children in that it is easier to write with some confidence about childhood than about children. The challenge is to tease out the relationship between ideas about childhood and the experience of being a child, and to see how it has changed over time. How can the relationship between the two be explored? The answer is that ideas about childhood can be shown to have had some impact in two distinct ways. First, manuals for parents provide us with ideals of child-rearing in the past, and although we know that they were hardly ever followed to the letter by those who read them, and that frequently the advice was totally ignored, we also know that sometimes they were taken seriously; changes in emphasis in the advice books may be both a symptom and a reflection of changes in practice.[5] Secondly, ideas about childhood fed through into the discourses and actions of philanthropists and governments; a major theme of the book will be that public action shaped the lives of innumerable children in the centuries with which we are concerned.

It would be a mistake to fall into a way of thinking which assumes that if we beaver away at the relationship between children and childhood we may come up with some satisfactory history. Childhood cannot be studied in isolation from society as a whole. It is arguable that the factors which have had most impact on it, both as a set of ideas and as a phase of life, have been primarily economic and demographic, and, in second place, political. It has been the economic development of the western world which has allowed for both the shift in the experience of childhood from work to school, and for the emergence of the idea that childhood should be a time of dependency. And concern for the present safety and future needs of the state has often provided the impulse for public action concerning children. If, as we shall see, one of the theories about the history of children and childhood is that they have become increasingly separate from adults and adulthood, that is in fact all the more reason why we need to embed their history in wider economic, social and political developments.

The historiography of childhood

Until the explosion of publications over the past forty years, someone in search of information about children and childhood in the past would have been dependent either on books which were essentially antiquarian in approach, for example R. Bayne-Powell's *The English Child in the Eighteenth Century* (1939), or on histories of social policy, many of them seeking to make a point about the present by study of the past. Some of the latter endure as scholarship, for example L. Lallemand's *Histoire des Enfants Abandonnés et Délaissés: Etude sur la Protection de l'Enfance aux*

Diverses Epoques de la Civilisation (1885), which sought to defend the part played by the Catholic Church in its policies toward abandoned children, or O.J. Dunlop and R.D. Denman's *English Apprenticeship and Child Labour* (1912), which, like many such studies in the early twentieth century in England, was inspired by the pioneering work of Beatrice and Sidney Webb on the history of the Poor Laws. Such books helped to build up a picture of the relationship between children and public authorities over time, and of the economic role of children. In 1926 R.H. Tawney highlighted the potential significance of such studies when he wrote that 'the treatment of childhood' in any society revealed more clearly than anything else 'the true character of a social philosophy'.[6]

In the past forty years historians have shown a burgeoning interest in children and childhood, but have rarely been in agreement with one another. There has been a reversal of opinion on some of the central issues. At the end of the 1970s most people agreed that the history of childhood was a history of progress, that the experience of being a child, and an understanding of the nature of childhood, had improved over time. A decade later the accepted orthodoxy was that, while obviously material circumstances had changed, the vast majority of children in the past had been brought up within nuclear families in which parents had loved their children; continuity replaced change as the *leitmotif* of the history of childhood.

Philippe Ariès's *L'Enfant et la vie familiale sous l'Ancien Régime* (1960), published in English as *Centuries of Childhood* (1962), launched the debates on the history of children and childhood which have lasted to the present day. His central theme had, however, been anticipated by Norbert Elias. In his volumes on *The Civilizing Process*, first published in Switzerland in 1939, and reaching an English readership only in the 1970s, Elias argued that 'The distance in behavior and whole psychological structure between children and adults increases in the course of the civilizing process.' This was the precise point underlying Ariès's book. For Elias 'the civilizing process' involved a control of the instincts, something which was hardly under way in the middle ages when, consequently, 'The distance between adults and children, measured by that of today, was slight.'[7] In the early modern period a plethora of advice books told adults how to behave, marking off the distance between adult and child. A French guide in 1714 urged readers to 'Take good care not to blow your nose with your fingers or on your sleeve *like children*; use your handkerchief and do not look into it afterward.' Of course children too were urged to control their instincts, another French advice book of 1774 noting how 'Children like to touch clothes and other things that please them with their hands. This urge must be corrected, and they must be taught to touch all they see only with their eyes.'[8] The assumption by the end of the eighteenth century was coming to be that adults, in the social classes who might be assumed to read the advice books, would already have acquired good manners, but that children needed to be taught them; the distance between the two was increasing. The recognition in the twentieth century that children should be allowed to develop the manners of the adult world at their own pace did nothing to decrease that distance.[9] For Elias the marking out of the world of childhood from adulthood was inseparable from 'the civilizing process'.

Ariès's book is an extended gloss on Elias's perception. He was not a professional historian, and the evidence on which he drew and the mode in which he presented it bore the marks both of the antiquarian tradition, and of the interest in the present embedded in the histories of social policy. What distinguished the book from the work of other antiquarians was its chronological range – for Ariès covered the period from the middle ages to the present – and Ariès's willingness to point to changes over that time-span in accordance with the arguments made by Elias. He set out hypotheses about the history of childhood, and these have become the benchmark for all subsequent students.

Ariès did not disguise the fact that he was seeking to understand the particularity of the present by comparing and contrasting it with the past. What struck him about the present was the way in which social life and the emotions were centred in the family. From the eighteenth century, first within the middle classes, 'the wall of private life' was raised 'between the family and society'. The old sociability of the community was lost. Children were at the centre of these families, in a privatised world where adults were 'obsessed by the physical, moral and sexual problems of childhood'.[10] Ariès's starting point, then, was his distaste for what he saw as the oppressive and intolerant nature of modern family life.[11] In seeking to understand how this had come about, he chose to focus on childhood for it was changes in ideas about childhood which, in his view, had been central to the making of the modern family. Crucial in this was the development of the idea that children should have an education, which Ariès saw as part of a 'moralization of society' promulgated by reformers in the sixteenth and seventeenth centuries; children came to be subjected to 'a sort of quarantine' before they were allowed to join adult society. Parents were taught that they had a duty to ensure that their children were sent to school.[12] In what, as we shall see in the next chapter, may have been a rather romantic view of the middle ages, Ariès pictured medieval children as merging naturally into adult society from about the age of seven, retaining only relatively loose ties with their families. By contrast, education, and the responsibilities of parents with regard to it, placed children at the heart of a family which was increasingly in isolation from the rest of society.

Given the importance which Ariès ascribed to education in defining modern concepts of childhood it is not surprising that he devoted roughly half of his book to a study of changes in 'Scholastic Life'. The key change was the development of the idea that schooling was for children only rather than for people of all ages; childhood and adulthood were being separated out. Once schooling became something confined to children, it became possible to impose on it an order and discipline, including corporal punishment, this discipline separating 'the child who suffered from it from the liberty enjoyed by the adult'.[13] Moreover, as schooling spread and was extended, childhood itself lasted longer. Ariès recognised that these changes were of long duration, and took effect on different timescales according to gender, class and nation, but he was in no doubt that the influence of moralists in spreading the idea and practice of schooling was fundamental to the emergence of modern ideas of childhood.

It has been necessary to stress this point because most commentary on Ariès's book concentrates on the essays which make up Part I of the book, entitled 'The Idea of Childhood'. These were exploratory and tentative in their conclusions. Ariès investigated in turn changes in concepts of age, the portrayal of childhood in pictures, children's dress, the history of games and pastimes, and the development of the idea that children were naturally innocent and should be protected from anything which might disturb their modesty. His overall conclusion was that by the seventeenth century there had developed in France two concepts of childhood. The first was to be found within families; parents began 'to recognize the pleasure they got from watching children's antics and "coddling" them'.[14] The second had its origins outside the family in moralists who stressed how children were fragile creatures of God who needed to be safeguarded and reformed. It was these moralists who were increasingly to argue that school must work with the family in carrying out this task.

Ariès stressed that 'it is not so much the family as a reality that is our subject . . . as the family as an idea'.[15] He was more interested in the history of childhood than in the history of children. He set out a trajectory of the development of ideas about childhood, mainly in France, but with references to other European countries. Parts of his argument, as we shall see in the next chapter, are widely criticised, but few would doubt that the task he set himself, without any body of established scholarship as a base, was a legitimate one: ideas or concepts of childhood have not remained constant, and do have a history. In pursuing this theme Ariès inevitably drew evidence from the reality of childhood, from the experience of schooling for example, and he certainly implied that changes in ideas about childhood had radically affected the experience of childhood. His immediate successors in the historiography of childhood tended to reverse the emphasis, stressing the experience of being a child rather than the development of ideas about childhood.

Ariès's book did not immediately achieve fame or even recognition. Few historical journals reviewed it. Within the social sciences, however, it became accepted as important and authoritative, a status it retains to this day.[16] Moreover, when social history began to enjoy a boom in the late 1960s and early 1970s, *Centuries of Childhood* was the only available text on its topic. This was soon to change. A trio of books are now often grouped together as marking a peculiarly 1970s' approach to the history of children and childhood: Lloyd de Mause (ed.), *The History of Childhood* (1974); Edward Shorter, *The Making of the Modern Family* (1976); and Lawrence Stone, *The Family, Sex and Marriage in England 1500–1800* (1977). These three are also often linked to *Centuries of Childhood*. At the time, however, it was the disagreements amongst these authors which were most striking, rather than the common ground which they were subsequently alleged to share.

De Mause's book is subtitled *The evolution of parent–child relationships as a factor in history*, and this accurately indicates the theme of the editor's seventy-page essay. The other contributions, it has often been noted, do not always fit easily into the schema outlined by de Mause, and are best seen as self-standing case studies in the history of children and childhood. The evolution of the relationship between parent and child was, however, central to what de Mause called the 'psychogenic' interpretation of history. This interpretation had ramifications far outside the history of childhood, for the quality of parent–child relations was seen as the motor force of history; as de Mause put it, 'the central force for change in history is neither technology nor economics, but the "psychogenic" changes in personality occurring because of successive generations of parent–child interactions'. De Mause outlined three ways in which adults can respond to children. In the projective reaction, adults use children as a vehicle for the projection of their own unconscious, that is the children become the repository of all the adults' unacknowledged bad feelings and fears about themselves. It is this projective reaction, de Mause argues, which is behind the idea of original sin. In the reversal reaction, adults use children as a substitute for an adult figure important in their own childhood, that is the parent becomes a child, and the child becomes a parent. Thus parents look for love from their children. Finally, in the empathic reaction adults empathise with children's needs, and attempt to satisfy them. It is quite possible for a parent to combine both projective and reversal reactions, this dual image of the child as both bad and loving being indeed 'responsible for much of the bizarre quality of childhood in the past'. The key to success in parenting for de Mause is to have the ability to regress to the psychic age of your child, and he believed that each generation of parents was likely to be better than its predecessors in this respect, though the mechanism which drives this evolution is not at all clear. But it followed that one could, in a rough and ready way, periodise parent–child relations, moving through six modes, the infanticidal, the abandonment, the ambivalent, the intrusive, the socialisation, and finally, from the mid-twentieth century, the helping mode. In short, things have got steadily better. Or as de Mause put it at the beginning of his chapter, 'The history of childhood is a nightmare from which we have only recently begun to awaken. The further back in history one goes, the lower the level of child care, and the more likely children are to be killed, abandoned, beaten, terrorized, and sexually abused.'[17]

The psychogenic theory of history has never won much of a hearing amongst historians, to a degree doubtless because of an instinctive hostility on the part of historians to concepts with which most of them are unfamiliar, but also because of the inherent implausibility of a theory which attempted to schematise and explain the course of human history by exploring parent–child interactions; its reach was too ambitious.[18] In any case de Mause acknowledged that his hypotheses were 'subject to proof or disproof by empirical historical evidence', and it is on that ground that historians have chosen to assess his work – and generally found it wanting.[19]

Where de Mause concentrated on the parent–child interaction, Edward Shorter returned to the central concern of Ariès, the rise of the modern family. Unlike Ariès, he did not see a new role for children as central to the making of the modern family, putting much more emphasis on the sexual behaviour of young people and adults. Indeed children, as distinct from babies, hardly feature in Shorter's book. It was Shorter's ambition to move away from reliance on evidence from the elites of society, and to 'find out about the representative experience of the average person'. Moreover, he argued that the shift from what he called the 'traditional' to the 'modern' family was associated with 'a surge of sentiment' in three areas, one of them of direct concern to us, the mother–baby relationship. In essence,

Shorter agreed with Ariès that the contemporary family was a recent phenomenon both in its internal relationships and in its privacy, but he took issue with the implicit chronology in which, for Ariès, the seventeenth and eighteenth centuries marked the turning point. For Shorter, with his emphasis on the mass of the people, the transition was later. In a form of words as much quoted and as notorious as that of de Mause on the history of childhood as a nightmare, Shorter claimed that 'Good mothering in an invention of modernization. In traditional society, mothers viewed the development and happiness of infants younger than two with indifference. In modern society, they place the welfare of their small children above all else.' For Shorter this transition did not begin to take place for the mass of the people until the last quarter of the eighteenth century, and in some regions and classes later than that. Using mainly French evidence, and acknowledging that French experience may have differed from that of other Europeans, Shorter found signs of a surge of sentiment amongst the middle classes in the mid-eighteenth century, marked by maternal breast-feeding and an end to the system of sending children off to a wet-nurse. Other indications were the abandonment of swaddling, allowing a freer interaction between mother and baby. But the revolution in sentiment for the mass of the people was not complete until the beginning of the twentieth century, taking root from about the 1860s.[20]

Shorter was inclined to explain his surges of sentiment by arguing that capitalism fragmented and broke up traditional society, and in matters of romantic love and sexual behaviour he accorded a leading and initiating role to proletarians. He recognised, however, that this pattern did not fit the mother–child relationship, and concluded that capitalism's input in this respect was to allow the possibility of time for well-off middle-class mothers to begin to look after their babies in a 'modern' way. Gradually, as capitalism brought improved family incomes for more and more sections of society, 'women could exchange the grim pressures of production for the work of infant care'.[21] In effect, there was a trickle-down of good mothering from the well-off to the less well-off, an explanation of change sharply at odds with Shorter's overall assessment of the impact of capitalism, and one which makes his account of mothers and infants conventional in its general outline.

Whereas Shorter focused his attention on the late eighteenth and nineteenth centuries, Lawrence Stone, like Ariès, searched for the key changes in the history of the family in the period 1500–1800. The difference is in large part explained by Stone's concentration on the middle and upper sections of society. Stone identified three types of family, the 'open lineage family' in the period 1450–1630, the 'restricted patriarchal nuclear family' in the period 1550–1700, and finally the 'closed domesticated nuclear family' in the period 1640–1800. Stone argued that one of the central features of the modern family, an 'intensified affective bonding of the nuclear core at the expense of neighbours and kin', was well established in 'the key middle and upper sectors of English society' by the middle of the eighteenth century. But he did not think that this and other features of the modern family spread up to the higher court aristocracy or downwards into the respectable working class until late in the nineteenth century.

For Stone, changes in parent–child relationships were a more important indicator of overall changes in the nature of the family than they were for Shorter, but neither children nor childhood had the centrality in his explanation that had been accorded to them by Ariès. In the 'open lineage family' Stone argued that relationships between parents and children were 'usually fairly remote', marked in the upper classes by sending off babies to wet-nurses, and in the upper bourgeois and professional classes by despatching them to boarding school at about the age of ten. Things were little better in the 'restricted patriarchal nuclear family' where Stone found, especially amongst Puritans, 'a fierce determination to break the will of the child, and to enforce his utter subjection to the authority of his elders and superiors, and most especially of his parents'. Both in the schools and in the home, corporal punishment, often very brutal, was the norm, the late sixteenth and early seventeenth centuries being 'the great flogging age'. Children were taught to behave with great formality in the presence of their parents, and to defer to them at all times.[22] Change came from about 1660, and over the ensuing century and a half there occurred 'a remarkable change in accepted child-rearing theory, in standard child-rearing practices, and in affective relations between parents and children'. England moved 'towards a child-oriented family type'. Stone did not pretend that this affected the whole of society; indeed he identified six different modes of child-rearing, only one of which, the 'child-oriented, affectionate and permissive mode' within 'the upper bourgeoisie and squirarchy' was fully modern. And even within that social strata there was an alternative 'child-oriented but repressive mode'.[23]

Like Shorter, Stone was concerned to find an explanation not for 'a change of structure, or of economics, or of social organization, but of sentiment'. In contrast to Shorter, he dismissed the idea that it had anything to do with industrial capitalism, finding the explanation in a rise of individualism linked to the decline in aristocratic society and 'the growth of a large, independent and self-confident middle class'. It was this which explains the emergence of the new mentality with respect to children first in England and New England.[24]

Although Stone used the language of 'evolution' with respect to the family, he also claimed that 'it is wholly false to assume that there can have been any such thing as straightforward linear development'. Rather, Stone was inclined to see 'an unending dialectic of competing interests and ideas' and development in cycles, rather than in a straight line – although with one crucial exception: 'The only steady linear change over the last four hundred years seems to have been a growing concern for children, although their actual treatment has oscillated cyclically between the permissive and the repressive.' Moreover, he argued that there were as many losses as gains in the rise of affective individualism.[25]

Ariès, de Mause, Shorter and Stone had one thing in common, and that was that they believed that there had been, over time, major changes in attitudes to and treatment of childhood. Other less wide-ranging studies, often focused on the eighteenth century as a crucial century of change, reached the same conclusion.[26] Where these writers disagreed was in their evaluation and explanation of that change, in its timing, and in the way they related it to social class. And the disagreements were profound; Ariès described an increasing distance between adult and child where de Mause saw convergence, the latter correctly noting that 'Ariès's central thesis is the opposite of mine'.[27] In the 1980s, however, that ubiquitous focus on a change in sentiment was highlighted to emphasise the common ground rather than the disagreements, and formed the basis for a criticism which seemed to sweep all before it.

Michael Anderson's *Approaches to the History of the Western Family 1500–1914* (1980) was perhaps the first to group these writings together as 'the sentiments approach' to the history of the family, in contrast to 'the demographic approach' and 'the household economics approach'. Although he accepted the validity of the common set of questions which they were addressing, he pointed to the problem in finding evidence to answer them, and to 'a style of writing in which speculation or even pure fantasy is glossed over as if it were clearly established fact'. Moreover, he noted the difficulty these writers had in arriving at explanations for the changes they described, and argued that their method encouraged too much decontextualisation in the sphere of culture, without close examination of economic structures.[28]

A full-blown critique of the existing histories of children and childhood came only with Linda Pollock's *Forgotten Children: Parent–child relations from 1500 to 1900* (1983). It was by this time clear that medievalists rejected Ariès's contention that 'in medieval society the idea of childhood did not exist',[29] and that English historians disagreed profoundly with Stone's characterisation of parent–child relationships in the seventeenth century. A head of steam was building up which was to criticise the key writings of the 1970s as methodologically unsound, technically incompetent, and in their conclusions wholly mistaken.[30] Pollock established a new paradigm for the 1980s. In its essence this new approach concentrated on the actuality of parent–child relationships, rather than on ideas about childhood, and its fundamental argument, as expressed by Pollock, was that continuity rather than change was the most important fact about those relationships. Thus, whereas Stone had argued that because infant mortality was so high, parents reduced 'the amount of emotional capital available for prudent investment in any single individual, especially in such ephemeral creatures as infants', Pollock found 'no change in the extent of parental grief over the centuries and no support at all for the argument that parents before the eighteenth century were indifferent to the death of their young offspring, whereas after the eighteenth century they grieved deeply'. Similarly on the issue of discipline, Pollock concluded that 'the evidence does not agree with the arguments of such writers as Ariès, de Mause, or Stone that children were harshly, even cruelly, disciplined, but reveals that brutality was the exception rather than the rule'.[31]

On what basis did Pollock reach these conclusions? First, she turned to evidence from sociobiology, studies of primates, and anthropology to argue that 'children require a certain amount of protection, affection and training for normal development', and that parents everywhere try to supply that.[32] The bulk of her evidence, however, was taken from a systematic study of diaries and autobiographies in Britain and North America concerning child-rearing in the period between 1500 and 1900. Pollock had to concede that 'diarists as a class may be exceptional rather than representative of society as a whole', and she was aware that at best she would only have access through this source to the literate; she tried to surmount this problem by turning, very briefly, to other evidence which suggested to her that lower-class child-rearing practices did not differ fundamentally from those of the higher classes. But overall she argued that diaries help to reveal 'the actualities of childhood rather than the attitudes to it'. This ambition indicates the shift that had occurred since Ariès declared his wish to understand the history of the idea of the family. Pollock went further to argue that 'there is little, if any, connection between attitudes and behaviour'. Historians who spend their time reading advice books, or sermons, or general treatises on childhood will, on Pollock's argument, learn little of use about the actualities of child-rearing or of child life. The history of childhood as an idea was thus sharply differentiated from the history of children.[33]

Pollock's refutation of the work of the 1960s and 1970s did not stand alone. Keith Wrightson, for example, in his widely-read *English Society 1580–1680* (1982) devoted fifteen pages to children, using, amongst other sources, wills, and concluded, directly contradicting Stone, that 'there seems no reason to believe that parental attitudes towards or aspirations for their children underwent fundamental change in the course of the seventeenth century'.[34] Ralph Houlbrooke, in his level-headed study of *The English Family 1450–1700* (1984), was alert to the variety of experience within and across social classes, but nevertheless noted that there 'is much direct evidence of the reality of loving care in some families and of parental grief in face of the loss of children'.[35]

The work of Ariès, de Mause, Shorter and Stone had placed the history of children and childhood firmly within the overarching category of the history of sentiment; their critics by and large responded within the same terms. Yet there were, as Anderson pointed out, other possible approaches to the history of children and childhood. One of these, the demographic, had at some level informed all these studies. The Cambridge Group for the History of Population and Social Structure had been arguing since the 1960s that certainly in England and probably elsewhere – at least in northern Europe – household size had typically been small, with a nuclear family as the dominant norm. This work undermined the old sociological assumption that there had been a transition, generally associated with industrialisation, from extended families to nuclear families; the nuclear family now became the norm. It thus became possible to argue that loving relationships within nuclear families had a perdurance in history and a power to withstand the onslaughts and intrusions of church, of state, and of economic change.[36] More generally, the work of demographers has provided crucial evidence on such factors as age of marriage, number of children born and surviving, the spacing of children, and the age at which they might leave home. These provide essential contours for the history of children and childhood, but, as has often been pointed out, the 'facts' on these matters do not unreservedly speak for themselves; we still need to try to find out what meaning people attached to them.

One way to do this is to locate families within particular economic and social structures, and this is the approach which Anderson described under the heading of 'household economics'. This can be linked to a wider body of studies which examines 'family strategy'. The underlying assumption is that families make rational responses to the situations in which they find themselves. For example, the number of children born to families may differ considerably according to their socio-economic situation. Thus it has been argued both that the age of marriage fell and the level of fertility within marriage rose in the conditions known as proto-industrialisation which offered considerable employment opportunities to all members of a family including its children. Similarly, as no one can doubt, fertility levels have fallen since the late nineteenth century and at the same time children have become more of an expense to their parents.

The family strategy or household economics approach thus places the emphasis on the economic more than on the sentimental value of children. The most far-reaching of such studies, which aims to bring the two approaches together, is Alan Macfarlane's *Marriage and Love in England 1300–1840* (1986). Macfarlane contrasted societies typically studied by anthropologists in which children are seen unreservedly as a benefit, both economically in their contribution to the family economy, and emotionally as supports to their parents and testimony to their status, and England (and with some reservations other parts of Europe) where, he argued, children have since the middle ages been a cost to their parents; hence the limitations on fertility in England achieved by late or non-marriage and spacing of children within marriage.

Macfarlane has argued for deeply-rooted habits and assumptions which have produced relatively constant behaviour over centuries. Others, with a shorter time focus, have argued that family strategies can respond quickly to changing circumstances. This is the approach of a number of recent studies to what used to be the central question in the history of childhood, the use of child labour in the industrial revolution. It is argued in one such study that it was families who made the crucial decisions about the participation of their children in the labour market, and who later, as economic circumstances improved, decided that it made more sense to invest in their children's education and so withdrew them from the labour market; the work of philanthropists striving to rescue children, or of laws which forbade the work of children, were at best of secondary importance.[37]

Such assertions suggest that it is timely to consider in more depth the role of philanthropy and the state in relation to children. The emphasis on studying the experience of childhood within the family – an emphasis common to the demographic, sentiments and household economics approaches – has led to neglect of the wider political and social structures which had an impact on childhood. A common starting point is the assumption that secular agencies in particular only began to play a crucial role in the nineteenth and twentieth centuries. This, as I shall show in Chapters 4 and 5, is a mistake; the strategies of the vast majority of poor families were shaped by their awareness of the facilities, services and sanctions operated by the state. At the same time, there is also little doubt that the introduction of compulsory schooling, normally in the late nineteenth century, did more than any other factor in these five centuries to transform the experience and the meanings attached to childhood by removing children, in principle if not immediately in fact, from the labour market, now reserved for those who were no longer 'children'. It was this which eventually brought about in the twentieth century an emotional valuation of children much greater than anything accorded to them in previous centuries.[38]

This book, then, will concentrate on three central interlocking themes: ideas of childhood; the actuality of adult–child relations; and the roles of philanthropists and states in regard to childhood. The underlying assumption will be that we will gain an understanding of these only if they are linked to the wider history of western society. As a working guide, 'children' will be taken to mean anyone under fifteen, though in actual fact in nearly all societies people have differed quite substantially in their thinking on the age at which childhood ends. I cannot, of course, hope to provide a history of children and childhood in each and every country of the western world, and make no pretence of so doing. The reason why I have chosen to study such a large geographical area is that, although I will frequently be drawing attention to different experiences in different parts of the west, there is nevertheless an important common pattern of change which concentration on minutiae can obscure. In Chapter 2 I shall be concerned to see what ideas and practices were inherited from or available as models from the classical and Christian traditions, and will then examine the debates about medieval childhood, sparked off by Ariès, as a background against which to measure childhood in the early modern period. Chapter 3 will argue that over the period 1500 to 1900 there was built up a set of ideas about childhood sufficiently coherent to be described as an ideology. In Chapter 4 I shall examine the experience of childhood and attitudes towards childhood in the mass of the populations of Europe and North America, arguing that the major transition that occurred in the centuries between 1500 and 1900 was that from early participation of children in contributions to the family economy to compulsory schooling. Chapters 5 and 6 will examine the relationship between families and children and both philanthropists and the state, paying particular attention to the ways in which states were drawn into setting up institutions aimed at preventing the death or impoverishment of children – though often achieving the opposite of what they intended. In Chapter 7 the focus will be on the twentieth century, the self-proclaimed 'century of the child'. Finally, in the Conclusion, I will take stock of the evidence as a whole and suggest ways in which the histories of childhood and children are interrelated.

Notes

1 Z. Filipović, *Zlata's Diary: A Child's Life in Sarajevo* (London, 1994), pp. 60, 122.

2 G. Boas, *The Cult of Childhood* (London, 1966).

3 C. Steedman, *The Tidy House: Little Girls Writing* (London, 1982), pp. 61–84.

4 A. Farge, *Fragile Lives: Violence, Power and Solidarity in Eighteenth-Century Paris* (Cambridge, 1993), pp. 46–51; L. Jordanova, 'New worlds for children in the eighteenth century: problems of historical interpretation', *History of the Human Sciences*, 3 (1990), esp. p. 82.

5 J. Mechling, 'Advice to historians on advice to mothers', *Journal of Social History*, 9 (1975–6), pp. 44–64 has perhaps induced in historians an excessive caution in utilising this source.

6 R.H. Tawney, *Religion and the Rise of Capitalism* (1926; Harmondsworth, 1937), p. 239.

7 N. Elias, *The History of Manners: The Civilizing Process, Vol. 1* (1939; New York, 1978), pp. xiii, 141.

8 Ibid., pp. 146, 203.

9 Ibid., p. 168.

10 P. Ariès, *Centuries of Childhood* (London, 1962), pp. 397, 395.

11 Ibid., pp. 395, 399.

12 Ibid., pp. 396–7.

13 Ibid., pp. 320–1.

14 Ibid., p. 127.

15 Ibid., p. 7.

16 R.T. Vann, 'The Youth of *Centuries of Childhood*', *History and Theory*, XXI (1982), pp. 279–97.

17 L. de Mause (ed.), *The History of Childhood* (1974; London, 1976), pp. 1, 3, 21.

18 M. Anderson, *Approaches to the History of the Western Family 1500–1914* (London, 1980), p. 15.

19 De Mause, *History of Childhood*, p. 3; for a critique of de Mause's use of evidence, see L.A. Pollock, *Forgotten Children: Parent–Child Relations from 1500 to 1900* (Cambridge, 1983), pp. 57–8.

20 E. Shorter, *The Making of the Modern Family* (London, 1976), pp. 11, 170, 192–6.

21 Ibid., p. 259.

22 L. Stone, *The Family, Sex and Marriage in England 1500–1800* (London, 1977), pp. 105–7, 161–74.

23 Ibid., pp. 405, 411, 449–78.

24 Ibid., pp. 658, 665–6.

25 Ibid., pp. 682, 683–7.

26 J.H. Plumb, 'The New World of Children in Eighteenth-Century England', *Past and Present*, 67 (1975), pp. 64–93; R. Trumbach, *The Rise of the Egalitarian Family: Aristocratic Kinship and Domestic Relations in Eighteenth-Century England* (New York, San Francisco and London, 1978).

27 De Mause, *History of Childhood*, p. 5.

28 Anderson, *Approaches to the History of the Western Family*, pp. 41, 61–4.

29 Ariès, *Centuries of Childhood*, p. 125.

30 A. Macfarlane, ' "The Family, Sex and Marriage in England 1500–1800" by Lawrence Stone', *History and Theory*, 18 (1979), pp. 103–26; A. Wilson, 'The Infancy of the History of Childhood: An Appraisal of Philippe Ariès', *History and Theory*, 19 (1980), pp. 132–54; E.P. Thompson, 'Happy Families', *Radical History Review*, 20 (1979), pp. 42–50.

31 Pollock, *Forgotten Children*, pp. 141–2, 199.

32 Ibid., pp. 33–43.

33 Ibid., pp. 71–3, 88, 270.

34 K. Wrightson, *English Society 1580–1680* (London, 1982), p. 118.

35 R.A. Houlbrooke, *The English Family 1450–1700* (London, 1984), p. 156.

36 F. Mount, *The Subversive Family* (London, 1982).

37 C. Nardinelli, *Child Labor and the Industrial Revolution* (Bloomington and Indianapolis, 1990).

38 See V.A. Zelizer, *Pricing the Priceless Child: The Changing Social Value of Children* (New York, 1985).

CHAPTER 2

Children and childhood in ancient and medieval Europe

In the early modern and modern centuries ideas about childhood and child-rearing were likely to have their origin in two sources: the classical inheritance and Christianity. The actual practice of child-rearing was likely to be influenced by the way children had been reared in medieval society. My aim in this chapter is to set out that classical and Christian inheritance, and to make an assessment of medieval thought and practice with regard to children.

The classical inheritance

The revival of interest in the classical world at the time of the Renaissance makes it particularly important to examine Greek and Roman thought and practice. First, we need to make an assessment of the practices of infanticide, sale of children, abandonment and wet-nursing. Some scholars see these as the hallmark of child-rearing in the ancient world, indicative of attitudes to all children, and leaving a legacy for later centuries. Secondly, much of our language about children and childhood is inherited from Greek or Latin and may carry with it some of the intellectual baggage with which it was associated in classical times. Thirdly, some legal structures were taken over into the medieval and early modern worlds from Rome, and we need in particular to see how far the *patria potestas*, the overriding power of the father, was still a factor to be considered in the early modern centuries. Finally, the ways of thinking about childhood and the advice given on child-rearing and education in the classical world carried an authority which would have been influential in the period up to at least 1900.

De Mause argued that the 'infanticidal mode' of child-rearing was dominant in the period up to the fourth century AD. It was not simply that many children were killed, but also that 'when parents routinely resolved their anxieties about taking care of children by killing them, it affected the surviving children profoundly'.[1] The evidence for infanticide – the act of killing a child – is hard to assess,[2] but no one can doubt that many children were exposed or abandoned, girls being more likely than boys to suffer this fate. De Mause assumed, and on the face of it this seemed plausible, that abandonment amounted to infanticide, and that the abandoned child died.[3] John Boswell challenged this interpretation in *The Kindness of Strangers: The Abandonment of Children in Western Europe from Late Antiquity to the Renaissance* (1988). Boswell noted that one of the anxieties of a Roman man when he visited a brothel was that the prostitute might be his own daughter; she might have been abandoned, but rescued and brought up by foster parents. Boswell did not deny the extent of abandonment; he estimated that perhaps a majority of women who had reared more than one child abandoned at least one, and that in the first three centuries AD between 20 per cent and 40 per cent of all children born were abandoned.[4] But he suggested, though without putting a figure on it, that many of these children survived, and that parents knew this to be the case, otherwise there would have been no cause for fathers to fear incest in the brothel, nor for the anxiety, widely expressed, that freeborn children might be being reared as slaves. Unlike the medieval, early modern and modern periods, there were no institutional arrangements, in the shape of foundling hospitals, for abandoned children; they owed their survival to 'the kindness of strangers', people who picked up these exposed children, and raised them.

Why should they have done this? Boswell admits that 'a large percentage of exposed or sold children doubtless became slaves'; there was nothing in Roman law to prevent either abandonment or sale, the latter 'widespread not only in Rome but throughout the Hellenistic Mediterranean', sometimes as payment of debts. It is clear also that both boys and girls were 'used to a considerable extent as prostitutes'. But Boswell goes on to suggest that 'there were many happier possibilities'.[5] An abandoned baby might be taken and passed off as the legitimate child of a woman who had been unable to conceive or who had had stillbirths or whose baby had died. The Romans emphasised procreation and the continuation of the family as the purpose of marriage and of sexual relationships, and couples who had been unsuccessful in producing children might have welcomed the opportunity of providing themselves with a child from amongst the exposed. On the other hand, someone looking for an heir would normally have adopted an adult rather than a baby whose chances of living to adulthood would always be in doubt.[6] Most children who were taken up by other families would have become 'alumni', a status which effectively gave them foster-parents who might well treat them like their own children, perhaps freeing them from slavery, and leaving them bequests. Inscriptions show that alumni often enjoyed close relationships with their foster-parents.[7]

Wet-nursing is another practice which was prevalent in the ancient world, and which has received much comment in the writing on early modern and modern childhood. If the exposed babies of the ancient world did indeed live it can only have been through wet-nursing. Moreover, wet-nursing was almost universal amongst the upper classes, and probably common for the children of slaves – in this latter case so that the mothers could return to productive work, or so that they might become pregnant again and breed another slave, for it was well known that breastfeeding had a contraceptive effect.[8] Until bottle-feeding became safe in the twentieth century, wet-nursing was undoubtedly the best alternative to mother's milk. And in numerous cases, for example where the mother had died, or was unable to produce milk, it was the obvious resort. But it is quite clear that, particularly in the upper classes, many mothers who could have breastfed, nevertheless hired wet-nurses. In this practice there is considerable continuity right through to the nineteenth century, a continuity which extends to the characteristics which should be looked for in a wet-nurse.[9]

Early modern and modern Europe inherited from the ancient world a practice of abandoning children, together with a commentary upon the practice which rarely condemned it. 'Most ancient moral writers', concludes Boswell, 'evince indifference toward or acceptance of abandonment.' Both Plato and Aristotle seem to have condoned it. The sale of freeborn children was condemned, but largely because it was likely to lead to slavery.[10] It is very difficult for modern readers not to assume from this that there was in the ancient world a level of indifference to childhood and to children which, as de Mause argues, places them at the opposite end of the spectrum to ourselves. Yet the emphasis of recent writing on the ancient family, much of it written with one eye on the debates on the early modern period, is that close and loving relationships between parents and children were the norm. As Mark Golden puts it, writing about the Greeks, 'the weight of the evidence seems overwhelmingly to favor the proposition that the Athenians loved their children and grieved for them deeply when they died'. On the analogy with abortion in modern times, and with anthropological evidence, Golden argues that abandonment of one child would not imply parental indifference to other children who were kept.[11] More cautiously, Beryl Rawson finds 'evidence to suggest that adult–child relationships could often be close and sensitive', and Suzanne Dixon concludes that in ancient Rome 'there was certainly a sentimental interest in children as such, and some parents were desolate at the death of small children'.[12] A typical example of the kind of evidence which supports such generalisations is a child's sarcophagus dating from the first or second century AD found at Agrigento in southern Sicily. It depicts the child at play, learning to read, and then the deathbed scene, with the parents and grandparents manifestly grieving over their loss.[13]

It is from evidence like this that classicists have to reconstruct the history of attitudes to childhood and treatment of children. Much of it is susceptible to more than one interpretation. The sarcophagus at Agrigento certainly tells us something about the Roman idealisation of childhood, but it is impossible to be certain that the actuality of the dead child's life was similar in spirit to its representation in sculpture. It is therefore tempting for classicists to argue by analogy, pulling on what seem to them well-substantiated conclusions from later history. But as we have seen, there has been fierce debate about children and childhood in the early modern world in particular. There is a danger that classicists will reach conclusions about the ancient world which are consonant with those in fashion for later centuries, but which cannot be substantiated from classical evidence on its own.[14]

The problem for classicists is made no easier by the ambiguities of language related to childhood. 'The term "child"', writes Richard Lyman, 'seems to refer to anyone, depending on context and literary convention, from infancy to old age.'[15] To which one might respond, which term? Neither Greek nor Latin had any equivalent to the word 'baby', but each had a variety of words signifying child, but rarely restricted to that.[16] Modern European languages have drawn on one Greek and two Latin words; from the Greek *pais* have come the English words, 'paediatrics' and 'pederasty'; from the Latin *infans*, literally 'not speaking', come the English 'infant' and the French 'enfant'; and from the Latin *puer*, the English 'puerile'. None of these words carried an unambiguous meaning in their original form. *Pueri* was sometimes thought to be derived from *puri*, indicating purity, but for the Romans that purity was not sexual innocence, but the lack of hair or down on the cheeks.[17] There is a particular difficulty in deciding whether the words relate to age or status. Just as in the age of modern imperialism an African adult might be called a 'boy', so in the ancient world a slave or a servant, of whatever age, could be *pais* or *puer*. Does this imply that children were held in low esteem, or does it simply refer to the fact that 'in terms of power and juridical standing' slaves and servants were in the same position as children?[18] In the home slaves and children were undoubtedly differentiated; fear of the whip was seen as fundamental in maintaining the authority of master over slave whereas moderation was the keynote for punishment of children.[19] Outside the home, however, no one doubted that the authority of teacher over pupil was maintained by the rod, the Latin word for teaching, *disciplina*, having the same meaning as punishment.[20] The linguistic association of slave and child meant that ambiguities and different layers of meaning attached to the words for childhood descended to the medieval and modern worlds.[21]

From Roman law came an apparently less ambiguous inheritance in the form of *patria potestas*, the power of the father. In Roman law the oldest living male in a family had far-reaching powers over all his descendants whatever their age and wherever they were living. These included not only rights over property, but also rights of life and death; it was he who decided whether a baby should be exposed, and it was he who could sentence and execute his own child. It has been argued that *patria potestas* 'was the fundamental institution underlying Roman institutions', private life providing a model for public.[22] As Aristotle had put it, a father 'rules his children as does a king his subjects'.[23] *Patria potestas* was well known to early modern scholars, and used as the main pillar in arguments for absolute government.[24] But in the Roman world *patria potestas* was less awesome in practice than in theory. The exercise of powers of life and death was extremely rare. Late age of marriage and low life expectancy meant that adult married sons were comparatively rarely under the theoretical jurisdiction of their own fathers. In addition, separate residences and allowances for sons helped to remove sources of tension between generations.[25] But even if the absoluteness of patriarchal power was moderated in practice, later centuries inherited the idea that absolute power within a family should reside in the father. As we shall see, these ideas were to be extremely influential in the early modern period.

The tenor of recent scholarship on children and childhood in the ancient world has been far removed from that of de Mause. Infanticide has been placed on the margin, the horrors of abandonment have been explained away by 'the kindness of strangers', *patria potestas* has become a mere theory which neither in practice nor advice writings precluded loving relationships between fathers and children, and the family has been portrayed as often a haven of affectionate relationships. Yet if this appears to add strength to the argument that continuity is the key to the history of children and childhood, a word of caution is in order. The overriding impression derived from ancient sources is that childhood was not seen as important for itself, but as part of a process towards producing a good citizen; and that in this process the years of youth, from about puberty to twenty-one, were the key ones.[26] Moreover, it was common to consider children, not as individual human beings, but in terms of the services they could render their parents, partly in continuing the line, but also as supports in old age, and in carrying out essential rituals at the time of the parents' death. In Euripides' *Medea*, Medea sends her two children away to their death, and exclaims, 'It was all for nothing . . . I once built many hopes on you. I imagined that you would care for me in my old age, and that you yourselves would prepare my body for burial when I was dead.'[27] Some evidence might seem to point in the opposite direction. Children were often seen as having powers of divination, and they played an important role in rituals; they were considered to be close to the divine world. But, it is argued, 'classical society saw children as especially associated with the divine world because they were unimportant', rather than this religious role being a testimony to high status. Children, and they shared this characteristic with women and slaves, were marginal to society, not fully part of it, and closer than adults to another world, the divine. Part of this marginality stemmed from the likelihood that they might die before reaching adulthood and becoming part of society; certainly if they died very young they were subject to quite different burial customs than older people, being buried inside the city walls rather than outside, sometimes in the foundations of buildings, and at night.[28]

There is therefore, compared to some of the later sources we will examine, a relative neglect of younger children. In so far as they are discussed they are seen in terms of their deficiencies, the adult qualities which they lack. In classical Athens 'children were regarded as physically weak, morally incompetent, mentally incapable', and, not surprisingly, Greeks 'were generally not nostalgic for childhood'.[29] If children who died were mourned, it was because they were perceived to have lived to no purpose, not having reached adulthood. Childhood itself cannot be praised, thought Cicero, only its potential.[30] Related to this was the idealisation of children who appeared to acquire adult characteristics, the *puer senex*, or 'old child'. Gravity, seriousness, studiousness were all valued qualities.[31]

The overriding Roman aim to continue the family and to produce good citizens has led to a considerable bias in the sources available to us: the bulk of the evidence concerns boys rather than girls, and we know hardly anything about children and childhood outside the upper classes. As Wiedemann admits, 'the vast majority of the population of the Roman empire has left no record of its feelings about children'.[32]

Ancient historians have been alert to the possibility that there may have been changes in attitudes to and treatment of childhood in the centuries between 500 BC and AD 400. Such changes are very hard to document. A naturalistic portrayal of children in the poetry and art of the Hellenistic period used to be taken as indicating new attitudes to children and childhood, but this is now discounted.[33] Dixon ascribes a 'sentimental interest in young children and enjoyment of their childish qualities' to 'a general ideological stress on the domestic comfort of the conjugal unit which emerges in Latin art and literature from the first century BC.' She cites Lucretius on the common lament of mourners for a young man: 'No more, no more will your happy house welcome you, nor will your excellent wife. No more will your sweet children run to greet you with kisses and cling to your chest in sweet silence.' She sees this 'sentimental ideal of family life' as comparable with our own, and argues that it continued into the period of the Empire.[34] Beryl Rawson is in broad agreement with this emphasis, arguing that the early Empire, from the latter half of the first century BC, provided Romans 'with greater leisure, stability, and affluence for at least two centuries, and thus a more sensitive and sophisticated atmosphere for interpersonal relations. Adult–child relations benefited from this . . . There seems to have been a particular concentration of child-oriented activity in the second century.'[35] Wiedemann's view of these centuries is much bleaker. His central theme is change in the first four centuries AD, but his starting point is not Dixon's 'sentimental ideal', but a low level of interest in children and childhood. He sees some move towards a more child-centred society over time, partly connected with the Christian view that all humans are equal in the eyes of God. Lyman, from a still later starting point and studying the period AD 200–800, argued that 'ideals about childhood underwent substantial change . . . the official and formal expectations about the treatment of children seem gentler to us after the fourth century', and, further, this was to some extent reflected in practice. Lyman ascribed these changes partly to Christianity, partly to the possibility that 'the barbarians' brought with them traditions of child-rearing rather more humane than anything the classical world had known.[36] Faced with these differences of emphasis, and with the paucity of the evidence on which they are built, one can only counsel scepticism, while noting the constancy with which historians of childhood are on the lookout for progress.

Christianity

The Christian belief in the need of every human being for salvation immediately implied a higher status for young children. They needed to be brought, as early as possible, into the Christian family of God. One way of doing this, though it did not command universal approval, was infant baptism.[37] Whether or not this had occurred, there was a perceived need to make young children aware that they had a soul, and that their life in the hereafter as well as on earth was dependent on the state of their soul; they could not be treated as of marginal importance to society as a whole until they had achieved adulthood.

In accordance with this, and in contrast to the Greeks and Romans, Christians acted on their belief, inherited from Judaism, that infanticide was murder. In 374 the Christian emperors Valentinian, Valens and Gratian decreed that 'If anyone, man or woman, should commit the sin of killing an infant, that crime should be punishable with death', an attitude considerably at variance with the Roman law code of the Twelve Tables (fifth century BC) where any child obviously deformed at birth was to be put to death.[38] This decree probably initially referred to pagan ritual killing of children, but, as Boswell notes, it 'would have been interpreted subsequently as constituting a blanket condemnation of infanticide'.[39]

Abandonment was judged less harshly. Valentinian ruled in 374 that all parents must support their children, and that those who abandoned them should be subject to the penalty 'prescribed by law'. But it is not clear what that penalty would have been, and the law seems to have had no impact on the practice of abandonment. Indeed Christian attitudes to abandonment are often scarcely distinguishable from those of pagan Romans except that, particularly from the fourth century, sympathy and understanding were held out to those who abandoned their children through poverty or other misfortune. As they knew from the story of Moses, there were circumstances which could justify the abandonment of a child, and which could work to the greater glory of God.[40]

It is not only in attitudes to abandonment that we can see some similarity between pagans and Christians. The Bible sanctioned a view of the proper relationships between parents and children which would have been widely shared in the pagan world. Children were commanded to honour and obey their parents.[41] Fathers were advised that 'He that spareth his rod hateth his son: but he that loveth him chasteneth him betimes', a verse frequently employed in justification of corporal punishment.[42]

But in other respects the Bible provided Christians with the possibility of a starkly different attitude to children and childhood. Whereas the gods of pagans had commanded their followers to sacrifice their children, the Christian God had given up his own son. Moreover, to be a child or child-like now came to be an honoured state. When his disciples tried to prevent children being brought to him, Jesus rebuked them, saying 'Suffer the little children to come unto me, and forbid them not; for of such is the kingdom of God', and warning that 'Whosoever shall not receive the kingdom of God as a little child, he shall not enter therein.'[43] God or his angels offered special protection to children: 'Take heed that ye despise not one of these little ones; for I say unto you, That in heaven their angels do always behold the face of my Father which is in heaven.'[44] Children, it came to be believed, had their special guardian angels. Moreover, there was a stress on parental duties and responsibilities. Fathers were told not to provoke their 'children to wrath', and it was parents who should lay up treasure for children, not children for parents.[45] Finally, there were passages which could be interpreted as meaning that the pursuit of a Christian vocation might mean the abandonment of the natural family for the family of God.[46]

These tensions between novelty and tradition in Christianity can be seen as coming to a head in the person of St Augustine (d. 430), the author of the first modern autobiography. In a famous controversy with Pelagius, who argued that infants are born with a clean slate and that salvation comes from a good life led by an adult, Augustine countered that humans are born with original sin inherited from Adam, and that baptism will remove this, though not an individual's own tendencies towards evil, exemplified for Augustine by his own memory of stealing pears without any reason other than a compulsion to do something bad. But these views, harsh as they can seem, particularly when associated with Augustine's endorsement of corporal punishment, had a further implication, that the child, as a human being, was on a par with an adult, not incomplete, and that its moral dilemmas needed to be taken as seriously as if it was six feet tall. The child had begun to move in from the margins of society.[47]

The middle ages

All studies of childhood in the middle ages since 1960 have had a common starting point in Ariès's claim that 'in medieval society the idea of childhood did not exist'.[48] Rarely can so few words have brought forth so many in refutation. Medievalists never seem to tire of proving Ariès to be wrong. They have set themselves the task of showing that the middle ages did have a concept of childhood, not perhaps the same as in later centuries, but a concept nevertheless. Ariès, they say, misused or ignored evidence. Shulamith Shahar's *Childhood in the Middle Ages* (1990), with its central thesis 'that a concept of childhood existed in the Central and Late Middle Ages [1100–1425], that scholarly acknowledgement of the existence of several stages of childhood was not merely theoretical, and that parents invested both material and emotional resources in their offspring',[49] has become the acknowledged authority on the period. Our own task is not only to assess these claims, but also to see how far medieval ideas and practice were in fact distinctly and exclusively 'medieval', and how much they had in common with those of later centuries.

We need at the outset to gloss Ariès's famous claim. The English translation fails to convey the meaning of the original, for the word translated as 'idea' was in French '*sentiment*', which carries with it the sense of a feeling about childhood as well as a concept of it. Further, Ariès was quick to point out that he was not claiming that there was no affection for children in the middle ages; he was trying to keep clear a distinction between a '*sentiment*' about childhood and the way adults treated children. Nevertheless, this lack of a '*sentiment*' meant that from about the age of seven children 'belonged to adult society'. This did not mean that a child of, say, ten had the same status and role as an adult of thirty, but that there was no boundary fence separating off the world of adults from that of children. Children found their place within this world, but, as Ariès indicated, it was a special place, dependent on their age: 'There is not a single collective picture of the times in which children are not to be found, nestling singly or in pairs in the *trousse* hung round women's necks; or urinating in a corner, or playing their part in a traditional festival, or as apprentices in a workshop, or as pages serving a knight, etc.'[50] The theme of his book is the growth of a '*sentiment*' about childhood, and of a separation of the worlds of adulthood and childhood. It has sometimes escaped the attention of medievalists that Ariès placed the origins and early development of these in the middle ages. Ariès's view of medieval childhood was thus rather more nuanced than might have been imagined from his stark opening sentence.

Ariès's use of pictorial evidence has attracted most comment. He claimed that 'medieval art until about the twelfth century did not know childhood or did not attempt to portray it'. Size alone indicated that a figure was a child. From about the thirteenth century, three developments can be traced. First, angels were portrayed as adolescents, 'round, pretty, and somewhat effeminate'. Secondly, the infant Jesus began to be painted naturalistically and sentimentally. Thirdly, in a genre in which the soul was depicted as a child, children were painted naked. It was in the second of these that there was most development in the fourteenth and fifteenth centuries, the pictures of the Virgin and Child becoming 'more and more profane', other holy childhoods being portrayed, and eventually, these themes being taken up in lay iconography. More recent scholarship has confirmed Ariès's emphasis on change, finding that 'Around 1300, images of children become more lively, more human, and more probable.' But it was only in the early modern period, in the sixteenth and seventeenth centuries, that there emerged any pronounced genre of depicting lay children in everyday life, and that dead children were portrayed, this, for Ariès, marking 'a very important moment in the history of feelings'.[51]

The criticism of Ariès on this point is twofold. First, it is said that he was unaware of other medieval sources showing a naturalistic portrayal of childhood. Forsyth, concentrating on the ninth to twelfth centuries, argues that 'children do appear in early medieval art and that their portrayal there, which is often handled with wit and understanding of a dramatic, even poignant sort, reflects a particular awareness of this phase of life and a keen rapport with its special qualities'. The pictorial evidence supports this claim.[52] The second criticism is that Ariès was wrong to try to read off attitudes to childhood from images which are relevant to the history of theology or of art, but not of childhood. Take the theological point. Jesus was the child most frequently portrayed in the middle ages. In the early middle ages the aim of painters was to show him as divine, hence his 'adult' appearance. In the later middle ages, the aim was to show how the divine had become human, fully human, hence a portrayal of the child Jesus as naked, with the eye drawn towards his genitals. The changing image tells us about changes in theology, not in attitudes to childhood.[53] Similarly it is argued that 'the different types of childhood portrayed in paintings through the centuries may have more to do with changes in art rather than changes in the way children were seen'.[54] Certainly these arguments point to the need to be careful in the use made of pictorial evidence, but it does not render it useless, any more than it can be argued that the novels of Dickens tell us nothing about childhood in the nineteenth century.

Ariès has also been criticised for the conclusions he reached about the valuation placed by people in the middle ages on the early years of life. He included a chapter on 'the ages of life', ways of describing and depicting different stages of human life. This was very common in medieval literature and thought, and took many forms, the number of ages being anywhere from three to twelve, though settling down at seven in the later middle ages.[55] All of them recognise childhood in some form, normally in two stages, *infantia* and *pueritia*, covering the ages from birth to fourteen, and succeeded by *adolescentia* and *iuventus*. They suggest some recognition of the characteristics of childhood, particularly as children are depicted as playing with toys.[56] Ariès did not deny this, but he argued that the age of life which was favoured above all others in this iconography was youth (*iuventus*), a period which might last from the mid-twenties to the fifties. Correspondingly childhood was, relative to the nineteenth century, under-valued. Sometimes the ages were linked to the months of the year, with January standing for the first six years of life; Ariès cited a fourteenth-century poem to suggest the relatively low value put on this age:

> *Of all the months the first behold*
> *January two-faced and cold.*
> *Because its eyes two ways are cast,*
> *To face the future and the past.*
> *Thus the child six summers old*
> *Is not worth much when all is told.*[57]

There is in fact a weight of evidence pointing in the opposite direction. There was grief for young children who died, movingly expressed by Gregory of Tours in the sixth century describing a famine which 'attacked young children first of all and to them it was fatal: and so we lost our little ones, who were so dear to us, whom we cherished in our bosoms and dandled in our arms, whom we fed and nurtured with such loving care. As I write I wipe away my tears.'[58] More substantially, there was, as Shahar has shown, a body of theory and practice in the middle ages in relation to pregnancy, childbirth, infant feeding, weaning and early child-rearing. Shahar is careful not to idealise childhood in the middle ages, but she notes that in some respects medieval thought and practice seem preferable to that of later centuries, and in particular to that model of enlightenment, the eighteenth century: she describes the medieval preference for warm rather than cold baths, and contrasts the medieval view that up to the age of seven a child should be treated with tenderness with the advocacy by a number of eighteenth-century writers of 'rigid discipline from the very earliest age and relentless battle even against infants to force them to obey parental commands'. She notes how the medieval view that birth should take place in a darkened room in conditions which ease the transition to the world outside the womb corresponds to some late twentieth-century theories.[59] Moreover, she is able to place before us examples of real adult–child interactions. Thus a fourteenth-century source describes a vision of St Ida of Louvain in which she was permitted by St Elizabeth to assist in bathing the infant Jesus:

When the Holy Infant was seated in the bath, he began to play as is the way of infants. He made noise in the water by clapping hands, and as children do, splashed in the water until it spilled out and wet all those around. He continued to splash while moving all of his tiny body. On seeing the water splashing all around, he began to shout with joy in a loud voice . . . and when the bathing was complete, she lifted the child from the bath, dried him, and wrapped him in his swaddling bands. She seated him on her lap and as mothers do, began to play with him.

This is a vision, but it is arguable that it is so realistic that it must be drawn from some memory. Moreover, it assumes a shared world, where the reader can respond to the phrases 'as children do' and 'as mothers do', and where the bath, unlike in the sixteenth and seventeenth centuries, was an everyday event. Play was also seen as essential for the proper growth and development of the child. 'Children should be allowed to play since nature demands it', wrote the otherwise strict Philip of Novare.[60]

What was the origin of ideas such as these? First, there was a substantial body of medical writing, derived from ancient and Arabic sources, which identified, described and offered remedies for a host of illnesses peculiar to children.[61] In addition, from the thirteenth century preaching manuals became available which contained model sermons specifically addressed to issues of childhood, and these recognised stages in childhood, urged the importance of encouraging learning, and stressed the desirability of moderation in punishment, a much-quoted exemplar being Anselm who in the eleventh century had emphasised a child's need 'of loving-kindness from others, of gentleness, mercy, cheerful address, charitable patience, and many such-like comforts'. These manuals became 'extremely popular over the following two centuries'.[62]

There is a difficulty in knowing how far this body of what is likely to strike us as enlightened precept affected practice. It is possible that in its very repetition it suggests that people's actual behaviour was at odds with it. Shahar argues that 'it seems abundantly clear that people did not internalize the exhortations of the preachers and didactic writers' that children should be kept innocent of any sexual knowledge or activity.[63] But in other respects she finds more concordance between precept and practice, with a general acknowledgement that children in their first seven years should be brought up by their mothers with kindness and with a degree of freedom from overbearing adult authority. She and other scholars have shown beyond any doubt that the medieval world recognised *infantia*, the first seven years of life, as a separate stage of life, and accorded it much greater importance than Ariès implied.

What of the second stage, *pueritia*, up to the age of twelve for girls and fourteen for boys? This was the time for education, with fathers having responsibility for sons, and mothers for daughters.[64] Education for the vast majority of the population did not mean school; it meant a gradual initiation into the world of adult work, whether through a formal apprenticeship, or simply through carrying out more and more skilled tasks within the home or on the land. It was a mark of the fact that this was an initiating and learning stage that children in it were not held to be fully criminally responsible, and if they did commit a crime their punishment was generally lighter than it would have been if they had been older. Similarly with regard to sins, their penance was likely to be light, some believing that confession and penance should not commence until the end of *pueritia*.[65]

Ariès would not have disagreed with these conclusions about *pueritia*. Yet the emphasis of his work on this age range was quite different. On the lookout for change rather than continuity, he saw in the development of schooling a key agency in the emergence of a separate world of childhood. In the cathedral schools of the middle ages, Ariès argued, 'as soon as he started going to school [probably between the ages of nine and twelve], the child immediately entered the world of adults'.[66] By contrast, in the modern world schooling is associated with childhood. Ariès deployed evidence of three kinds to show this beginning to happen from the fifteenth century. First, school began to replace apprenticeship as a means of socialisation, the characteristic of apprenticeship being that children mixed with adults. Ariès is at pains to emphasise the importance of this change, though he acknowledges that it did not take full effect until the end of the eighteenth century.[67] He has been criticised on the grounds that apprenticeship was associated with adolescence or youth, not childhood, but in fact apprenticeship normally began in the period of *pueritia*, at the age of eleven or twelve, and in some cases, where it lasted only three years, would have been completed before the third stage of life had begun.[68] Secondly, there is evidence of age-grading in schools, so that adults and children were separated, and children themselves put in different classes according to age. And thirdly, there was an imposition of discipline by teachers. Together these changes began to forge the modern linkage between childhood and school, and to create a separate world of childhood. Ariès was quite right to stress the influence of schooling on concepts of childhood, but although he was keen to root the origin of this in the middle ages, it is perfectly possible to read his long central section on 'the scholastic life' as pointing to the nineteenth century rather than the seventeenth century, far less the middle ages, as the period in which the most fundamental change occurred.[69] Schooling in the middle ages was only for a minority. Didactic writers, it is true, stress the unity of the period from seven to fourteen, and see it as one in which the upper classes at least will be receiving an education; but the important point is that even for them not all of it would be in a school, the latter being primarily reserved as a training place for the clerical profession.[70] In Ariès's account the chronology of the shift to a situation where childhood is spent in an age-graded and disciplined school is not always clear; but he was entirely correct in latching onto the linkage between schooling and both concepts and experience of childhood.

In stressing the gradualness of the process of growing up, Shahar found herself in agreement with Ariès on one important point. Children from an early age, even before the age of seven, were not cut off from adult society. Living conditions in medieval houses gave little opportunity for privacy, whether for adults or for children, and in the outside world children were immediately part of a society in which the ages mixed, and in which neighbours played their part in looking after children.[71] Children often took part in processions, and were thus socialised into communal life. They played a particularly important role in boisterous celebrations around Christmas time when, in most West European countries from the twelfth century onwards, Boy Bishops reversed the age order and mocked their elders in a licensed world turned upside down.[72] Some writers, it is true, wanted to protect the innocence of the child, but in other respects there was no feeling, as there was to be in later centuries, that the world of childhood should be kept separate from that of adults.

Shahar has given us a picture of medieval childhood which is very much more positive than that common in the literature only a few years ago. Her account is the more convincing as she does not attempt to hide negative aspects which suggest to her overall a degree of ambivalence towards children. The negative image of childhood stemmed in large part from Augustine's stress on original sin, combined with a high valuation of those who either never had sexual relationships or who were willing to give up their children for the sake of dedication to God, a common theme in the lives of female saints. The *puer senex*, joined by the *puella senex*, was much praised, with the difference that whereas in classical literature the child combined the freshness of youth with the maturity of old age, in medieval sources the child 'is old in everything but years'. Hagiographers, moreover, reserved their praises for those displaying the virtues of old age rather than the innocence of infants.[73] But to set against this there are numerous images of childhood and of children as pure and innocent, and with an ability to seize on truths hidden from adults which Shahar compares to the images projected by nineteenth-century Romanticism. This positive image of medieval childhood is reinforced by Nicholas Orme, who is fiercely critical of Ariès, and sets out powerful evidence of a culture of childhood, with play, toys and books specially written for children. 'Children's literature in England', he writes, 'in terms of both content and readership, begins in the middle ages', a firm rebuke to those who have conventionally dated it from the 1740s.[74]

Shahar, and other scholars, thus build up a picture of childhood in the middle ages which suggests that there were some distinctively medieval attitudes to childhood, as well as a degree of continuity, much of it imposed upon us by biology. Her most signal contribution may have been the stress on the early years of childhood as a time for growth and play. Three caveats are in order.

The first is that Shahar covers a period of over three centuries without suggesting that much changed within this time. She does acknowledge that towards the end of the middle ages there began to be an emphasis on the importance of learning in early childhood, but in other respects she stresses continuity, in opposition to those who have argued for a growing maternal tenderness in iconography and in life from the twelfth century onwards or for a more positive image of childhood after the plagues of the fourteenth and fifteenth centuries.[75] There is a danger that 'medieval childhood', perhaps stretching back by inference prior to the twelfth century, and covering the whole of Europe, will be set up as something which can be compared and contrasted with childhood in other eras, with the nuances, ambivalences and changes within the period being forgotten.[76] There is one change which needs particular emphasis. It was in the middle ages that the family began to assume a structure which we can recognise. In the ancient world a *familia* would include slaves and other non-kin, ruled over by a father who was not seen as part of it. The Christian insistence on exogamy and monogamy, and the control which the Church exercised over marriage, combined with an identification of a particular family with a particular piece of land, began to make the family not only an economic unit but also a location for affection and sentiment. The 'child-oriented family', argues Jack Goody, was 'intrinsic to the religious ideology of the Christian Church from a very early period'.[77] In the fourteenth and fifteenth centuries, wracked by plague and taxes, people began to look to the family as a refuge against a hostile external world. And children were at the centre of these families. Thomas Aquinas wondered whether parents loved children more than children loved parents, and concluded that they did. Such love, thought the Archbishop of Florence in the mid-fifteenth century, was leading to a situation where parents 'because of disordered love for their children, earn damnation! Oh how many are they, who serve their children like idols!'[78]

Secondly, Shahar is not entirely immune from the wish to point up the modernity of medieval people, and may have missed aspects in which they differed from us in most fundamental ways. A study of childhood in the German middle ages from 1100 to 1350 argues that there was indeed a concept of childhood in the middle ages, but that it differed fundamentally from anything we instinctively think. Childhood, in this perspective, was important not in itself but for what observation of childish traits (courage, modesty, and so on) might tell you about the adult to be. How you treated the child would have little effect on its adult future (the very opposite of most twenty-first-century thinking). The child was a person lacking in adult attributes, marked by her or his deficiencies.[79]

The third caveat is that we need to remind ourselves, as Shahar does, that there are many things we do not know; she acknowledges, for example, that 'there is almost no direct evidence on small children from the peasantry',[80] who comprised the vast majority of society. Scholars have been ingenious in trying to surmount this problem. Barbara Hanawalt has used coroners' records from London, Oxford, Bedfordshire and Northamptonshire, and has been able, from the pattern of accidents, to identify four stages in childhood. In the first year of life the most common accident was for the baby to be burned in its cradle, perhaps indicating that children were left alone. Children aged two were the most prone to have accidents, falling into wells and ponds, and scalding themselves, boys generally suffering accidents outside the house, girls inside. In the third stage, from age four to seven, children spent more time with their parents, but the accidents they suffered suggest that play was their chief occupation. From ages eight to twelve, children were more likely to be independent from adults, starting work. Studies of miracles in which children were cured from illnesses or healed after accidents reach similar conclusions, together with a marked gender difference. Sixty per cent of the 134 children whose accidents (over half of them near-drowning) are recounted in records from the shrines of English saints and martyrs were boys. Even more telling with respect to gender, over Europe as a whole, boys were much more likely than girls to be taken to shrines for cures from birth problems or illnesses.

Hanawalt's records 'do not indicate one way or another a sentimental attachment to the state of childhood', but Gordon feels able to conclude that 'medieval youngsters, like their modern counterparts, were inquisitive, adventurous, inexperienced, and often poorly supervised', and further that 'parents loved their offspring dearly and often exhibited grief, guilt, or remorse over the accident'. Finucane also finds plenty of evidence of parental, particularly maternal, anguish and grief, combined with a recognition of the 'childishness' of children; but this has to be taken in conjunction with what appears to be a greater concern for boys than girls.[81]

Local studies, too, can sometimes reveal details of child care. In Montaillou, a village in the French Pyrenees, there is evidence, from the late thirteenth and early fourteenth centuries, of care for children, of enjoyment of their company, and of grief if they died. One woman described how her brother's baby was dying, and 'he sent for me when I was going to the woods to gather firewood, so that I could hold the dying child in my arms. So I did hold it from morning until evening, when it died.' All this, claims Le Roy Ladurie, 'shows that there was not such an enormous gap, as has sometimes been claimed, between our attitude to children and the attitude of the people in fourteenth-century Montaillou and upper Ariège'.[82] Le Roy Ladurie confirms that children were generally with their parents until the age of twelve or soon after, sometimes helping with work, often used as messengers. But at twelve boys began to keep sheep, either their father's or someone else's, and girls were soon preparing for marriage.[83] Evidence of this kind is helping historians to make tentative generalisations about medieval childhood amongst the mass of the population.

In conclusion, it is clear that Ariès's rash assertion that 'in medieval society the idea of childhood did not exist' cannot be sustained. Nor would such a claim be true of the ancient world. The impact of Christianity meant that the middle ages accorded more importance to young children than had the ancient world, but the evidence is overwhelming that in both periods childhood was recognised as a separate stage of human existence. Moreover, the rather smaller body of evidence on actual child-rearing indicates a concern for even very young children, and provides examples of close and loving relationships, especially between mothers and children. Infanticide undoubtedly existed, but again the impact of Christianity had been to make it unmistakably a crime; and attempts to measure its extent are beset with difficulties in these as in all periods.[84] The practice of abandonment has left us with more evidence than infanticide, but, closely studied, it is not so obviously an indication of a lack of parental feeling as de Mause claimed.

The problem which remains is that most medieval scholars have been too content to score an easy goal by disproving Ariès in his least defensible mode. They have avoided the more complex task of identifying the contradictions and changes over time and place in medieval thought and practice. Ariès was alert to those issues, even if unsystematic in dealing with them.

Notes

1 L. de Mause (ed.), *The History of Childhood* (1974; London, 1976), p. 51.

2 See, e.g., D. Engels, 'The problem of female infanticide in the Greco-Roman world', *Classical Philology*, 75 (1980), 112–20; W.V. Harris, 'The theoretical possibility of extensive infanticide in the Graeco-Roman world', *Classical Quarterly*, 32 (1982), 114–16.

3 De Mause, *History of Childhood*, pp. 25–9.

4 J. Boswell, *The Kindness of Strangers: The Abandonment of Children in Western Europe from Late Antiquity to the Renaissance* (1988; London, 1989), p. 135; for an authoritative survey of the evidence, see W.V. Harris, 'Child-exposure in the Roman Empire', *Journal of Roman Studies*, LXXXIV (1994), 1–22.

5 Boswell, *Kindness of Strangers*, pp. 65–71, 111–14.

6 S. Dixon, *The Roman Family* (Baltimore and London, 1992), p. 112.

7 Boswell, *Kindness of Strangers*, pp. 116–31; for a more cautious assessment of alumni and of exposed children in general, see B. Rawson, 'Children in the Roman *familia*', in B. Rawson (ed.), *The Family in Ancient Rome: New Perspectives* (London, 1986), pp. 173–86, 196.

8 K.R. Bradley, 'Wet-nursing at Rome: a study in social relations', in Rawson, *Family in Ancient Rome*, pp. 210–13.

9 V. Fildes, *Wet Nursing: A History from Antiquity to the Present* (Oxford, 1988), pp. 1–25.

10 Boswell, *Kindness of Strangers*, pp. 66–7, 81–5, 88.

11 M. Golden, *Children and Childhood in Classical Athens* (Baltimore and London, 1990), pp. 87–9.

12 B. Rawson, 'Adult–child relationships in Roman society', in B. Rawson (ed.), *Marriage, Divorce, and Children in Ancient Rome* (Canberra and Oxford, 1991), p. 7; Dixon, *Roman Family*, p. 130.

13 The sarcophagus is displayed in the Museo Nazionale at Agrigento. For a full consideration of the representation of children in the ancient world, see B. Rawson, *Children and Childhood in Roman Italy* (Oxford, 2003), pp. 17–92.

14 See e.g. Bradley, 'Wet-nursing at Rome', pp. 201–29.

15 R.B. Lyman, 'Barbarism and religion: late Roman and early medieval childhood', in de Mause, *History of Childhood*, p. 77.

16 Dixon, *Roman Family*, p. 104; Golden, *Children and Childhood in Classical Athens*, pp. 12–16; T. Wiedemann, *Adults and Children in the Roman Empire* (London, 1989), pp. 32–4.

17 Wiedemann, *Adults and Children*, p. 180; S. Shahar, *Childhood in the Middle Ages* (London, 1990), p. 17.

18 Boswell, *Kindness of Strangers*, pp. 27–8.

19 R. Saller, 'Corporal punishment, authority, and obedience in the Roman household', in Rawson, *Marriage, Divorce, and Children*, pp. 144–65.

20 Wiedemann, *Adults and Children*, pp. 28–30.

21 Boswell, *Kindness of Strangers*, pp. 28–36.

22 W.K. Lacey, '*Patria potestas*', in Rawson, *Family in Ancient Rome*, pp. 121–44, quoting p. 123.

23 Aristotle, *Politics and the Athenian Constitution* (London: Everyman Edition, 1959), p. 23.

24 R. Saller, '*Patria potestas* and the stereotype of the Roman family', *Continuity and Change*, 1 (1986–7), 8–9.

25 Ibid., 7–22; see also E. Eyben, 'Fathers and sons', in Rawson, *Marriage, Divorce, and Children*, pp. 114–43.

26 Dixon, *Roman Family*, p. 100.

27 Wiedemann, *Adults and Children*, pp. 32–43, quoting p. 40.

28 Ibid., pp. 176–85, quoting p. 185.

29 Golden, *Children and Childhood in Classical Athens*, pp. 4–5; cf. Wiedemann, *Adults and Children*, p. 19.

30 Wiedemann, *Adults and Children*, pp. 24, 41–2.

31 Dixon, *Roman Family*, pp. 104–5; Wiedemann, *Adults and Children*, passim.

32 Wiedemann, *Adults and Children*, p. 204.

33 Golden, *Children and Childhood in Classical Athens*, pp. 169–80.

34 Dixon, *Roman Family*, p. 103; S. Dixon, 'The sentimental ideal of the Roman family', in Rawson, *Marriage, Divorce, and Children*, pp. 99–113.

35 Rawson, 'Adult–child relationships in Roman society', pp. 29–30; Rawson, *Children and Childhood in Roman Italy*, pp. 4–9.

36 Wiedemann, *Adults and Children*; Lyman, 'Barbarism and religion', pp. 76–7.

37 Wiedemann, *Adults and Children*, pp. 188–93.

38 Ibid., p. 37.

39 Boswell, *Kindness of Strangers*, p. 163, n. 86; Lyman, 'Barbarism and religion', p. 90.

40 Boswell, *Kindness of Strangers*, pp. 162–79.

41 Deut. 5:16; Matt. 15:4; Mark 7:10; Eph. 6:1–2.

42 Proverbs 13:24.

43 Mark 10:14–15; cf. Luke 18:16–17.

44 Matt. 18:10.

45 Eph. 6:4; 2 Cor. 12:14.

46 Matt. 10:34–7; Luke 18:29–30; Mark 3:31–5.

47 Wiedemann, *Adults and Children*, pp. 102–6; J. Sommerville, *The Rise and Fall of Childhood* (Beverly Hills, London, New Delhi, 1982), pp. 52–6; Lyman, 'Barbarism and religion', pp. 88–90; Saint Augustine, *Confessions*, ed. H. Chadwick (Oxford, 1991), pp. 28–34.

48 P. Ariès, *Centuries of Childhood* (London, 1962), p. 125.

49 Shahar, *Childhood in the Middle Ages*, p. 1.

50 Ariès, *Centuries of Childhood*, p. 125.

51 Ibid., pp. 31–41, 327–52; Andrew Martindale, 'The child in the picture: a medieval perspective', in D. Wood (ed.), *The Church and Childhood* (Oxford, 1994), p. 197.

52 I.H. Forsyth, 'Children in early medieval art: ninth through twelfth centuries', *Journal of Psychohistory*, 4 (1976), 31–70.

53 L. Steinberg, *The Sexuality of Christ in Renaissance Art and in Modern Oblivion* (New York, 1983).

54 L.A. Pollock, *Forgotten Children: Parent–Child Relations from 1500 to 1900* (Cambridge, 1983), quoting p. 47; see also Shahar, *Childhood in the Middle Ages*, p. 95.

55 E. Sears, *The Ages of Man: Medieval Interpretations of the Life Cycle* (Princeton, 1986); J.A. Burrow, *The Ages of Man: A Study in Medieval Writing and Thought* (Oxford, 1986).

56 Ariès, *Centuries of Childhood*, p. 21; Sears, *Ages*, Figures 50, 56, 65–7, 70, 71, 78.

57 Ariès, *Centuries of Childhood*, pp. 13–30, quoting p. 20.

58 Quoted in S. Wilson, 'The myth of motherhood a myth: the historical view of European child-rearing', *Social History*, 9 (1984), 193.

59 Shahar, *Childhood in the Middle Ages*, pp. 2, 3, 40–1, 84.

60 Ibid., pp. 96, 85, 99. See also M.M. McLaughlin, 'Survivors and surrogates: children and parents from the ninth to the thirteenth centuries', in de Mause, *History of Childhood*, pp. 112–19.

61 L. Demaitre, 'The idea of childhood and childcare in medical writings of the Middle Ages', *Journal of Psychohistory*, 4 (1977), pp. 461–90.

62 J. Swanson, 'Childhood and childrearing in *ad status* sermons by later thirteenth century friars', *Journal of Medieval History*, 16 (1990), pp. 309–31, quoting p. 310; J. Kroll, 'The concept of childhood in the middle ages', *Journal of the History of the Behavioral Sciences*, 13 (1977), p. 390.

63 Shahar, *Childhood in the Middle Ages*, p. 102.

64 Ibid., p. 174.

65 Ibid., pp. 24–5.

66 Ariès, *Centuries of Childhood*, p. 150.

67 Ibid., pp. 186–8, 278–9, 353–5, 357, 383; see also Ariès, 'Préface à la nouvelle édition', *L'enfant et la vie familiale sous l'ancien régime* (Paris, 1973), pp. iii, vi–ix.

68 N.Z. Davis, 'The reasons of misrule: youth groups and charivaris in sixteenth-century France', *Past and Present*, 50 (1971), pp. 41–75; Shahar, *Childhood in the Middle Ages*, pp. 232–3.

69 Ariès, *Centuries of Childhood*, e.g. pp. 229–30.

70 Shahar, *Childhood in the Middle Ages*, pp. 162–224; see also, N. Orme, *From Childhood to Chivalry: The Education of the English Kings and Aristocracy 1066–1530* (London, 1984).

71 Shahar, *Childhood in the Middle Ages*, pp. 2, 102, 112. B.A. Hanawalt, *Growing Up in Medieval London: The Experience of Childhood in History* (Oxford, 1993), p. 67. But see also B.A. Hanawalt, *The Ties That Bound: Peasant Families in Medieval England* (New York, 1986), p. 44 for the suggestion that there was greater privacy in the medieval house than many scholars imply, and that there was also 'almost an obsession' with securing privacy.

72 Shahar, *Childhood in the Middle Ages*, pp. 179–82; Hanawalt, *Growing Up in Medieval London*, pp. 79–80.

73 Shahar, *Childhood in the Middle Ages*, pp. 9–16, quoting p. 15; Burrow, *Ages of Man*, pp. 95–123; cf. Lyman, 'Religion and barbarism', pp. 79–80.

74 Shahar, *Childhood in the Middle Ages*, pp. 17–20, 101; N. Orme, *Medieval Children* (New Haven and London, 2001), quoting p. 274.

75 Shahar, *Childhood in the Middle Ages*, pp. 13–14, 116; McLaughlin, 'Survivors and surrogates', pp. 101–82.

76 For an attempt to tease out the attitudes to and experience of childhood in
    a particular medieval society, see S. Crawford, *Childhood in Anglo-Saxon
    England* (Stroud, 1999). For the argument that there was no discontinuity
    between medieval and early modern childhood, see L. Haas, *The Renaisssance
    Man and His Children: Childbirth and Early Childhood in Florence
    1300–1600* (Basingstoke, 1998), pp. 8–9, 180.

77 J. Goody, *The Development of the Family and Marriage in Europe*
    (Cambridge, 1983), p. 153; D. Herlihy, *Medieval Households* (Cambridge,
    Mass. and London, 1985), and 'Family', *American Historical Review*, 96
    (1991), pp. 1–16.

78 Herlihy, 'Family', pp. 11–15.

79 J.A. Schultz, *The Knowledge of Childhood in the German Middle Ages,
    1100–1350* (Philadelphia, 1995).

80 Shahar, *Childhood in the Middle Ages*, p. 108.

81 B.A. Hanawalt, 'Childrearing among the lower classes of late medieval
    England', *Journal of Interdisciplinary History*, VIII (1977–8), pp. 1–22;
    E.C. Gordon, 'Accidents among medieval children as seen from the miracles of
    six English saints and martyrs', *Medical History*, 35 (1991), pp. 145–63;
    R.C. Finucane, *The Rescue of the Innocents: Endangered Children in
    Medieval Miracles* (Basingstoke, 1997), esp. pp. 9–10, 151–63. See also
    Shahar, *Childhood in the Middle Ages*, pp. 139–44.

82 E. Le Roy Ladurie, *Montaillou: Cathars and Catholics in a French Village
    1294–1324* (Harmondsworth, 1980), pp. 210–13, quoting p. 212.

83 Ibid., pp. 190, 215–16.

84 E. Coleman, 'L'infanticide dans le Haut Moyen Age', *Annales, ESC*, 29
    (1974), pp. 315–35; R.C. Trexler, 'Infanticide in Florence: new sources and
    first results', and B.A. Kellum, 'Infanticide in England in the Later Middle
    Ages', *History of Childhood Quarterly*, I (1973), pp. 98–116, 367–88; R.H.
    Helmholz, 'Infanticide in the Province of Canterbury during the fifteenth
    century', *History of Childhood Quarterly*, II (1974–5), pp. 379–90.

CHAPTER 3

The development of a middle-class ideology of childhood, 1500–1900

By the middle of the nineteenth century an ideology of childhood had become a powerful force in middle-class Europe and North America. Its precepts were by no means fully integrated into middle-class practices in child-rearing, and as a set of beliefs it was not without powerful rivals. But it operated as an ideal across wide stretches of western culture. At the heart of this ideology lay a firm commitment to the view that children should be reared in families, a conviction that the way childhood was spent was crucial in determining the kind of adult that the child would become, and an increasing awareness that childhood had rights and privileges of its own.

The development of this set of beliefs did not proceed smoothly along a single track with a destination clearly in view. What holds the period together is a heightened sense of the importance of childhood which manifested itself in a variety of ways: in a belief in the importance of early education; in a concern for the salvation of the child's soul; in a growing interest in the way children learn; and in a sense that children were messengers of God, and that childhood was therefore the best time of life. Each of these can be linked to major movements in European and American history, the Renaissance, the Reformation and Counter-Reformation, the Enlightenment and Romanticism; and they are associated, too, with individuals whose fame stretches beyond their writings about childhood: Erasmus, Locke, Rousseau and Wordsworth.

Humanism

Our starting point is the Renaissance and in particular fifteenth-century Florence; in its culture children held a 'special and exalted place'.[1] They were thought to hold the key to the future of the state, and their proper upbringing was crucial to that future. But more than this, the family was itself a prototype of the state, and properly-ordered and harmonious relationships within it would themselves be manifested in similar virtues in the state. The state was dominated by men, and it followed from this that fathers had a crucial role to play in the family. Here we can see the first break with medieval thought and practice where, as we have seen, mothers were thought to have primary if not exclusive responsibility for the first seven years of life. The father–child relationship vied with, if it did not replace, the mother–child relationship as the most intense of all relationships. 'Who would believe', asked Alberti in a widely-known book on the family, 'except by the experience of his own feelings, how great and intense is the love of a father toward his children?' A father's responsibility, and his authority, were unlimited:

He ought . . . to watch over and guard the family from outsiders, to check over and consider the whole company, to examine the practices of every member, inside and outside the house, and to correct and improve every bad habit. He ought preferably to use reasonable rather than indignant words, authority rather than power . . . He ought in every thought always to put first the peace and the tranquillity of his entire family. This should be the kind of goal toward which he, using his intelligence and experience, guides the whole family with virtue and honor.[2]

It was the father, in advice books of this kind, who should take responsibility for choosing and hiring a wet-nurse if the preferred option of maternal breastfeeding was not followed – and there is evidence that they did do this. Fathers should watch over their children, thoughtfully interpreting 'every little action, word, and gesture' so as to understand the nature and probable future destiny of their child, but they should also enjoy the company of the child who 'laughs very happily and changes a thousand times per hour'.[3]

The second change from medieval advice was the stress on early learning, and again it was fathers who had the primary role, teaching children their letters soon after weaning, with liberal use of fruits and cookies both to form letters and as a reward – an idea probably taken from Horace – and maintaining their authority 'by love'. Corporal punishment might be necessary, but it was de-emphasised as the fifteenth century progressed.[4]

Historians are rightly wary of assuming that advice was put into practice; we might do better to assume that the advice was necessary only because practice was to the contrary. Why otherwise would the advice books warn against adults teaching a child to put its thumb between its two fingers and point it at its mother, amidst adult laughter?[5] There are, however, two reasons for taking seriously these Florentine advice books. First, there is good evidence that they were read and approved within the great merchant families, and second, as we have seen, they mark a departure in significant respects from medieval advice books. A new ideal of child-rearing was being formulated, the model for it being derived from classical culture.[6]

The new humanist approach to childhood was not confined to Florence or Italy. It found its most famous representative north of the Alps in the Dutchman, Desiderius Erasmus. Italian humanist thought was well known in Paris and elsewhere in northern Europe at the turn of the fifteenth century, and Erasmus himself spent the years 1506 to 1509 in Italy. In the 1520s he wrote a series of books and pamphlets which brought together his lifelong interest in upbringing and education. Their common characteristic was that they were founded on ancient authorities, interlaced, though to a much lesser extent, with Italian humanist writings, and that they drew on his own experience.

Erasmus placed considerable emphasis on early education, directly attacking those who, 'out of a false spirit of tenderness and compassion', allow children 'to be pampered by their dear mothers and spoiled by nurses'. A child ought 'to imbibe, as it were, with the milk that he suckles, the nectar of education', for 'he will most certainly turn out to be an unproductive brute unless at once and without delay he is subjected to a process of intensive instruction'. It was a much greater crime, he claimed, to neglect early education than to commit infanticide.[7] Erasmus made great play with the time and money people spent on training their dogs or horses compared with the neglect of their children. And he believed that nature had implanted in children the seeds of a desire for knowledge, and a power of memory greater than at any other age. But they needed to be shaped: 'The child that nature has given you is nothing but a shapeless lump, but the material is still pliable, capable of assuming any form, and you must so mould it that it takes on the best possible character. If you are negligent, you will rear an animal; but if you apply yourself, you will fashion, if I may use such a bold term, a godlike creature.'[8] Like many other writers, Erasmus compared a child to wax, to be moulded while it is soft. Anselm in the twelfth century had also used the wax image, but he had described young children as like wax which was too nearly liquid to mould into shape; one had to wait until the time of *adolescentia*.[9]

The 'you' whom Erasmus addressed was a father. 'To be a true father', he wrote, 'you must take absolute control of your son's entire being.' A mother had a nurturing role, but a father had to be responsible for that part of a boy's 'character which distinguishes him from the animals and comes closest to reflecting the divine'.[10] It is true that in other writings Erasmus addressed parents when he was referring to educational responsibilities, and that Christian humanists did in general accord some role to the mother in education, but the overriding responsibility lay with the father, particularly, as in these passages, where the child was a son; and it was on the education of sons that Erasmus concentrated, leaving it unclear how far he thought daughters should share in the education he advocated.[11]

The method of teaching should be one in which the child learned by encouragement and in which there was an admixture of play. As early as 1497 he had written that 'a constant element of enjoyment must be mingled with our studies so that we think of learning as a game rather than a form of drudgery, for no activity can be continued for long if it does not to some extent afford pleasure to the participant'. A good example was an English father who, noting his son's liking for archery, 'had a beautiful set of bow and arrows made, decorated all over with the letters of the alphabet', and with the Greek and Latin alphabets as the target. If the boy hit the target and pronounced the letter, he might be rewarded with a cherry, or a competition might be set up with other boys. 'It was by means of this stratagem that the boy in question learnt in a few days of fun and play to identify and pronounce his letters – something which the majority of teachers, with all their beatings, threatenings, and insults, could scarcely have accomplished in three years.'[12] Erasmus had a horror of beating, partly built on his own experience, and placed a corresponding emphasis on the high importance of the teaching profession – for he recognised that fathers could hardly be expected to be responsible for the entire education of their offspring. 'To be a schoolmaster', he wrote, 'is an office second in importance to a king.' The reality was far different: 'Schools', he lamented, 'have become torture-chambers; you hear nothing but the thudding of the stick, the swishing of the rod, howling and moaning, and shouts of brutal abuse.'[13]

The curriculum which Erasmus suggested was built around and largely confined to the classics, just as his own approach to education was derived from classical authorities, for example from Plutarch's tract *On the Education of Children* and from the writings of Quintilian, who in the first century AD had stressed the importance of starting education early, building on the child's natural wish to learn, and who had been unusual in the ancient world in his opposition to corporal punishment.[14]

Erasmus did not confine himself to the more formal aspects of child-rearing and schooling. He also wrote, and it was the piece which received the widest circulation of all his writings, a guide to manners for children, addressed to the eleven-year-old Henry of Burgundy, but meant to set out rules for all boys. Erasmus recommended modesty and decorum in everything a boy did, giving advice on body language, sneezing, spitting, urinating, table manners, and on interactions with others. With its stress on 'training in good manners right from the very earliest years', the tract is consonant with Erasmus's belief in the importance of a balanced education from an early age, and a clue to the kinds of behaviour which would be set up as a model for children for some centuries – for the book remained popular in the nineteenth century.[15]

Erasmus may be taken as the voice of humanism, but it was a humanism inseparable from Christianity. Erasmus himself was caught up in the struggles of the Reformation, holding on with some difficulty to the Catholic Church. He was in no doubt, as he expressed it in his tract on manners, that the most important part of 'fashioning the young' was 'implanting the seeds of piety in the tender heart'. God gave us 'children to be raised in the ways of religion', and to neglect that was 'more than simply a venial sin'.[16] Erasmus, however, was at pains to set a distance between his own beliefs and those which put an emphasis on original sin. Although acknowledging that we were born with 'a disposition to evil', he thought this was often much exaggerated, and that it was mainly adults 'who corrupt young minds with evil before we expose them to the good'. As another humanist, John Earle, wrote in 1628, 'A child is a man in small letter, yet the best copy of Adam before he tasted of Eve or the apple . . . His soul is yet a white paper unscribbled with observations of the world . . . he knows no evil.' Good habits, learned early, would conduce to piety.[17]

Protestantism

Erasmus wrote in Latin, but his works were quickly translated into every main European language, and were enormously influential amongst both Catholics and Protestants. Protestants in particular looked to the Bible more than to the classical authorities who were Erasmus's main inspiration, but the conclusions they reached about child-rearing were very similar, and drew on Erasmus's authority. One historian has recently concluded that 'in regard to the family, the biblicism of Erasmus led to many of the same conclusions which Protestant biblicism would derive, and the common classical sources of humanists and protestants produced common assumptions and ideals'.[18]

True as this is as a point about origins and influences, it nevertheless fails to give due weight to the significance of the 'spiritualization of the household' within Protestantism. It was Christopher Hill who first drew attention to this process, and he perhaps underestimated the humanist input to it. But no one doubts that he was identifying a new emphasis in family relationships, and one which had particular resonance within Protestantism. At the heart of this was a belief in the family as a microcosm of the church and the state, both in the sense that in its internal government it should mirror those larger institutions, and in the sense that the family should be a nursery of both church and state, training the young for service.[19] As Justus Menius put it, 'The diligent rearing of children is the greatest service to the world, both in spiritual and temporal affairs, both for the present life and for posterity.'[20] The family was the stem organisation for all other organisations, and on its good government much depended. Above all, in actively Protestant circles, the family should be a community of worshippers, with family prayers and Bible readings built into the structure of the daily round.

It went almost without saying that fathers headed these families: 'Every man's a king in his own house.'[21] Scholars differ in the emphasis they give to this, some seeing in the ideal Protestant family a patriarchal tyranny, others pointing to passages in advice books, and even more reports of actual family life, which suggest a degree of companionship and joint rule between husband and wife.[22] What no one could doubt was that the children's position was a subordinate one. Marriage was now praised, most famously by Luther, as a state superior to celibacy, and one of its prime purposes was procreation, but the child was a source of anxiety as well as joy. According to the writers of advice books, the temptation to be avoided was over-indulgence of the child. As Conrad Sam wrote about Ulm's lords and Junkers:

As soon as the child can move about, one throws a ragged frock on him and treats everything he does in the same [unjudgmental] way. Soon there are outbursts and tantrums, but these only delight the old, since they come from a dear little son who can do no wrong. Where one sows thorns and thistles in this way, how can anything other than weeds be expected to grow?

Too many parents, it was claimed, thought childhood 'only a time for fun, joy, and amusement'.[23] There were much more serious matters at stake, not only the future good order of the church and state when the children grew up, but more immediately the condition of the child's soul. Success would bring its rewards to the dutiful parent: 'Is there anything on earth more precious, friendly, and lovable', wrote a mid-sixteenth-century reformer, 'than a pious, disciplined, obedient, and teachable child?'[24] There we have it, the model child of the Protestant Reformation.

What was the way to produce such a paragon? Training by parents from an early age in good habits. The analogies and metaphors which pervade the books are not ones of natural growth, but of horticulture, of preparing good soil, of rooting out weeds, of training young shoots in the direction you want them to go; or they are of the instilling of obedience into puppies or colts. Left to themselves, children will turn out bad. Their wills must be broken. Biblical authority could be found in Proverbs 22:15: 'Foolishness is tied in the heart of a child, but the rod of discipline shall drive it away.' So far as possible this training should be done rationally and calmly, but there might be occasion for inflicting corporal punishment; if so, it must not be too severe, and it must not be administered in anger.[25] Frequently it seemed to affect the father as much as the children. Thomas Cawton, a minister in London and then in Rotterdam, 'was often so moved with compassion, his fatherly bowels did so yearn over them, that the tears would trickle apace from his eies when he was correcting them: nothing ever wrought upon me like this sight, which did plainly convince his Children of his unwillingness to chastise, but that he was forced to it'.[26]

Some of this concern stemmed from a belief in original sin, a matter which, as we have seen, Erasmus tended to downplay. But in the Protestant literature it was marked. 'What is a child, or to be a child?' asked Thomas Becon in 1550, only to reply, 'A child in Scripture is a wicked man, as he that is ignorant and not exercised in godliness.' Becon went on to produce a catechism for his five-year-old son which ran to 271 folio pages.[27] A Nuremberg catechism, translated under Cranmer's authority in England, asserted that even unborn babies in the womb had 'evil lusts and appetites'.[28] A German sermon of the 1520s argued that

just as a cat craves mice, a fox chickens, and a wolf cub sheep, so infant humans are inclined in their hearts to adultery, fornication, impure desires, lewdness, idol worship, belief in magic, hostility, quarreling, passion, anger, strife, dissension, factiousness, hatred, murder, drunkenness, gluttony, and more.[29]

What could a concerned parent do, why indeed would anyone have children? Infant baptism now offered no sure route to salvation as it did amongst Catholics. Faith alone could save. Some argued that God might 'infuse the gift of faith into the soul of a child',[30] but the concerned Protestant parent was naturally anxious to bring children as early as possible to a conscious awareness of the necessity of salvation. John Robinson, the pastor for the Pilgrim Fathers, wrote that

surely there is in all children . . . a stubborness, and stoutness of mind arising from natural pride, which must, in the first place, be broken and beaten down; that so the foundation of their education being laid in humility and tractableness, other virtues may, in their time, be built thereon. For the beating, and keeping down of this stubborness parents must provide carefully . . . that the children's wills and wilfulness be restrained and repressed, and that, in time.[31]

Printed catechisms, question and answer sessions between parent and child, were the ideal way to do this, though they might equally be used by church ministers. They were produced in great numbers, over 350 in England alone between 1549 and 1646.[32] It was impossible to start too early. It was an 'idle concept', insisted Thomas Gataker, that 'Religion and Godlinesse is not for children', he himself producing a catechism for children 'that are not past the breast yet'.[33] In some, though not all, commentary, only a father could be relied upon to undertake this religious instruction, mothers being castigated as too unstable and fanciful.[34] Thus Thomas Cawton 'took a great deal of pains to instruct and catechise [his children], to bring them up in the nurture and admonition of the Lord'.[35]

In their emphasis on original sin the Protestant conduct books were at some distance from Erasmus; they were much closer to him in their belief in the importance of good manners. Convinced that outward body language revealed inward thoughts and emotions, they laid great stress on demeanour and behaviour. William Gouge's seventeenth-century 'Prayer for a Childe to Use' urged children not only to obey their parents but also to show them reverence,

in refraining much speach before them, in patient hearkening to them, in giving reverend titles to them, and humble and ready answers, without pride or stoutnesse . . . To my reverend speech, let my dutifull carriage towards my Parents be answerable, by hasting to meete them when they are comming to me, by rising up to them, by standing before them, by yeelding all due obeisance to them, giving place to them, and by asking them blessing: Avoiding all unmannerly rudenesse, disdainfull statelinesse, toyish wantonnesse, over-much boldnesse, and high-mindednesse.

Gouge had doubtless witnessed much 'unmannerly rudenesse' and so on, but he held up a quite different standard for a Christian child.[36]

If the godly household was the foundation block of good order in church and state, the school built on that. And although Puritans valued learning only so far as it conduced towards godliness, they accepted with little question the classical curriculum of the humanists.[37] They made their distinctive mark in three ways. The first was in the founding of new schools or in charitable donations for education. Thus the 1607 statutes of Wakefield grammar school state in their preamble that 'For as much as this school is principally ordained a Seminarie for bringing up of Christian Children to become in time Ambassadors of Reconciliation from God to his Church, and generally is intended a School of Christian instruction for vertue, and manners therein to be learned of all the Scholars thereof . . .' The second was in the choice of schoolmasters. They should be, wrote Thomas Becon, 'men of gravity, wisdom, knowledge, learning, of an honest and godly conversation, of an approved life, of uncorrupt manners, diligent and painful in their office, favourers of true and pure religion, earnest lovers of Gods word, haters of idolatry and superstition . . .' William Gouge thought that lack of piety was reason enough to dismiss a teacher.[38] Thirdly, in those families where schooling beyond an elementary level became a norm, a sharp wedge was driven between the experience of boys and that of girls: for the schools were for boys only, and inculcated a version of masculinity in which the stress was on discipline and control of the emotions; girls, by contrast, received a less demanding form of education at home, with the emphasis on modesty and obedience.[39]

The conduct books, catechisms and school ordinances set out an ideal of child-rearing in the Protestant mode. Their sheer quantity, associated of course with the spread of print, makes it implausible that they existed purely in the realm of ideals. People bought these books, and at least at some level of their being, used them as a model. It is, however, difficult to know how far the ideal became reality. Even for the literate and well-to-do with whom we are concerned in this chapter, the sources are patchy; they consist of written documents, diaries, autobiographies, letters and wills; and of the remnants of the material culture of the age, tombstones, toys, clothes and pictures. From these sources historians have endeavoured to reconstruct the reality of childhood in the sixteenth and seventeenth centuries in the Protestant heartlands of Northern Europe and North America.

We may ask first how a birth was greeted. The answer seems to be with anxiety, and then if all went well, with thanksgiving. In the Dutch Republic, 'with the birth of a child, the happy family entered a sort of state of civic grace'. Signs were posted on the door, the father donned a paternity bonnet, and the household was exempt from certain taxes and duties. Parties and feasts marked the early stages of the child's life.[40] The birth was indeed a semi-public event, female relatives, neighbours and friends all being present.[41] Although conduct books provided a multiplicity of ways of predicting the sex of a child, and although Lady Mordaunt may not have been alone in her thoughts when she entered in her diary when pregnant in the 1650s, 'if it be thy blessed will let it be a boy', there are no signs of outright rejection of a baby if it turned out to be of the wrong sex.[42]

Both humanist and Protestant writings firmly advocated breastfeeding, and in society as a whole it was undoubtedly the norm. If there were exceptions they were to be found mainly amongst the rich, but there are numerous records of mothers in this group who did breastfeed and took pride in it. Swaddling was advocated, and almost certainly practised, though there is no record of it among the early American colonists.[43] The rationale was that it would help the bones to set straight, and protect a baby from the cold. It does not seem to have been used for more than a few months.[44]

It was of course not unlikely that a baby or child would die, perhaps between one-fifth and one-quarter of all children dying before they reached the age of ten.[45] How did parents cope with this possibility or eventuality? A seventeenth-century Dutch print shows the gruesome figure of death dragging off a crib with a swaddled baby inside while the mother sleeps; it must have been a picture to haunt the dreams of parents.[46] The consensus of recent opinion is that the emotional withdrawal from young babies in conditions of high mortality posited by Stone finds no support from the primary evidence. Parents grieved. They tried to protect themselves by seeing it as the will of God, and by persuading themselves that their offspring had gone to a better place, but their grief is unmistakable. We can see it most poignantly in Luther, two of whose six children died during his lifetime, Elizabeth at eight months and Magdalene at the age of thirteen. Elizabeth's death left Luther 'exquisitely sick, my heart rendered soft and weak; never had I thought that a father's heart could be so broken for his children's sake'. When Magdalene died, Luther and his wife knew that she was now 'free of the flesh, the world, the Turk, and the Devil', but, as he wrote to a friend, 'The force of our natural love is so great that we are unable to do this without crying and grieving in our hearts . . . The features, the words, and the movement of our living and dying daughter, who was so very obedient and respectful, remain engraved in our hearts; even the death of Christ . . . is unable to take all this away as it should'.[47] Or consider the response of the Essex clergyman, Ralph Josselin to the illness and death of his eight-year-old daughter Mary:

my little Mary, very weake, wee feared shee was drawing on, feare came on my heart very much, but shee is not mine, but the Lords, and shee is not too good for her father, shee was tender of her mother, thankefull, mindefull of god, in her extremity, shee would cry out, poore I, poore I . . . it was a pretious child, a bundle of myrrhe, a bundle of sweetnes, shee was a child of ten thousand, full of wisedome, woman-like gravity, knowledge, sweet expressions of god, apt in her learning, tender hearted and loving, an obedient child to us. It was free from the rudenesse of litle children, it was to us as a boxe of sweet ointment, which now its broken smells more deliciously then it did before, Lord I rejoyce I had such a present for thee . . . [48]

But beneath this determination to submit to the will of the Lord, this will to accept, lay a sorrow and a sense of loss which burns in Josselin's tortured prose.

Both Luther and Josselin had clearly enjoyed the company of their children. And there are plenty of expressions of this in happier circumstances than reminiscence on the death of the child. In seeking to explain the profusion of depictions of children in the art and culture of the Dutch Republic, Simon Schama finds the key in 'the polarity between the ludic and the didactic, between play and learning, between liberty and obedience, between independence and safety', and suggests that, whatever the apparent moral message of much Dutch art, it is often and increasingly overborne by a delight in children. Schama even suggests that 'as a culture the Dutch were genuinely besotted with the children'. They painted them, in hundreds of family groupings, and often on their own, the personality of the individual child shining through. In Caesar van Everdingen's portrait of a *Child Holding An Apple* (Plate 1) a moral lesson is inscribed: the boy has a pet bird on his left index finger and it seems to have been feeding on the apple in his right hand; the ability to tame and teach a bird was a metaphor for child-rearing, for children, too, needed to be tamed and taught. But neither these symbols, nor the curious tiled floor and classical pedestal in a rural setting, nor the elaborate clothing in which the boy has been dressed for the occasion, detract from the artist's ability to capture the personality of a particular boy.[49] Dutch paintings constantly depicted children at play, perhaps to make a moralising point about the folly of the world's ways, but perhaps also because they simply delighted in the play. And moralists defended play, van Beverwijck writing in 1643 that 'children should not be kept on too tight a rein, but allowed to exercise their childishness . . . Let them freely play and let school use play for their maturing . . .' In contrast to the classical association of discipline and education, the Dutch word for education, *oproeding*, is rooted in the verb *voeden*, meaning to nourish or feed, and the attitudes implicit in that seem to have been embodied in Dutch child-rearing.[50]

Schama perhaps exaggerated in the extent to which he saw these attitudes and forms of behaviour as peculiarly or exclusively Dutch. They are to be found throughout the Protestant world, and beyond it. The Duchess of Buckingham in 1623 sent her husband a full description of their young daughter, ending 'I wood you were here but to see her for you wood take much delight in her now shee is so full of pretye playe and tricks . . .'[51] Parental pride shines through. Adam Martindale recorded of his son John who died in 1663 that 'He was a beautifull child, and very manly and courageous, for his age . . . We had a wanton tearing calfe, that would runne at children to beare them over. This calfe he would encounter with a sticke in his hand, when he was about two yeares old . . . stand his ground stoutly, beat it backe, and triumph over it, crying *caw, caw*, meaning he had beaten the calfe. I doe not think one child of 100 of his age durst doe so much.' Not to be outdone, John Saffin of Boston remembered his seven-year-old son as 'as witty and towardly a Child as one Shall See Amongst A thousand'.[52]

It would be a mistake to suppose that there was a single uniform Protestant mode of child-rearing. Philip Greven has helpfully identified three such modes in America, each with a long projection from the seventeenth to at least the mid-nineteenth century. He describes these as 'evangelical', 'moderate' and 'genteel', each producing a different type of family, 'authoritarian', 'authoritative' and 'affectionate'. His categories can with minor adjustment be applied to Protestant Europe. To some extent each can be associated with particular social circumstances, a genteel mode of child-rearing being found especially amongst those who could think of themselves as 'gentry'.[53]

But this can take one only so far; at bottom Greven is looking at matters of belief. Thus the 'authoritarian and rigorously repressive' child-rearing he finds in Evangelical families stemmed from a belief in original sin, and a corresponding emphasis on breaking the will of the child. Jonathan Edwards, the most famous preacher of the eighteenth century, and not obviously in other respects an unkindly man, nevertheless thought that children 'are young vipers, and are infinitely more hateful than vipers'. Beliefs such as these were bound to have consequences in parental action. Of the Edwards children it was written that 'they were uncommonly respect[ful] to their parents. When their parents came into the room, they all rose instinctively from their seats, and never resumed them until their parents were sated; and when either parent was speaking, no matter with whom they had been conversing, they were all immediately silent and attentive.'[54] In this kind of household what some parents then and later delighted in as the natural high spirits of children found no favour. Susanna Wesley, mother of the founder of Methodism, was to write of her own children that

when turned a year old (and some before) they were taught to fear the rod and to cry softly, by which means they escaped abundance of correction which they might otherwise have had: and that most odious noise of the crying of children was rarely heard in the house, but the family usually lived in as much quietness as if there had not been a child among them.[55]

If children of such families died they were praised for their obedience and respectfulness (Luther), or their 'woman-like gravity' and obedience (Josselin). Discipline and punishment, ideally without use of the rod, were a necessary accompaniment of such childhoods. William Caton, born in England in the 1630s, recalled how he had 'a fear upon me of reproof and chastisement from my parents, who according to their knowledge endeavoured to educate me in virtue and godliness'.[56] No serious parent could act otherwise. As the English Primer of 1553 put it, 'To have children and servants is thy blessing, O Lord; but not to order them according to thy word deserveth thy dreadful curse.'[57]

Family relationships of this kind, once taken as symptomatic of all families, have been downplayed in recent writing. They were to be found in their full rigour only among the stricter Puritans and later Evangelicals, and even there some parents found it difficult to stick to the task of breaking the will. Greven's second category of moderate parenting may have been more typical of Protestantism amongst the well-to-do, at least in the eighteenth century. Such parents were much less exercised about original sin, and although they were insistent on the need for obedience from their children, they believed that it could be achieved by treating children 'with Tenderness and Patience'.[58] Families of this kind were less intense than the evangelical, with grandparents often welcomed as partners in child-rearing whereas they were suspect as too soft amongst the Evangelicals.[59]

It could be said that in many respects moderate parenting bore the imprint more of Locke than of the Bible, and certainly it is difficult to see anything specifically Protestant in Greven's final 'genteel' category. We are left asking whether the Protestant family may have dissolved before our eyes. Two historians have addressed this issue. Steven Ozment, focusing on sixteenth-century Germany, both attacks the 'great, self-serving myth of the modern world that the children of former times were raised as near slaves by domineering, loveless fathers who owed them nothing', and insists that child-rearing in the sixteenth century was driven by objectives quite different from those current in the late twentieth century. 'In the sixteenth century', he writes, 'children were raised and educated above all to be *social* beings; in this sense they had more duties toward their parents and society than they had rights independent of them.'[60] The parental behaviour which Ozment describes as 'breaking their children's selfish, antisocial behavior by regular discipline, using verbal threats and corporal punishment when love and reason failed to persuade' had as its rationale, he claims, the building of a society where there would be a measure of 'social cohesion and harmony'.[61] Certainly Protestants insisted that good order in the state was dependent on good order in the family, but there was of course a higher motive for discipline – it was to bring the child to a sense of the necessity for salvation. Ozment, one cannot help feeling, disliking the individualism he sees encouraged by contemporary child-rearing, is trying to read back into the sixteenth century more than the sources will allow. The stricter the family discipline the more evidence there is of its social isolation, and possibly of the likelihood of antagonism with neighbours.[62]

Patrick Collinson is more cautious, aware of the difficulty of finding evidence about 'the Protestant family', and of the current of scholarship which stresses continuity both in child-rearing, and in advice about it. He does not deny that so far as the family is concerned the Protestant Reformation was 'not a point of wholly new departure'. Yet he sees it as elevating certain features of the western European family 'to a high point of explicit consciousness and of emulation and perpetuation in successive generations. It was here that the family as we know it experienced its birth.'[63]

Catholicism

What, then, of the Catholic family? If the humanist influence had an essential impact on the making of the Protestant family, then of course that influence was even more available within Catholicism for it was in

Catholic Italy that it had its origin. And we need to remember that when Ariès was looking for the origins of the modern family he took most of his evidence from largely Catholic France. And yet the 'Catholic family' is even more likely to dissolve before our eyes than its Protestant counterpart; indeed it is not clear that we have for it, as we have for Protestantism, an ideal type. Partly this is a matter of sources. The French *livres de raison*, family record books, convey very little of the intimate reality of family life such as can be found in a diary like that of Ralph Josselin.[64] Perhaps this difference in source material is more than accidental, and indicates that Catholic family life was less intense, less self-scrutinising than Protestant. Relieved by infant baptism of the obsession with original sin, Catholic parents were not so immediately brought face to face with the question of their child's salvation. Moreover the strain within Protestantism which had elevated the responsibility of the father within the household was in part due to the removal of the authority of the priest as the intermediary between God and man.[65] Within Catholicism this, of course, did not happen. There was therefore likely to be much less sense of the family as a mini-church in itself, and less need for family devotions.

There was, however, in Catholic thinking a growing emphasis on the duties of parents towards their children. Although there was an inheritance from Roman law, reinforced by absolutism, that emphasised that 'we should consider fathers as gods on earth', and even some call for a restoration to them of the powers of life and death over children, Catholic conduct books and confession manuals from the end of the sixteenth century began to refer to the responsibilities of parents. The Fourth Commandment, 'Honour thy Father and thy Mother', wrote Cardinal Richelieu, 'imposes obligations not only on children towards their fathers, but also on fathers and mothers towards their children, inasmuch as love should be reciprocal.' Children were exhorted to love their parents, and in the eighteenth century that love began to take on positive attributes rather than consisting, as it appears to do in the catechisms of the sixteenth and seventeenth centuries, of an absence of hatred. In Catholic thinking there was some shift between the sixteenth and eighteenth centuries towards an ideal of a family which was the location for affectionate emotions; but that shift appears to lag behind Protestant thinking.[66]

It is very difficult to know how far this reflected or was reflected in actual changes in the family life and child-rearing of the well-to-do in Catholic Europe. There was much that can scarcely be distinguished from Protestant Europe, including grief at the death of children. In Paris in 1591 'grief-stricken parents' erected a funerary inscription for their six-year-old daughter 'whom death stole as a little child from their sight, but not from their memory'. Henri de Campion wrote of his daughter Louise-Anne who died at the age of four in 1653, that 'I loved her with a tenderness that I cannot express.'[67]

Henri de Campion went on to say that he used to spend his time 'at home very agreeably . . . playing with my daughter, who, despite her tender age, was so amusing to those who saw her'. Here again is a common theme. As within Protestant Europe, we find increasing expression being given to parents' enjoyment of their children. It is difficult to know whether this reflects anything more than a tendency to give written expression to such feelings, and to the survival of such writings, but the fact that it is accompanied by a body of writing complaining about such coddling suggests that there may be something new in it. Mme de Sévigné in 1672 described playing with her grand-daughter: 'I am reading the story of Christopher Columbus's discovery of the Indies, which is entertaining me greatly; but your daughter entertains me even more. I do so love her . . . she strokes your portrait and caresses it in such an amusing way that I have to kiss her straight away.'[68] Moralists deplored parents who appeared to 'value their children only in so far as they derive pleasure and entertainment from them'.[69] Painting provides further evidence of an accretion of sentiment around childhood; the sixteenth-century practice of portraying children who had died was followed in the seventeenth century by portraits of living children either singly or with their siblings.[70]

There is one French child of the late sixteenth and early seventeenth centuries about whom our knowledge is extensive: the young Louis XIII, every day of whose life is recorded in the journal kept by his doctor, Jean Heroard. The journal was of course atypical both in its existence and in its subject, for the upbringing of a future king was likely to be very different from that of anyone else. And yet when all allowances have been made, including an obsessive concern with the future of the Bourbon dynasty, this document still retains the power to surprise and shock. At the age of one, 'in high spirits', and to the amusement of all his attendants, the future king 'made everybody kiss his cock'. Engagement at this age to the Infanta of Spain gave scope for many games and much innuendo. 'Where is the Infanta's darling?' he would be asked, and put his hand on his penis. Before getting dressed he would declare that he wanted to give everyone some milk from his penis, and they would all hold out their hands. It is Ariès's argument that this adult encouragement and enjoyment of a child's sexuality disappeared over the course of the seventeenth century to be replaced by a strong sense of the child's innocence and of the necessity to protect it.[71]

The evidence for this change, however, comes not from within families, but from outside them. And it is here that we come to the true significance of the Catholic Counter-Reformation to the history of childhood. As well as working through the family, spiritualising the household, it set up institutions for child-rearing outside the family, the most prominent of which were schools. Schools were of great importance within the Protestant Reformation, but they were seen as working alongside the family rather than as repairing its deficiencies or as a substitute for it. Within Catholicism schools became a centre of power and authority often rivalling and threatening to displace the family. Thus one adolescent girl, aspiring to saintliness, began to 'think seriously of satisfying God rather than my father', and when she entered a convent sought to exclude her father from it.[72] The Jesuits in the late sixteenth and seventeenth centuries took the lead in establishing boarding colleges where boys of a similar age would lead a highly disciplined life. But perhaps the showpiece in France of the new education was Port-Royal, a boarding school for girls under a famous headmistress, Jacqueline Pascal. Pascal had a high sense of vocation in looking after children; it was so important, she wrote, 'that we are bound to prefer that duty to all others when obedience imposes it on us, and what is more, to our personal pleasures, even if these are of a spiritual nature'. Children must be kept under constant surveillance and supervision, for example when girls had retired for the night their 'beds are faithfully inspected to see if they are lying with fitting modesty, and also to see if they are covered up in winter'. But 'this constant supervision should be exercised gently and with a certain trustfulness calculated to make them think that one loves them . . .' If this sounds manipulative, it must be set alongside a new positive evaluation of childhood, associated with a devotion to the childhood of Jesus, and a self-perception on the part of teachers that 'we are only impelled by the desire to render [the children] such as God wishes them'.[73]

The Catholic Reformation shared with its Protestant counterpart a sense of the importance of childhood, but it worked in different ways to express it. The balance shifted from the family to the Church and its schools as the primary institution for rearing good Christians.[74] It was, it must be stressed, a matter of a difference of emphasis, for, from the point of view of the history of childhood, the two movements had more in common than separated them. Both placed importance on early childhood in the making of a Christian, and both had that as their most important aim. Nevertheless the differences did have important implications for family life. One of the least satisfactory parts of Ariès's book is that in which he seeks to connect the changes in educational institutions with the emergence of a modern family, for in many ways for the child the school became a substitute for the family; it served to separate him (for the schools were almost exclusively for boys) from his family.[75] This in turn removed from the family that intense concern for children which characterised the Puritan or Evangelical family. In Greven's terms, we may see Catholic child-rearing as 'moderate' or 'genteel', modes of child-rearing which were not exclusively Protestant.

The eighteenth century

Ariès emphasised the seventeenth century as the crucial one in the transformation of ideas about childhood, but for most historians the eighteenth century holds pride of place. Framed by the writings of John Locke at its beginning and of the Romantic poets at its end, and with the strident figure of Rousseau at centre stage, there seems in the eighteenth century to be a degree of sensitivity to childhood and to children lacking in previous centuries. Some people began to see childhood not as a preparation for something else, whether adulthood or heaven, but as a stage of life to be valued in its own right. Children can be classed alongside slaves and animals as the recipients of the sentimentalism and humanitarianism that characterised the latter part of the eighteenth century. Even when all caveats have been made, it is difficult for historians to avoid thinking of the century as one of progress, to be followed by a period of reaction in the first half of the nineteenth century when parent–child relationships became more distant and formal, only for this in turn to be set aside in the second half of the nineteenth century with the triumph of the view that childhood was not only a separate stage in life, but the best of those stages.

The key to these changes is the long-term secularisation of attitudes to childhood and children. It was not that people suddenly ceased to be Christian, but that for many their Christianity narrowed in its range, became less all-embracing as an explanation for natural phenomena and as a guide to action. There were numerous and important exceptions to this generalisation; Christianity did not give up its claims without a fight, and was on the resurgence in the late eighteenth and early nineteenth centuries. But there was a long-term, if interrupted, decline in belief in original sin, so that by the mid-nineteenth century it flourished only on the margins of Christianity; and with that decline children were transformed from being corrupt and innately evil to being angels, messengers from God to a tired adult world. They also came to be seen to a greater degree as endowed with a capacity for development and growth the motor for which was more Nature than God. The art of child-rearing became one of hearkening to Nature, giving free rein to growth, rather than bending twigs to a desired shape.

The increasing privacy and comfort of upper- and middle-class family life was part and parcel of this focus on the individuality of the child. The community and the extended family lost their role as arbiters of moral issues; their resolution became concentrated within the nuclear core of the family, as at the same time did the strongest affections. The love between parents and children, and in particular between mother and child, long sanctified in western iconography, now became imbued with a new intensity as it became secular. And this love could more easily be expressed within the design of houses where there were now many more private spaces.

The move towards a more child-oriented society was challenged at every stage, and never completed. Both in attitudes to childhood and in behaviour towards children we are confronted at every turn by ambivalences and contradictions. There remain what we may increasingly see as subcultures of child-rearing apparently untouched by change. But the evidence is powerful that a change of some magnitude occurred, one which may be summarised as the shift from a prime focus on the spiritual health of the child to a concern for the development of the individual child.

John Locke's *Some Thoughts Concerning Education* (1693) has attained the status of a classic in this process, though it is not immediately obvious why this should be so. Asked originally for some advice from a gentleman on the upbringing of his son, Locke found his letters in such demand that he was prevailed on to publish them. So what we have is not a systematic treatise on education, but sometimes repetitious reflections on child-rearing enlivened by examples of Locke's own experience in gentry houses. The book in many ways belongs to a genre with a pedigree stretching back to the Renaissance, the book of the courtier, or, in this case, how to raise a boy who will turn out to be a model English gentleman. Moreover, much of the advice offered would have had a familiar feel to anyone acquainted with that literature. Anyone who followed Locke to the letter would have been engaged in a form of child-rearing which was quite as much conservative as innovative.

The issue to which Locke obsessively returned was an old one: what place should corporal punishment have in child-rearing? The answer was very little. 'I am very apt to think', he wrote, 'that *great Severity* of Punishment does but very little Good; nay, great Harm in Education.' But that is less than a blanket condemnation of corporal punishment, and Locke went on to allow its legitimacy for children who display 'obstinacy' or 'rebellion', for he was convinced that a young child must become used to submitting 'his Will to the Reason of others'.[76] This sounds like a Puritan emphasis on breaking the will, but in Locke it has a different purpose: it is to produce an adult who will 'submit to his own Reason, when he is of an Age to make use of it', and who will recognise 'that the Principle of all Vertue and Excellency lies in a power of denying our selves the satisfaction of our own Desires, where Reason does not authorize them'.[77] This power can be attained by habit formation instilled from an early age. Corporal punishment might on occasion need to be used to attain that end of the submission of the will, a process the internalisation of which was the key to the creation of a successful and moral adult.

Put this way, Locke seems to be laying out a blueprint for the production of capitalist man, repressing his desires and deferring if not denying gratification. But there is another side to Locke. Locke is perhaps best known for something he did not believe in, that is the view that a child is to be 'considered only as white Paper, or Wax, to be moulded and fashioned as one pleases'. Locke acknowledges that that is the view he has taken in his book, but, as his argument in *An Essay Concerning Human Understanding* makes clear, a child is a *tabula rasa* or blank slate with respect to ideas only, not to abilities or temperament.[78] This was not a new idea, but Locke's statement of it carried an authority unmatched by his predecessors. The implications for child-rearing were enormous, bestowing colossal power and responsibility on the educator, who must write on the paper or mould the wax. As Locke put it trenchantly, 'Nine Parts of Ten are what they are, Good or Evil, useful or not, by their Education.'[79] But whatever might be said about a child's mind, Locke is at pains to point out that no two children are alike; they have their 'various Tempers, different Inclinations, and particular Defaults', and these must be discovered by watching their play, and adjusting a system of education to fit their 'natural Genius and Constitution'. While therefore one may be able to set out the general principles which should govern child-rearing, the application of them must be suited to the individual child: 'Few of *Adam's* Children are so happy as not to be born with some Byass in their natural Temper, which it is the Business of Education either to take off, or counterbalance.'[80]

Here is an important step towards a child-oriented society, a recognition of the individuality of each child. There is much else which has a similar tendency. Children, said Locke, should 'be treated as rational

Creatures', their curiosity should be encouraged, their questions carefully answered. Everything possible should be done to make learning 'a Play and Recreation to Children', and at the same time 'All their innocent Folly, Playing, and *Childish Actions, are to be* left perfectly free and *unrestrained*, as far as they can consist with the Respect due to those that are present; and that with the greatest Allowance.'[81]

But for Locke this incipient child-centredness was continually blunted by his stress on the overall purpose which was to produce an adult who conformed to the role expected of someone in his or her rank. It is that ultimate goal, the adult, which dominates the book. 'I suppose a wise Father had rather that his Son should be able and useful, when a Man, than pretty Company, and a Diversion to others, whilst a Child.'[82] It was women, Locke wrote, who might harm the child 'by *Cockering* and *Tenderness*', a fear echoed by Defoe who thought that women might have too much influence over young children 'when the most early hints are to be given to the mind, when the genius, like a piece of soft wax, may be moulded up to what form, and to receive what impressions, they please, and when, a few obstinacyes, and meer incapacityes of nature excepted, a child may be form'd to be a man of sense or a brute which they please'.[83]

If what is present in Locke does not always conform to what many textbooks say, so too what is absent can escape attention. God plays little part in this book. There is not the slightest indication that the prime purpose of child-rearing is to produce a Christian. It is true that as part of the acquisition of 'vertue', 'there ought very early to be imprinted on his Mind a true Notion of *God*, as of the independent Supreme Being, Author and maker of all Things, from whom we receive all our Good, who loves us, and gives us all Things'; and further that children should learn the Lord's Prayer, the Creeds and the Ten Commandments by heart. But the overriding purpose in this, as in carefully selected Bible reading, was to learn 'easy and plain moral Rules . . . ready at hand in the whole Conduct of his Life'.[84] That is to say, an adherence to Christian moral precepts went into the making of an English gentleman. In part this downplaying of Christianity within child-rearing may be explained by the genre to which Locke's book belongs, but it becomes of much greater significance when account is taken of the fact that Locke became the guide for innumerable middle-class families. There had been more than a dozen English editions by the mid-eighteenth century, and several editions in French, German, Italian, Dutch and Swedish in the course of the eighteenth century. Locke's ideas can be traced in the fiction and poetry of the century; for example in Samuel Richardson's *Pamela* Mr B. gives his wife a copy of

Some Thoughts Concerning Education and invites her comments, which are given at length.[85] Did readers notice this absence of an emphasis on Christianity? We cannot tell, but we must note the fact that the premier child-guidance book of the eighteenth century is dominantly secular in tone and content.[86]

Rousseau acknowledged Locke as his predecessor, and almost certainly had him in mind when he wrote in the Preface to *Émile* (1762) that 'The wisest writers devote themselves to what a man ought to know, without asking what a child is capable of learning. They are always looking for the man in the child, without considering what he is before he becomes a man.' Rousseau, declaring robustly that 'We know nothing of childhood',[87] was determined to reverse this, to consider a child as a child, and it is that which made his book a landmark and an inspiration for other writers and thinkers, as well as for parents. The radicalism of Rousseau is apparent from the outset. He attacks that tradition established at the time of the Renaissance that fathers must take charge of child-rearing: 'You say mothers spoil their children, and no doubt that is wrong, but it is worse to deprave them as you do. The mother wants her child to be happy now. She is right, and if her method is wrong, she must be taught a better. Ambition, avarice, tyranny, the mistaken foresight of fathers, their neglect, their harshness, are a hundredfold more harmful to the child than the blind affection of the mother.'[88] How then can the happiness of the child be attained? By bringing up a child in the ways of nature; this means, first of all, maternal breastfeeding and no swaddling, but more radically it means that a child should learn from things rather than from people; he should learn by experience that stones are hard and that fire burns, and not by being told these things. Education in the early years, up to the age of twelve, should be 'merely negative'. 'Leave childhood to ripen in your children . . . beware of giving anything they need to-day if it can be deferred without danger to to-morrow.' In short, 'Reverse the usual practice and you will almost always do right.'[89] For 'childhood has its own ways of seeing, thinking, and feeling'; childhood 'is the sleep of reason', and therefore you should abandon Locke's advice to reason with a child ('in the height of fashion at present'), and allow a child to discover the secret of true happiness which is to achieve an equilibrium between the power and the will.[90]

Other writers had been condescendingly indulgent towards children's games and playfulness, but always with an ulterior motive; 'All the Plays and Diversions of Children', wrote Locke, 'should be directed towards good and useful Habits . . .'[91] Rousseau discards this manner of thinking. He points out that many children will die young, having spent their lives preparing for an adulthood which they never achieved; and he asserts the right of a child to be a child, and to be happy in it. Moreover we find the first expression of the view that childhood may be the best time of life, something to be looked back to with nostalgia:

Love childhood, indulge its sports, its pleasures, its delightful instincts. Who has not sometimes regretted that age when laughter was ever on the lips, and when the heart was ever at peace? Why rob these innocents of the joys which pass so quickly, of that precious gift which they cannot abuse? Why fill with bitterness the fleeting days of early childhood, days which will no more return for them than for you.[92]

Rousseau, as he admitted, wrote in paradoxes, many of them, such as 'reading is the curse of childhood',[93] designed to shock. And he is not without inconsistencies. It comes as something of a surprise to find that when he reaches adolescence he writes that 'The way childhood is spent is no great matter; the evil which may find its way is not irremediable, and the good which may spring up might come later.'[94] But it would be a perverse reader who carried away this as the message of the book. Although Rousseau is in many ways as concerned as any other writer on education to produce the good adult, his radicalism lay in thinking that the way to do this was to allow children to grow up in accordance with nature, and without the imposition upon them of moral rules and learning. The child-nature link was being forged, with enormous implications for future thinking on the nature of childhood and on the proper manner of child-rearing.

Émile differs from other educational tracts in the form which the book takes. Émile is the book's hero, the boy being brought up in the way that Rousseau recommends. His gender is no accident, for in the second half of the book Rousseau introduces us to Sophy who completes Émile's education, and does so as a foil to Émile's carefully fostered masculinity. 'The man should be strong and active', wrote Rousseau; 'the woman should be weak and passive.'[95] The book then ends as a romance. It may be said to start as a utopia. 'You will tell me', wrote Rousseau, ' "This is not so much a treatise on education as the visions of a dreamer with regard to education." '[96] Like Locke, Rousseau accords special importance to the choice of a tutor, but whereas Locke's tutor has the straightforward task of education in its widest sense, Rousseau's is a sometimes invisible manipulator of events designed to bring home to Émile the lessons of nature. Ideally Émile would be brought up without other human contact at all, simply learning from nature. Rousseau recognises the impossibility of this: 'I am showing what we should try to attain, I do not say we can attain it, but I do say that whoever comes nearest to it is nearest to success.'[97]

There is plenty of evidence that people did aspire to bring up their children on Rousseau's principles. We know, for example, that Jean Ranson, a merchant from La Rochelle in Brittany, purchased numerous books on child-rearing and education 'saturated with Rousseauism', that he called his second son Émile, and that he ascribed his children's virtues to the application of Rousseauian principles.[98] In 1788 Mme de Staël was confident that 'Everyone has adopted Rousseau's physical system of education: A sure success has permitted no disagreement . . . He has succeeded in restoring happiness to childhood.'[99] Evidence of this from America comes from a significant change in the clothes that children wore and the furnishings of the household; whereas in the seventeenth and first half of the eighteenth centuries the aim was to get the child upright at an early age, to progress as rapidly as possible to adulthood, in the period 1750 to 1830 the emphasis was on the child growing up in accordance with the precepts, and on the timescale, of nature.[100] In England there were at least 200 treatises on education published before the end of the century, all in some way influenced by Émile.[101] Richard Edgeworth tried to bring up his first son on Rousseau's principles – with disastrous consequences which came to a head when the boy was introduced to Rousseau himself and was extremely rude. There were other absurdities bordering on scandal. Thomas Day, author of the best-selling children's book Sandford and Merton, sought to find himself a Sophy by selecting an eleven-year-old girl from the Shrewsbury Orphanage, and bringing her up in an approved Rousseauian manner, hardening her to pain, for example, by pouring hot sealing wax on her arms. To her credit, the girl failed to live up to expectations.[102] Events such as these provided plentiful ammunition for Rousseau's critics of whom there were many – the book had been condemned by the Roman Catholic Church because of Rousseau's rejection of the Church's authority. But the voice of the critics was in its way a testimony to the success of the book.

The most immediately influential parts of the book were those dealing with maternal breastfeeding and swaddling, the parts which had least claim to novelty, and which Rousseau had added as an afterthought, virtually plagiarising another book.[103] Rousseau was both contributing and giving further publicity to a new sensibility surrounding motherhood. In the thought patterns which dominated from the Renaissance through to the Enlightenment fathers played the key role in the rearing of children. With Romanticism, mothers regained the predominance they had held in the middle ages; child-rearing became a female occupation, and fathers were relegated to a subordinate position. The consequences were striking. In the third quarter of the eighteenth century the death rate of English aristocratic children under the age of five dropped by 30 per cent. The only plausible explanation for this seems to be that aristocratic mothers were spending more time with their children, breastfeeding them from the late 1760s. 'Children survived', writes Randolph Trumbach, 'less because they were immune from disease or better nourished, and more because they were better loved.'[104]

Survival of this kind was clearly all to the good. It is less easy to be so unambiguously positive about some of the other consequences of the bonding together of childhood and nature. The effect of them was to mark off childhood as a separate and special world. Perhaps the most striking evidence for this is the development of a special genre of literature for children. We have seen that catechisms and other religious literature had been produced mainly, if not exclusively, for children since the Reformation, but it was only in the eighteenth century that there emerged a more secular literature, distinct from the cheap chapbooks which were read by people of all ages. In England John Newbery's publications of the 1740s are the conventional starting point. By the second half of the eighteenth century children's literature was a well-established genre, marked in France, for example, by the sixty volumes for children written by Madame Le Prince de Beaumont between the 1750s and 1770s, and by the twenty-four volumes of Arnaud Berquin's *The Children's Friend* in the 1780s.[105]

Children were also making their mark in the arts aimed at adults. Poets mourned the death of children, or worried about their future,[106] and in prose children loomed large in the novels of the second half of the century. They were symbols or icons, rather than protagonists in their own right, standing for 'innocence, emotion, and simplicity'.[107] The depiction of children changed too. A study of American family portraits shows that before 1750 men and breeched boys (aged over six) tended to dominate a subordinate group of women and children in petticoats; thereafter the composition of portraits was more complex, and children, in their dress and the props with which they were surrounded, became more clearly demarcated from adults of both sexes.[108] Similar changes towards naturalism and to a more prominent position for children can be seen in the paintings by Jean-Baptiste Greuze and Étienne Aubry in France; or in the work of Gainsborough and Reynolds in England of upper- and middle-class children enjoying 'what was and is thought of as a "natural" childhood, surrounded by the evidence of parental care, fenced off from certain kinds of painful experiences, in an arena of innocence and therefore of happiness'.[109] Reynolds, indeed, entitled his portrait of his great-niece, Offy, *The Age of Innocence* (Plate 2). Seated in the countryside (the 'natural' setting for children), Offy, about six years old, is a reminder to the adult viewer that the age of innocence (not least sexual innocence) is to be treasured for it will pass. Although the child is in the light, the background is dark, a hint of things to come. This painting, and others like it, were much reproduced in the nineteenth and twentieth centuries, setting out ways of depicting children which inscribed into modern consciousness a romantic vision of childhood.[110]

These images of innocent and natural childhood did not enjoy a wholesale and uncontested triumph. The challenge to them came from three directions. First, the Puritan emphasis on original sin remained alive. It made adults anxious about children, an anxiety they projected onto the children themselves. Isaac Watts made them sing:

> *There is an hour when I must die,*
> *Nor do I know how soon 'twill come.*
> *A thousand children, young as I,*
> *Are call'd by death to hear their doom.*

This legacy from the Puritans was reinforced by the evangelical revival at the end of the eighteenth century. In 1799 the *Evangelical Magazine* advised parents to teach their children that 'they are sinful polluted creatures', and in the same year Hannah More, one of the leading figures in the evangelical revival, warned against the prevalence of treating children as if they were innocent.[111] Such beliefs were perhaps on the increase in the early nineteenth century, and there are some striking documents testifying to their implementation. In the United States, a Baptist recorded how he had kept his son locked up without food for forty-eight hours until he acknowledged his wrongdoing.[112] In Britain, Samuel Butler in his autobiographical novel, *The Way of All Flesh*, and Edmund Gosse in *Father and Son*, his account of his relationship with his father, describe in detail evangelical childhoods. In the United States it was not until the 1860s that expressions of belief in original sin disappeared from popular literature, and not until the early twentieth century that the Presbyterian Church formally abandoned the doctrine of infant damnation.[113] But in this the Church was behind the more popular advice books, and almost certainly behind popular belief. 'Don't tell children they are sinners', advised Jacob Abbott in 1871.[114]

A second threat to Rousseauian ideas was more nuanced, coming from those who acknowledged some indebtedness to him. It is to be found in a moralising literature for children, both in France and in England, which was above all concerned to instruct, to teach. This was far from what Rousseau would have approved, but it had another feature to which he had lent the authority of his support: it had no time at all for imaginative literature. These books, of which the most famous example is Mrs Barbauld's *Early Lessons*, bear the mark more of Locke than of Rousseau; they are sensible, moral, and adapted for the most part to a child's mode of understanding, but they have their eye fixed on the production of a useful adult.[115] The same can be said of the toys which proliferated in the eighteenth century; taking their cue from Locke, they were designed to teach. An American asked a friend in England to buy for her young son 'the new toy, the description of which I enclose, to teach him according to Mr Locke's methods – which I have carefully studied – to play himself into learning'.[116]

The third threat to the success of Rousseauian ideas lay in what critics saw as a growing tendency for parents to treat children almost as objects testifying to their own status. Ariès found in seventeenth-century France a vein of criticism of parents who coddled and spoilt their children, and saw them as creatures made for the amusement of adults. This continued into the eighteenth century but to it was added a concern that 'children had become luxury objects upon which their mothers and fathers were willing to spend larger and larger sums of money . . .' We must see this in the context of a growing consumerism in society as a whole, and a corresponding availability of books, toys, and entertainment for children in forms which simply did not exist at the beginning of the eighteenth century. 'In 1730', writes J.H. Plumb about England, 'there were no specialized toy-shops of any kind, whereas by 1780 toy-shops everywhere abounded.' Literature for children similarly expanded exponentially from the 1740s. There were sane Lockeian voices deploring this excess expenditure on and over-indulgence of children, but they did nothing to stop the expansion of the market.[117]

The Romantic poets had no time for any of these trends, but the one at the centre of their target was the second. 'Damn them! I mean the cursed Barbauld Crew, those Blights and Blasts of all that is Human in man and child', wrote Charles Lamb to Coleridge.[118] Romanticism sought to recover for childhood a freedom of imagination which utilitarianism would have quashed. This meant access to the whole of literature, and there is much evidence that chapbook tales of magic, courage, cunning, strength and endurance, a literature which the polite world would have consigned to oblivion, fed the imagination of many children in the eighteenth century. The common-sense, utilitarian education which became fashionable was denounced by Wordsworth as 'an evil which these days have laid / Upon the children of the land – a pest / That might have dried me up body and soul'.[119]

Wordsworth shared with Locke the view that the mind was at birth a *tabula rasa*, but whereas Locke wanted it imprinted from the outset with habits which would go to the making of a gentleman, Wordsworth urged that it should be wide open to feelings and sensations, above all those from nature. In this he seems close to Rousseau, but for Rousseau what the child would learn from nature would be experience – that fire burns – whereas for Wordsworth nature would implant the foundations of moral virtue and of beauty; and these in turn would shape the adult life:

> *The Child is father of the man,*
> *And I could wish my days to be*
> *Bound each to each by natural piety.*[120]

The romantics in this way set out an ideal of childhood in which it was transformed from being a preparatory phase in the making of an adult to being the spring which should nourish the whole life. If adults do not keep the child in them alive, they will become dried up and embittered, Scrooges.

This was the central message of Romanticism, first articulated by William Blake, but it was quickly confused with another to which Wordsworth had given expression in his *Ode on Intimations of Immortality from Recollections of Early Childhood*. There he had envisaged the child as being born

> *Not in entire forgetfulness,*
> *And not in utter nakedness,*
> *But trailing clouds of glory do we come*
> *From God who is our home:*
> *Heaven lies about us in our infancy!*

This not only seemed to put paid to original sin, but to replace it with the idea of an infancy positively endowed with blessings from God. Children came to be thought to have keener perceptions of beauty and of truth than adults. In a world much concerned with the ways in which 'luxury' could blunt sensibilities or corrupt morality, childhood began to replace 'savagery' as the location and repository of virtue. Life could be seen, not as an ascent to maturity, but as a decline from the freshness of childhood. For Wordsworth himself the Ode was an attempt to understand what he saw as his declining poetic powers, and at odds with much else in his writing, but it came to encapsulate what was thought of as a romantic attitude to childhood: that is, that childhood was the best part of life.

The influence of Romanticism

It is difficult to exaggerate the influence of Wordsworth's Ode. It had, claims Barbara Garlitz, 'as powerful an influence on nineteenth-century ideas of childhood as Freud has had on present-day ones'. Christians happily accepted that a child was, as the future Cardinal Newman expressed it in the 1830s, a being come 'out of the hands of God, with all lessons and thoughts of Heaven freshly marked upon him'. The children who climb onto our knees, claimed Rev. Stopford Brooke in 1872, 'are fresh from the hand of God, living blessings which have drifted down to us from the imperial palace of the love of God'.[121] A romantic sensibility towards childhood dominated the nineteenth and much of the twentieth centuries. It was probably at its height between about 1860 and 1930. Dickens's childhood heroes did much to fix in the public mind the idea of a child as both pitiable (Oliver Twist), and, 'fresh from God', as the embodiment of a force of innate goodness which could rescue embittered adults.[122] But the child was central to much other nineteenth-century fiction. Consider, for example, George Eliot's *Silas Marner*, where the old miser is rescued by the girl, Eppie:

There was love between him and the child that blent them into one, and there was love between the child and the world – from men and women with parental looks and tones, to the red lady-birds and the round pebbles . . . In old days there were angels who came and took men by the hand and led them away from the city of destruction. We see no white-winged angels now. But yet men are led away from threatening destruction: a hand is put into theirs, which leads them forth gently towards a calm and bright land, so that they look no more backward; and the hand may be a little child's.[123]

The red lady-birds and round pebbles signified that link between childhood and nature which was central to the romantic vision, and little children were increasingly given the task of rescuing adults. 'Childhood hath *Saved* me', the American transcendentalist Bronson Alcott confided to his Journal in 1835. 'Infancy', claimed his compatriot Emerson, 'is the perpetual Messiah, which comes into the arms of fallen men, and pleads with them to return to paradise.'[124]

In this kind of thinking we can see a transformation in the way adults imagined their lives. Until the later eighteenth century they had not accorded much importance to childhood as they looked back over their life course. Now all was changed. Rousseau in his *Confessions* (1783) had said that 'Who wants to know me as an adult, has to know me as a child.' Increasingly those who reminisced about their lives accorded importance to childhood. In Dutch autobiographies those born around 1780 were the first to do so. In Germany the interest in the formation of the self in childhood and its subsequent influence came a little earlier.[125] People began to think of the self as an interior personal space to which they alone had access, and in its formation childhood and the memories of it were crucial. Childhood, and all it came to stand for, began to have placed upon it a new significance, marked by a new interest in children's bodies and minds and the way they developed. Adult interference with natural development was regarded with horror, the archetypal such child in European culture in the nineteenth and early twentieth centuries being Goethe's Mignon, a child disfigured by training as an acrobat. Mignon evoked intense pity as a child figure, and was at the same time a symbol of the childhood which the adults who observed her had lost.[126]

Under the impact of Romanticism 'the child' was no longer thought of as a boy as had been the case with Erasmus and Locke. Childhood was coming to be a special time of life in which gender was no longer stressed as an attribute; rather it was the childlike quality of the child which needed to be preserved. In the 1830s knee-length dresses and long white trousers, with hair cut short, were recommended for both boys and girls, the aim being explicitly to blur sexual distinctions. Advice books between the 1820s and 1840s stressed that both boys and girls should avoid anger. This was perhaps the highpoint of the idealisation of the ungendered child for thereafter, until the early twentieth century, there was more differentiation between the genders in advice on emotional behaviour.[127] Science, however, continued to lend some backing. 'The child', wrote Krafft-Ebing, 'is of the neuter gender.'[128] If anything people were more likely to imagine the romantic child as female rather than male, perhaps because boys in the flesh were never sufficiently socialised into acting in harmony with ideas of nature. A striking example of this imaginative feminising of childhood is Thomas Gotch's *The Child Enthroned* (Plate 3) which Gotch painted as 'the personification of childhood'. The religious symbolism is overpowering, and some viewers at the Royal Academy in 1894 took it to be a picture of Jesus; in actuality the child Jesus had become a girl, and the viewers were being asked to worship at her feet.[129]

Romanticism could lead all too easily to a maudlin sentimentalism. Philipp Otto Runge in the first decade of the nineteenth century had invested children in his paintings with energy and vitality, and had forced viewers to see the world from a child's perspective, but it was an example which does not seem to have been followed until the very end of the century.[130] A sweetened romanticism was the dominant force in the way children came to be pictured in the nineteenth century. As Ruskin expressed it, writing about the depiction of children in the 1880s, 'you have the radiance and innocence of reinstated divinity showered again among the flowers of English meadows by Mrs Allingham and Kate Greenaway'.[131]

In literature there was a high death rate for child heroes and heroines for there was no acceptable life for them after childhood. People began to look back to their childhoods as the best part of their lives, perhaps even to wish that, like fictional characters, they had never grown up. In Louisa Alcott's *Little Women* (1868), fifteen-year-old Jo hates to 'think I've got to grow up', a view endorsed by her mother who thinks that 'children should be children as long as they can'.[132] It was an attitude which had many imitators in fiction, and probably struck a chord in real life.

The language and sensibility of Romanticism crept into advice books and literature about children. In the United States the *Christian Advocate*, recommending music in schools in 1898, did so in words which owed much more to Wordworth than to Hannah More: 'These little hearts are to be taken, while still fresh with the dew of heaven, and set to beating in harmony with the highest laws.'[133] An Edinburgh doctor, writing a best-selling guide to child-rearing at the very beginning of the twentieth century, allowed, referring to Wordsworth, that 'the selective emotion of a poet [may] sometimes discover traits which are hidden from the cold-blooded scrutiny of science'.[134]

It is at this point, however, that we need to note the limits of Romanticism's influence. Much of what we have been describing operated as a fantasy appealing especially to adult males. And in the middle-class world, adult males, though often doting fathers, had little to do with the day-to-day business of child-rearing.[135] For many mothers, by contrast, looking after babies and young children was a full-time occupation in which they were expected to find fulfilment, but which often provoked anxiety. While Romanticism did suggest conditions in which children should be reared – in the country for example – it did not provide a manual for child-rearing which mothers could follow. Children could more easily be reared in the spirit of Romanticism than by the letter of it. Romanticism did affect the way in which children were reared, above all in opening up for them a body of imaginative literature which would have been denied them if the spirit of Locke had retained complete dominance. But the overall influence of Romanticism, while all-pervading, was short on specifics. And there were many other sources of advice of a more traditional kind pouring in on mothers from every side. 'Books do so differ', lamented Mrs Gaskell, the novelist, confronted in the 1830s by different advice on how to cope with children's tears.[136] Mothers' worries were not simply how their children should or would behave, but whether they would live. And in face of that, there was an emphasis on hygiene and on routine, and, as the nineteenth century progressed, an increasing confidence that sensible child-rearing could reduce the dangers. 'In all but the most evangelical of families, Americans gradually supplemented reliance on Divine Providence with faith in the power of human agency.'[137] This faith operated in practice much more on the principles of Locke than of Rousseau or of the romantics; middle-class child-rearing remained essentially a training in habit formation. Further, there were powerful forces which paid little attention to the ideal of the romantic child, for example those which endorsed the separation from parents and the education in 'manliness' of the English public schools for boys.

Romanticism, then, was much more influential as a body of ideas than as an active force in day-to-day child-rearing within the middle-class home. Its importance was that it gave rise to ways of thinking about childhood, and ways of organising the lives of children, which we will explore further in subsequent chapters. At its heart was a reverence for, and a sanctification of childhood which was at total odds with the Puritan emphasis on the child as a sinful being. Romanticism embedded in the European and American mind a sense of the importance of childhood, a belief that childhood should be happy, and a hope that the qualities of childhood, if they could be preserved in adulthood, might help redeem the adult world. In becoming more child-oriented in this way, society had radically changed its ideas on the relationship between childhood and religion. As Wordsworth wrote of the child,

> *Mighty prophet! Seer blest,*
> *On whom those truths do rest*
> *Which we are toiling all our lives to find.*[138]

They are lines which indicate the truly revolutionary impact of Romanticism on thinking about childhood; from being the smallest and least considered of human beings, the child had become endowed with qualities which make it godlike, fit to be worshipped, and the embodiment of hope.

Notes

1 P. Gavitt, *Charity and Children in Renaissance Florence: The Ospedale degli Innocenti, 1450–1536* (Ann Arbor, 1990), p. 275.

2 Quoted in ibid., pp. 278–9.

3 Ibid., pp. 278–81.

4 Ibid., pp. 281–4; *Collected Works of Erasmus* (Toronto, Buffalo, London, 1985), Vol. 25, p. xxiii.

5 Gavitt, *Charity and Children*, pp. 282, 284.

6 Ibid., pp. 273–5.

7 'A declamation on the subject of early liberal education for children', in *Collected Works*, Vol. 26, pp. 299, 301, 307.

8 Ibid., pp. 297, 301–2, 305.

9 S. Shahar, *Childhood in the Middle Ages* (London, 1990), pp. 100–1.

10 *Collected Works*, Vol. 26, pp. 299–300.

11 M. Todd, *Christian Humanism and the Puritan Social Order* (Cambridge, 1987), pp. 107–8; for Erasmus's views on the education of girls, see W.H. Woodward, *Desiderius Erasmus Concerning the Aim and Method of Education* (1904; New York, 1964), pp. 148–53. I suspect that the 'pueri' in the title of his declamation would have conveyed to his readers the sense of 'boys' rather than 'children'.

12 *Collected Works*, Vol. 25, p. xxii; Vol. 26, pp. 324, 339.

13 Ibid., Vol. 25, pp. xxxv–vi, xvii; Vol. 26, p. 325.

14 Ibid., Vol. 25, pp. xiii–xvii; G. Kennedy, *Quintilian* (New York, 1969), pp. 41–4.

15 'On good manners for boys', *Collected Works*, Vol. 25, pp. 269–89; J. Revel, 'The uses of civility', in R. Chartier (ed.), *A History of Private Life III: The Passions of the Renaissance* (Cambridge, Mass. and London, 1989), pp. 168–81.

16 *Collected Works*, Vol. 25, p. 273; Vol. 26, p. 307.

17 Ibid., Vol. 26, pp. 312, 321; Earle quoted in J.E. Illick, 'Child-rearing in seventeenth-century England and America', in L. de Mause (ed.), *The History of Childhood* (1974; London, 1976), p. 317.

18 Todd, *Christian Humanism*, p. 97.

19 C. Hill, 'The spiritualization of the household', in *Society and Puritanism in Pre-Revolutionary England* (London, 1964), pp. 443–81.

20 Quoted in S. Ozment, *When Fathers Ruled: Family Life in Reformation Europe* (Cambridge, Mass. and London, 1983), p. 132.

21 Quoted in P. Collinson, *The Birthpangs of Protestant England: Religious and Cultural Change in the Sixteenth and Seventeenth Centuries* (London, 1988), p. 60.

22 See J. Morgan, *Godly Learning: Puritan Attitudes Towards Reason, Learning, and Education, 1560–1640* (Cambridge, 1986), pp. 143–4.

23 Quoted in Ozment, *When Fathers Ruled*, pp. 133–4.

24 Quoted in ibid., p. 132.

25 R.V. Schnucker, 'Puritan attitudes towards childhood discipline', in V. Fildes (ed.), *Women as Mothers in Pre-Industrial England* (London, 1990), pp. 108–21.

26 Quoted in Morgan, *Godly Learning*, pp. 169–70.

27 Collinson, *Birthpangs of Protestant England*, p. 78; P. Tudor, 'Religious instruction for children and adolescents in the early English Reformation', *Journal of Ecclesiastical History*, 35 (1984), p. 394.

28 Tudor, 'Religious instruction', pp. 393–4.

29 Quoted in Ozment, *When Fathers Ruled*, p. 164.

30 Quoted in ibid., pp. 164–5.

31 Quoted in J. Demos, *A Little Commonwealth: Family Life in Plymouth Colony* (New York, 1970), pp. 134–5.

32 Ozment, *When Fathers Ruled*, pp. 170–2; Tudor, 'Religious instruction'; I. Green, ' "For Children in Yeeres and Children in Understanding": the emergence of the Elizabethan catechism under Elizabeth and the early Stuarts', *Journal of Ecclesiastical History*, 37 (1986), pp. 400–1.

33 Quoted in Morgan, *Godly Learning*, p. 153.

34 R.P. Hsia, *Social Discipline in the Reformation: Central Europe 1550–1750* (London, 1989), pp. 147–8; but see also Morgan, *Godly Learning*, p. 143.

35 Quoted in Morgan, *Godly Learning*, p. 169.

36 W. Gouge, *Of Domestical Duties: Eight Treatises* (1634 edn).

37 Morgan, *Godly Learning*, pp. 177–82.

38 Ibid., pp. 185–6, 205–7.

39 A. Fletcher, 'Prescription and practice: Protestantism and the upbringing of children, 1560–1700', in D. Wood (ed.), *The Church and Childhood* (Oxford, 1994), pp. 335–45.

40 S. Schama, *The Embarrassment of Riches: An Interpretation of Dutch Culture in the Golden Age* (1987; London, 1991), p. 521.

41 P. Crawford, 'The construction and experience of maternity in seventeenth-century England', and A. Wilson, 'The ceremony of childbirth and its interpretation', in Fildes, *Women as Mothers*, pp. 3–38, 68–107.

42 S.H. Mendelson, 'Stuart women's diaries and occasional memoirs', in M. Prior (ed.), *Women in English Society 1500–1800* (London, 1985), p. 196.

43 Demos, *A Little Commonwealth*, p. 133.

44 Schama, *Embarrassment of Riches*, pp. 537–8; R.A. Houlbrooke, *The English Family 1450–1700* (London, 1984), p. 132; see also the evidence from France in E.W. Marvick, 'Nature versus nurture: patterns and trends in seventeenth-century French child-rearing', in de Mause, *History of Childhood*, pp. 270–1.

45 Houlbrooke, *English Family*, p. 136.

46 Schama, *Embarrassment of Riches*, p. 517.

47 Ozment, *When Fathers Ruled*, pp. 167–8.

48 A. Macfarlane (ed.), *The Diary of Ralph Josselin 1616–1683* (London, 1976), pp. 201–3; for other examples of parental grief, see J.J.H. Dekker and L.F. Groenendijk, 'The republic of God or the republic of children? Childhood and child-rearing after the Reformation: an appraisal of Simon Schama's thesis about the uniqueness of the Dutch case', *Oxford Review of Education*, Vol. 17 (1991), pp. 325–6.

49 J.B. Bedaux and R. Ekkart (eds), *Pride and Joy: Children's Portraits in the Netherlands 1500–1700* (Ghent and Amsterdam, 2000), esp. pp. 262–3.

50 Schama, *Embarrassment of Riches*, pp. 481–561, quoting pp. 495, 557, 559.

51 Quoted in Houlbrooke, pp. 135–6.

52 *The Life of Adam Martindale, Written by Himself*, Chetham Society, old series, 4 (1845), p. 154; P. Greven, *The Protestant Temperament: Patterns of Child-Rearing, Religious Experience, and the Self in Early America* (1977; New York, 1979), p. 158.

53 Greven, *Protestant Temperament*, passim.

54 Ibid., pp. 31, 47.

55 Quoted in ibid., p. 36.

56 Quoted in ibid., p. 47.

57 Quoted in Hill, 'The spiritualization of the household', p. 447.

58 Greven, *Protestant Temperament*, pp. 37, 162, 164–7.

59 Ibid., pp. 26–7, 153–5.

60 Ozment, *When Fathers Ruled*, p. 177.

61 Ibid., p. 163.

62 Greven, *Protestant Temperament*, pp. 25–6.

63 Collinson, *Birthpangs of Protestant England*, pp. 81–93, quoting p. 93.

64 M. Foisil, 'The literature of intimacy', in Chartier, *A History of Private Life III*, pp. 345–8.

65 Hill, 'The spiritualization of the household'. For Catholic denunciation of the Protestant obsession with original sin as corrupting the innocence of children, see Hsia, *Social Discipline in the Reformation*, p. 147.

66 J-L. Flandrin, *Families in Former Times: Kinship, Household and Sexuality* (Cambridge, 1979), pp. 130–40, 158–60.

67 P. Ariès, *The Hour of Our Death* (London, 1981), p. 231; Foisil, 'The literature of intimacy', p. 348.

68 P. Ariès, *Centuries of Childhood* (London, 1962), p. 127; but note that the girl's mother had rejected her for her failure to be a boy, Marvick, 'Nature versus nurture', p. 283.

69 Quoted in Ariès, *Centuries of Childhood*, p. 128.

70 Ibid., pp. 40–1.

71 Ibid., pp. 98–124.

72 Marvick, 'Nature versus nurture', p. 289.

73 Ariès, *Centuries of Childhood*, pp. 111–12, 118–19; Marvick, 'Nature versus nurture', p. 283.

74 For an elaboration of this argument, see L. Chatellier, *The Europe of the Devout: The Catholic Reformation and the Formation of a New Society* (Cambridge, 1989).

75 Ariès, *Centuries of Childhood*, pp. 357–8.

76 J. Locke, 'Some Thoughts Concerning Education', ed. J.W. and J.S. Yolton, *The Clarendon Edition of the Works of John Locke* (Oxford, 1989), pp. 105, 111, 138.

77 Ibid., pp. 105, 107.

78 Ibid., p. 265, and Introduction, p. 38; J. Locke, *An Essay Concerning Human Understanding*, ed. P.H. Nidditch (Oxford, 1975), pp. 85, 95, 106–7, 116–17.

79 Locke, 'Some Thoughts Concerning Education', p. 83.

80 Ibid., pp. 122, 198, 265.

81 Ibid., pp. 115, 119, 182–3, 208.

82 Ibid., p. 185.

83 Ibid., p. 84. Defoe quoted in M.J.M. Ezell, 'John Locke's images of childhood: early eighteenth century response to *Some Thoughts Concerning Education*', *Eighteenth-Century Studies*, 17 (1983), p. 150.

84 Locke, 'Some Thoughts Concerning Education', pp. 195, 212, 213–14.

85 Ibid., p. 65; Ezell, 'John Locke's images of childhood', pp. 139–55, esp. pp. 146–7; J.A. Leith (ed.), *Facets of Education in the Eighteenth Century, Studies on Voltaire and the Eighteenth Century*, CLXVII (1977), pp. 18–19; S.F. Pickering, Jr., *John Locke and Children's Books in Eighteenth-Century England* (Knoxville, 1981).

86 J.H. Plumb, 'The new world of children in eighteenth-century England', *Past and Present*, 67 (1975), p. 69.

87 J-J. Rousseau, *Émile*, ed. P.D. Jimack (London, 1974), p. 1.

88 Ibid., p. 5.

89 Ibid., pp. 57–8.

90 Ibid., pp. 44, 53–4, 71.

91 Locke, 'Some Thoughts Concerning Education', p. 192.

92 Rousseau, *Émile*, p. 43; for other expressions of nostalgia for childhood, see P. Coveney, *The Image of Childhood* (1957; Harmondsworth, 1967), p. 52.

93 Rousseau, *Émile*, p. 80.

94 Ibid., p. 193; see also p. 378.

95 Ibid., p. 322.

96 Ibid., p. 2.

97 Ibid., p. 59.

98 R. Darnton, *The Great Cat Massacre, and other Episodes in French Cultural History* (1984; Harmondsworth, 1985), pp. 209–49.

99 Rousseau, *Émile*, pp. xxiii–xxvi; see also R. Trumbach, *The Rise of the Egalitarian Family: Aristocratic Kinship and Domestic Relations in Eighteenth-Century England* (London, 1978), pp. 210–11, 214.

100 K. Calvert, *Children in the House: The Material Culture of Early Childhood, 1600–1900* (Boston, 1992).

101 Coveney, *Image of Childhood*, p. 46.

102 G. Summerfield, *Fantasy and Reason: Children's Literature in the Eighteenth Century* (London, 1984), pp. 119–20, 149–53.

103 Rousseau, *Émile*, pp. xxiv–xxv; T. Zeldin, *France 1848–1945*, Vol. I (Oxford, 1973), p. 317.

104 Trumbach, *Egalitarian Family*, pp. 187–233, quoting p. 208.

105 L. Hunt, *The Family Romance of the French Revolution* (Berkeley and Los Angeles, 1992), p. 27. For a good general survey of children's books in England, wider in scope than its title suggests, see Pickering, *John Locke and Children's Books.*

106 R. Lonsdale (ed.), *Eighteenth-Century Women Poets* (Oxford, 1989), pp. 115, 135, 270–1, 459, 506–7.

107 Hunt, *Family Romance*, p. 26; see also P. Stewart, 'The child comes of age', *Yale French Studies*, 40–1 (1968), pp. 134–41.

108 K. Calvert, 'Children in American family portraiture, 1670 to 1810', *William and Mary Quarterly*, XXXIX (1982), pp. 87–113.

109 Hunt, *Family Romance*, p. 36; for Aubry, see, e.g., his *L'Amour Paternel* in the Barber Institute of Fine Arts, University of Birmingham; P. Crown, 'Portraits and fancy pictures by Gainsborough and Reynolds: contrasting images of childhood', *British Journal for Eighteenth-Century Studies*, 7 (1984), pp. 159–67, quoting p. 159.

110 M. Pointon, *Hanging the Head: Portraiture and Social Formation in Eighteenth-Century England* (New Haven and London, 1993), pp. 177–226; A. Higonnet, *Pictures of Innocence: The History and Crisis of Ideal Childhood* (London, 1998), pp. 15–35; J.C. Steward, *The New Child: British Art and the Origins of Modern Childhood, 1730–1830* (Berkeley, 1995).

111 T.W. Laqueur, *Religion and Respectability: Sunday Schools and Working Class Culture 1780–1850* (New Haven and London, 1976), pp. 5–20; P. Sangster, *Pity my Simplicity: The Evangelical Revival and the Religious Education of Children 1738–1800* (London, 1963); H. More, 'Strictures on Female Education', in *The Works of Hannah More*, 18 vols (London, 1818), Vol. 7, p. 67.

112 W.E. McLoughlin, 'Evangelical child-rearing in the age of Jackson: Francis Weyland's view on when and how to subdue the willfulness of children', *Journal of Social History*, 9 (1975), pp. 21–43. For the argument that there was an increase in discipline in the early nineteenth century, see L. Stone, *The Family, Sex, and Marriage in England 1500–1800* (London, 1977), pp. 669–73; L.A. Pollock, *Forgotten Children: Parent–Child Relations from 1500 to 1900* (Cambridge, 1983), pp. 184–5.

113 B. Wishy, *The Child and the Republic: The Dawn of Modern American Child Nurture* (Philadelphia, 1968), pp. 22, 109.

114 Ibid., p. 96; cf. Bronson Alcott in 1831, 'This is, indeed, the sin, which is unpardonable – the belief in the original and certain depravity of infant nature', quoted in C. Strickland, 'A transcendentalist father: the child-rearing practices of Bronson Alcott', *History of Childhood Quarterly*, I (1973), p. 11.

115 Summerfield, *Fantasy and Reason*, pp. 100–10; Coveney, *Image of Childhood*, pp. 50–1.

116 J. Brewer, 'The genesis of the modern toy', *History Today*, 30 (Dec. 1980), pp. 32–9, quoting p. 37.

117 Plumb, 'New world of children', p. 90; see also Locke, 'Some Thoughts Concerning Education', p. 191; for toy shops in late seventeenth-century Amsterdam, see R. Dekker, *Childhood, Memory and Autobiography in Holland: From the Golden Age to Romanticism* (Basingstoke, 2000), p. 79.

118 Quoted in Pickering, *John Locke and Children's Books*, p. 150. Pickering himself rescues Mrs Barbauld from attempts by romantics and later commentators to consign her to oblivion, a process taken further in the essays in J.H. McGavran (ed.), *Romanticism and Children's Literature in Nineteenth-Century England* (Atlanta, 1991) which downplay the opposition between the didactic and the romantic.

119 Summerfield, *Fantasy and Reason*, pp. 23–71, 269–73, quoting p. 271.

120 Coveney, *Image of Childhood*, pp. 68–83, quoting Wordsworth, p. 68.

121 B. Garlitz, 'The Immortality Ode: its cultural progeny', *Studies in English Literature*, 6 (1966), pp. 639–49. Brooke's 'imperial palace' was lifted directly from the Ode.

122 A. Wilson, 'Dickens on children and childhood', in M. Slater (ed.), *Dickens 1970* (London, 1970), pp. 195–227; M. Andrews, *Dickens and the Grown-Up Child* (London, 1994), esp. p. 9.

123 G. Eliot, *Silas Marner* (1860), ch. 14.

124 Quoted in Strickland, 'A transcendentalist father', pp. 8, 45.

125 Dekker, *Childhood, Memory and Autobiography in Holland*; J. Schlumbohm, 'Constructing individuality: childhood memories in late eighteenth-century "Empirical Psychology" and autobiography', *German History*, 16 (1998), pp. 29–42.

126 C. Steedman, *Strange Dislocations: Childhood and the Idea of Human Interiority, 1780–1930* (London, 1995); see also A. Fletcher and S. Hussey, 'Introduction', in A. Fletcher and S. Hussey (eds), *Childhood in Question: Children, Parents and the State* (Manchester, 1999), pp. 6–7.

127 Calvert, 'Children in American family portraiture', p. 105; P.N. Stearns, 'Girls, boys, and emotions: redefinitions and historical change', *Journal of American History*, 80 (1993), pp. 36–74.

128 Quoted in J.R. Kincaid, *Child-Loving: The Erotic Child and Victorian Culture* (London, 1992), pp. 64–5; see also pp. 13–16, 106–7.

129 P. Fuller, 'Uncovering childhood', in M. Hoyles (ed.), *Changing Childhood* (London, 1979), pp. 93–6.

130 R. Rosenblum, *The Romantic Child from Runge to Sendak* (London, 1988).

131 J. Ruskin, 'Fairyland' (1883), in *The Library Edition of the Works of John Ruskin* (39 vols, London, 1903–12), Vol. XXXIII, pp. 339–40.

132 L. Alcott, *Little Women* (1868; Harmondsworth, 1953), pp. 21, 88; see also on the theme of the desire not to grow up, A. Birkin, *J.M. Barrie and the Lost Boys* (London, 1979).

133 Wishy, *The Child and the Republic*, pp. 162–3.

134 W.B. Drummond, *The Child: His Nature and Nurture* (1901; London, 1909), p. 19.

135 See L. Davidoff and C. Hall, *Family Fortunes: Men and Women of the English Middle Class, 1780–1850* (London, 1987), pp. 329–35; J. Tosh, *A Man's Place: Masculinity and the Middle-Class Home in Victorian England* (New Haven and London, 1999), esp. pp. 79–101; R. Habermas, 'Parent–child relationships in the nineteenth century', *German History*, 16 (1998), pp. 43–55.

136 J. Uglow, *Elizabeth Gaskell: A Habit of Stories* (London, 1993), pp. 94–5.

137 N.S. Dye and D.B. Smith, 'Mother love and infant death, 1750–1920', *Journal of American History*, 73 (1986–7), pp. 329–53, quoting p. 338; Davidoff and Hall, *Family Fortunes*, pp. 338–43.

138 Quoted in Drummond, *The Child*, p. 19.

CHAPTER 4

Family, work and school, 1500–1900

The majority of children in these four centuries were born into and grew up in families. Families were part of larger communities, but the child's most formative experiences took place within the family. Over the last forty years historians have tried in two rapidly converging ways to write the history of families. The first of these is known as 'family reconstitution'; using census returns of various kinds, methodologies have been established which enable historians to speak with some confidence of the size and composition of both households and families. The second approach is variously referred to as 'household economics' or 'family strategy'. The aim is to understand the particular form which households or families took, and to explain changes over time. It is argued that family strategies may change in response to changing external conditions, or indeed that changing family strategies may themselves alter the external environment. Thus whereas the first approach can give us profiles of communities at certain points in time, the second explores the dynamics of change. The distinction between these two approaches has become blurred as it has become obvious to practitioners that both are necessary for an understanding of the history of the family.

The role of children within the family changed considerably within these four centuries. At the beginning of the period childhood for most children from about the age of seven consisted of a slow initiation to the world of adult work. At the end of the period in nearly every country regular schooling was compulsory for all children. Many historians see compulsory schooling as the end point of a journey in which children and their families had moved from a peasant economy, often via a proto-industrial one to an industrial one. Each of these economies suggested or enforced different family strategies, and consequently different roles for children.

The importance of compulsory schooling, and its extension up the age range, was that it delayed into the distant future the point at which children could become an economic asset to their families, if indeed they ever could become so. The balance shifted, with enormous consequences, from a situation where parents could reasonably suppose that children, whatever other benefits or disadvantages they might bring, would be an economic asset, to one where they knew that they would be a liability. Economic goods began to flow from parents to children rather than from children to parents.

Historians of the mass of the population, as distinct from the elites, of Europe and North America adopt concepts and a language derived from the disciplines of demography, economics, and anthropology. The more literary sources, such as conduct books or diaries, which form the bulk of our evidence about the elites, are either not present, or are thought to be irrelevant: peasants did not read conduct books. Demography tells us about the behaviour of this mass of the population, the age at which they got married, the number of children they had, and so on; economics enables us to deduce their family strategies; and anthropology seeks to explain the meanings which people attached to their behaviour. In none of this do we have the illusion of intimacy which can be gained from reading a diary. Individual children and their families rarely come alive for us. In some ways there are more vivid pictures of children's lives in the late medieval world, in Le Roy Ladurie's *Montaillou* or Hanawalt's *The Ties That Bound* and *Growing Up in Medieval London*, than exist for the early modern period. Church court records of the seventeenth century have provided an insight into family life, but they have more to tell us about aspects of adult life than about children or childhood. There simply do not exist sources which enable us with any confidence to write about the emotional life of families in the mass of the population. Lawrence Stone, who had tried to tackle this question in the first edition of *The Family, Sex and Marriage in England 1500–1800*, omitted it entirely in the shorter version of the book, so heavily had he been criticised for the inadequacy of his evidence. In the disciplines which dominate the field, children are more likely to be seen as assets or liabilities than as individuals who might or might not be loved; or indeed who might have some feelings of their own. The history of the family is parent-centred.

Flesh-and-blood children emerge more clearly in the sources when they step outside the privacy of the home into the community and school. The evidence is nearly all from adults, but it gives some insight into the way children behaved, and suggests that there may have existed a children's culture with its own customs, morals, and language.

The peasant family

Family reconstitution work has transformed our knowledge of the structure of families in early modern Europe. In northern and central Europe the norm was the two-generational nuclear family (parents and children) living in a separate household; under 10 per cent at any one point of time were three-generational, and many peasant families never passed through a three-generational phase, or if they did so it was only for a short time.[1] In southern and eastern Europe multi-generational households were much more common. The origins of the nuclear family system are disputed, Macfarlane arguing a uniquely English adherence to the nuclear family form dating back to the Germanic invasions. Few historians are persuaded by this case, but there is agreement that in the north and central parts of Europe the nuclear family was established by the end of the middle ages, its emergence owing much to the power of the medieval Church in enforcing rules about monogamy and exogamy in marriage.[2]

A key accompaniment to the nuclear family was late age of marriage. With women marrying in their mid-twenties, and men in their late twenties, it was likely that one or other, if not both, of their parents would be dead at the time they married or soon after. On demographic grounds alone, multi-generational households were unlikely. Moreover when multi-generational households did exist, they were not dominated in a patriarchal fashion by the grandfather; authority rested with the middle generation, their parents having negotiated retirement arrangements which allowed them maintenance in old age, but deprived them of powers of decision over the land.[3]

Land had an overriding influence on the nuclear family form and the age of marriage. Peasants had access to land in a wide variety of forms, most of them stopping short of outright unencumbered ownership, but all of them giving rights of inheritance. Simplistically it can be said that there were two main forms of inheritance, partible, where the land could be split among surviving children, and impartible where it went to the eldest son. In practice there were many variations on these two forms, all of which affected the structure of the household and the prospects of children. Peasant families had to evolve a strategy which would ensure both the handing down of the land to the next generation, and the successful management of it. The key to success in the latter was to ensure that labour supply was adequate to work the land. At times labour would have to be hired, but newly-married peasants could look forward to a situation where the workforce would be comprised of their children. This almost certainly meant that there should not be too many of them, something which was achieved by late marriage, and by weaning babies late since suckling had a contraceptive effect. If there were too many children, those surplus to the labour needs of the land would be hired out as servants to other families.

For those studying family strategy in peasant families, children feature in two ways: as potential labour, and as the inheritors of the land. Of course the investment in children, if that is the way to regard it, was one slow to yield any return. Economists, many of them working on contemporary peasant societies, disagree about the 'value' of children, but in no possible scenario could there be anything but a net loss on the investment in the first six or seven years. At that age the eldest child might begin to perform minor but useful tasks within the household or on the land, looking after younger siblings, herding livestock or scaring birds off crops. Thus in sixteenth-century Castile, both boys and girls helped to collect firewood, to herd livestock, to assist with ploughing, to collect or destroy aphids or worms on the vines, and to rear silkworms. The English evidence suggests that it was not until they were at least ten that children were expected to do more than simple tasks which rarely took up all of a child's time.[4] It was only in their late teenage years that children's labour input began to equal that of adults, and there is much evidence, certainly in English sources, of underemployment or unemployment of children in the agricultural sector of the economy.[5] Agricultural work was by nature seasonal, and it is difficult to think of any agrarian economy that offered full-time work throughout the year for children; as we shall see, schooling tended to be concentrated in the winter months, when it was difficult to find ways in which children could contribute to the family economy. Historians have rigorously guarded themselves against a romanticism of family life in the past with the one exception that they still imagine a peasant family work unit in which all members contributed according to their age, strength and gender. In fact many children, unless there was a local industry, were frequently idle. Probably the labour input of the eldest child did not outweigh the costs of feeding, clothing and housing it until it was fifteen, and the family as a whole might not be a net gainer from having children until the eighteenth year of the marriage.[6] But if children were an expense, they were also crucial to the peasant economy, as the labour force in embryo and as the future inheritors of the land. And the delicate balance of that economy dictated late marriage and an ideal of about four or five surviving children, the eldest of whom might have left the family home by the time the youngest was born.[7]

For those who would not inherit land, marriage was the riskiest of ventures, and normally avoided. In an area of Austria with impartible inheritance, the eldest son employed his siblings as servants on the farm. They had little opportunity to marry, but did not remain sexually inactive, as is shown by an illegitimacy rate of over 80 per cent.[8] Marriage was closely associated with inheritance of land. Historians have speculated about the impact of systems of this kind upon relationships within the family. There was clearly plenty of scope for inter-generational rivalry as eldest sons waited for fathers to die or retire so that they could have access to land, and for sibling rivalry if the eldest son treated his siblings as servants; or in situations of partible inheritance, if the share-out was thought to be inequitable. It was also important for a family to achieve a gender balance among its children, so that the labour supply matched the customary gendered division of tasks. But work on these issues is at a most rudimentary level. In a survey of work on 'The European peasant family and economy', Richard Rudolph wrote that 'the comparison of extended families, stem families, and nuclear families of various forms with respect to the types of affective relations and especially the attitudes toward children would be extremely rewarding'.[9] Indeed, but it has not been done, perhaps cannot be done. And one should note the assumptions on which, in Rudolph's view, such a study should be based; it is assumed that the form of the family, itself determined by eco-systems and inheritance practices, will be the key to unlocking differences in attitudes toward children. Students of the peasant family tend towards economic determinism.

Does it make sense to talk of 'the peasant family'? Certainly there were vast differences not only from one region to another, or between northern and central Europe on the one hand and eastern Europe on the other (in the latter peasants were becoming more unfree), but also within regions, with a hierarchy of rank and status among peasants. And throughout Europe, but particularly in the economically more advanced areas, there was a growing number of people living in rural areas who were landless, dependent on wages, or otherwise scraping a living. Their children, as we shall see in the next chapter, gave rise to a problem of enormous proportions. Nevertheless, despite all these cautions, peasant families can be seen as constituting the majority, though a diminishing majority, of Europe's population throughout these four centuries, and falling into two distinct types, depending on where they lived. Within these families children's lives were dominated by the necessity to contribute by their labour to the family economy from an early age, and by their prospects or otherwise of inheriting land, directly or by marriage. Children were essential to the peasant economy, but no one knows whether their economic value was replicated in the realm of the emotions, or whether affection within the family may have been divorced from considerations of economic utility.

Proto-industrialisation

There were many peasant families which were not purely peasant. Sometimes, surplus family members moved into other sectors of the economy. Sometimes, work on the land was seasonal, giving scope for other work in the rest of the year, often through migration. And, with increasing frequency in the seventeenth and eighteenth centuries, the household became the centre for industrial production. The rural industry of the early modern period has long been a familiar mark of the landscape in historians' accounts of these centuries, but in recent years its importance has been heightened under the rubric of 'proto-industrialisation'. We need not follow the debates about the precise character of proto-industrialisation, but we do need to consider the impact of rural industry on age of marriage and on the role of children. In the initial formulation of theories of proto-industrialisation in the 1970s, it was argued that families which became dependent on industry no longer had hung around their necks the problem of inheritance, nor was there a limitation on the number of children who could easily be absorbed within the labour demands of the land they farmed. The barrier to early marriage was thereby removed, and with it family size increased. Marriage itself could take place whenever a young couple decided to set up a separate home/workplace, and this required only minimal capital. Children naturally followed, and could be put to some form of useful labour at an earlier age than they could in agriculture. As Hans Medick argued, proto-industrialisation 'favoured a form of reproductive behaviour which, by "producing" a maximal number of child labourers, raised the productive capacity of the family and thereby its survival possibilities beyond that critical threshold of poverty on the margins of which the family often began its existence'.[10] There was nothing new about children's industrial work. Archaeological evidence from near Bonn, dating back to the early thirteenth century, shows children's fingerprints on pots, indicating children's role in carrying freshly turned pots to drying areas in a business which was exporting to England, Scandinavia and Poland.[11] But the amount of industrial work for children was on the

increase – as it was for adults. In the textile districts of England Defoe, as
is often noted, delighted to find children of four apparently earning their
keep. He may perhaps have exaggerated the youthfulness of these workers,
but employment for children, year long in duration, certainly became a
possibility from the age of about six.[12] These children in turn might at a
relatively young age break free from the family, and from effectively forced
contributions to its upkeep, marry, and set up their own home and unit of
production.

It is now recognised that forms of rural industry existed not only in
marginal agricultural areas, but also in those of high productivity; and
further that not all forms of rural industry followed the prototype set
out above. In some, for example the arms-related cottage industries in
Belgium, a degree of training was required before the work could be done,
and this dampened down any tendency towards the formation of new
households.[13] Moreover the demographic consequences were sometimes
more complex than was first thought. It was only when the capital
required for setting up a new unit of production was indeed minimal, as in
framework knitting in Leicestershire where the machinery was rented, and
only when the incomes to be gained from proto-industrialisation were
clearly greater than in agriculture, that there ensued rapid demographic
growth linked to a lower age of marriage. Elsewhere forms of rural industry existed more as by-employments than as the major feature of a local
economy, or the work in them was dominated by females. In both cases the
demographic effects were much less striking; in an area of Normandy
where men continued to be employed in agriculture, and women constituted the industrial workforce, first in spinning and then in weaving,
the age of marriage remained at the high peasant level.[14]

The growth of rural industry was, however, of enormous importance
for children because it undoubtedly increased their economic usefulness.
Rural industries could help to absorb the surplus child labour supply. In
the canton of Zurich in Switzerland the children of farmer and craftsmen
families often worked in the proto-industrial textile industry; proto-
industrialisation offered regular work to children in ways that neither
agriculture nor traditional craft industries could match.[15]

The Zurich example points to a further conclusion: in conditions of
proto-industrialisation it was by no means certain that children would be
working in their own homes or with members of their own family. In a sense
they became available to earn some portion of a living wherever it could be
found. As Richard Wall concluded from a study of Colyton in Devon in
1851, 'many families were not functioning as integrated work units'.[16]

Industrialisation

The links between proto-industrialisation and industrialisation are complex and need not detain us, except in one respect. Proto-industrialisation had accustomed people to seeing young children in regular work. With few exceptions the response to it on the part of middle- and upper-class observers had been positive, and they had indeed invested much effort in attempts to create industries in which children could work. John Locke, in the same decade that he published his *Some Thoughts Concerning Education* as a guide to the education of a gentleman, also advised the Board of Trade that working schools should be set up in each parish for children from the age of three, and that there they should be instructed in the textile industries; by the age of fourteen, he reckoned, they would more than have paid off the initial expenses.[17] When in the late eighteenth century industrialisation began to shift the location of the textile industries from home to factory, it was natural to look to children as a key component of the workforce.

Potentially industrialisation offered a solution to a problem which had long irked the elites of Europe: the idleness of children. There is much less evidence that this advantage was recognised by working families. It is at this point in time, the onset of industrialisation, that the limitations of a 'family strategy' approach become most apparent. The phrase 'family strategy' conveys a sense of a family rationally, if perhaps hard-heartedly, considering a range of options open to it: of a family in control of its own destiny and making a choice.[18] Of course it is recognised that families did this within certain parameters, institutional, economic, geographic, and moral, but nevertheless choice is of the essence of family strategy; it makes the people the agents more than the subjects of history. Few families undergoing the process of industrialisation would have greeted this with anything other than a hollow laugh. In truth there comes a point where the 'parameters', 'constraints' and 'delimiting factors' affecting 'choice' are so paramount that the notion of 'choice' becomes meaningless. If families had been told that they had 'chosen' as part of a 'family strategy' to put their children to work exorbitantly long hours in unhealthy factories, they would have replied that it was not a choice but a necessity, and one which they deeply regretted.

No one now claims that the process of industrialisation transformed the nature or size of the family. The old view of a shift from extended to nuclear families as a consequence of industrialisation belongs to the historian's dustbin; if anything family size increased slightly. Nor can it be said that the family disintegrated under the pressures of industrialisation; again, the opposite can be argued, the family becoming a more central mechanism for survival, a resource which one abandoned at one's peril. For the family not only provided a home, it was also the means by which people found jobs, much early industrial work being organised around the structure of the family.

It is, however, easy to exaggerate the extent to which industrialisation can be seen as involving simply a shift of workplace from home to factory. And however much it is the continuities in family experience which now receive emphasis, for children the change in experience was considerable. First, in contrast to agricultural work, and to a lesser extent proto-industrial work, their work had a regular quality extending throughout the year; the trade cycle might bring with it periods of slump and lay-off, but in principle work achieved a regularity on a daily, weekly and annual basis far removed from pre-industrial practice. Secondly, entry into the labour market was no longer phased; one day you were not a worker, and the next day you were. Thirdly, it was by no means certain that children would be working under the supervision of members of their own families, a point which was also true under proto-industrialisation, but which had added impact in a work unit as large as a factory. Add to this the fact that children often started work under the age of ten, and the industrial revolution period begins to regain the reputation it had until recent years as a black moment in the history of childhood. The family as an institution may have survived the industrial revolution, but many individual children did not.[19]

Family strategy left many families with little if any option but to put their children to work in factories; the income they could bring in was essential. In surveys of Belgian families, children were found to be contributing 22 per cent of family income in 1853 and 31 per cent in 1891. In the United States in the 1880s, by the time the adult male head of household was in his fifties, children were contributing about one-third of family income. In a textile town in Catalonia it was higher than that, over half when the head of the household was in his late fifties, more than two-thirds when he was over sixty. The alternative to the child working in the factory was for the mother to do so, but normally 'children were preferred to their mothers as family wage-earners'.[20] Since in addition adult male employment became more difficult with the textile industry's predilection for juvenile labour, there might have been a transformation of family relationships, particularly as the children grew into their teen years; in practice few children seemed to exercise the power that was notionally there through their earnings. The family held together.

The work of children in factories eventually led to state interference to control it in all countries, a theme we shall take up in Chapter 6. What we need to note at this point is that the situation governments faced as they surveyed child labour in factories was indeed a novelty. Although there were people within the middle and upper classes who defended it, it is hard to find any within the working class who saw it as anything better than an unavoidable necessity; and there were many who condemned it outright. It is not surprising that the labour of children in factories was one key factor, though not the only one, leading to that transformation of childhood from being a time of initiation to the workforce to being a time for schooling.

Demography

Demography enables us to map out the contours of children's lives with some accuracy. The demographic profile of Europe retained a remarkable constancy until the latter half of the nineteenth century. That is not to say that the level of population did not change – of course it did. But certainly by comparison with what was to come in the twentieth century the changes in overall demographic structure were minimal.

We may start by asking what chances children had of survival. As a rough generalisation, somewhere between one in four and one in five of all children born died before they reached their first birthday. In England between 1600 and 1749 it is probable that the infant mortality rate (deaths per thousand births of those under one) was between 250 and 340. In France in the last third of the seventeenth century it was between 200 and 400, the chances of survival being greater in the country than in towns; the infant mortality rate seems to have dropped in France in the course of the eighteenth century in association with a decline in fertility.[21] In Sweden in the second half of the eighteenth century the average annual infant mortality rate was exactly 200. In the nineteenth century, when statistics for infant mortality become more available, there were some major contrasts, with predominantly rural countries like Ireland and Norway losing only about one baby in ten, while Germany lost more than double that number. But the main theme is one of continuity. Comparing the average infant mortality rate in nine countries in 1840–4 and 1895–9, we find that in three countries (Belgium, England and Wales, and France) the rate rose slightly, and in the remaining six (Austria, Denmark, Germany, Netherlands, Norway and Sweden), it fell, but again normally by only a small amount. Overall in these nine countries the infant mortality rate fell from

177 to 156 deaths per one thousand live births.[22] What was striking was how high it remained.

Mortality rates dropped after the age of one, but the child remained extremely vulnerable. In some areas nearly half of all children failed to live to the age of ten, but in favourable conditions, as English evidence shows, the rate could drop below one-quarter. In colonial New England, the situation was even better, with between 80 and 90 per cent of those born in Andover, Massachusetts between 1640 and 1729 surviving to the age of ten. By the late eighteenth century, however, North America was coming closer to the European norm.[23]

Deaths of children constituted the majority of all deaths; in a Florence parish in the second half of the seventeenth century, nearly two-thirds of all deaths were of children under the age of five.[24] The younger they were the greater the likelihood of death; it was in the first hours and days of life that children were most vulnerable. Epidemics or famines could alter these figures for the worse, good times for the better, but the variations are much less important than the contrast between these four centuries, and the almost uninterrupted improvement so far as mortality is concerned in the twentieth century. Nevertheless child mortality began to drop before infant mortality. In England and Wales the trend was downwards for one- to four-year-olds from the mid-1860s and for five- to nine-year-olds from the 1840s. For white Americans child mortality was in decline from the 1880s.[25]

This high mortality rate, which affected all classes, has been seen as indicating a low regard for children. We have seen that there are reasons to doubt this so far as the well-to-do are concerned. Does the same hold true for the lower classes? To answer this we must take account of two factors which bear on the mortality rate: abandonment and wet-nursing. Abandonment was closely linked to the availability of foundling hospitals and to the admission policies they operated. Broadly speaking, foundling hospitals were to be found in Catholic areas, that is to say largely in southern Europe. In Florence decennial averages for the sixteenth and seventeenth centuries suggest that never less than 12 per cent of babies were abandoned, some at least of these being legitimate children. There was perhaps a dip in the level of abandonment in Europe in the late seventeenth and early eighteenth centuries before it began a sustained rise in the later eighteenth and early nineteenth centuries.[26] In Paris the number of children abandoned was about 1,700 per year between 1700 and 1720, but had risen to 5,000–6,000 per year between 1760 and 1789. In Toulouse abandonments as a proportion of recorded births rose from a mean of 10 per cent in the first half of the eighteenth century to a mean of

17 per cent in the second half, sometimes reaching over 25 per cent. In Milan an abandonment rate of 16 per cent at the beginning of the eighteenth century had risen to 25 per cent by the century's end.[27] Abandonment rates continued to rise in the first half of the nineteenth century and even beyond. David Kertzer has summarised the situation in the early nineteenth century as follows:

babies were being abandoned in vast numbers in France, Belgium, and Portugal, and the situation was even worse in Spain, Ireland, Poland, and in most of the Austrian provinces. In Madrid, Dublin, and Warsaw, up to a fifth of all babies were being abandoned, while Milan had reached a third, Prague two-fifths, and Vienna a half.

Overall it is reckoned that in the mid-nineteenth century over 100,000 babies were abandoned every year in Europe.[28] The increases over previous centuries are marked. France as a whole abandoned six times as many babies in the decade 1820–9 as it had in 1740–9. The Ospedale degli Innocenti in Florence in the decade 1841–50 received 38 per cent of births in Florence compared to a percentage which was below 9 per cent in the fifteenth century. Although abandonment was most common at or soon after birth, it could happen later. Entry records for orphanages for girls in seventeenth- and eighteenth-century Rome show frequent admissions of older children if one parent died.[29]

There was also in France in the later eighteenth and nineteenth centuries an increase in the number of babies who were sent to the countryside to be wet-nursed for the first year of life. In the late eighteenth century in Paris the Bureau des Nourrices, the official wet-nurse agency created in 1769, was placing out nearly half of the 21,000 infants born each year, and a further 45 per cent were placed out through private agencies; that is, 95 per cent of all the babies born were wet-nursed. This was an exceptionally high rate; in 1801–2 it stood at 49 per cent, a rate which had dipped only slightly by 1869 when it was 41 per cent.[30]

Both abandonment and wet-nursing were associated with high mortality levels. Just how high it would be was dependent on the speed with which the baby was transferred to a rural wet-nurse: the sooner the better. In bad conditions as many as nine out of every ten abandoned babies died before they reached their first birthday. Where policies were in place to put children out quickly, even where abandonment rates were high, as in mid-nineteenth-century Florence, the rate of mortality dropped, to a rate of about 300 deaths per thousand live births.[31] Even so, abandoned children faced a distinctly uncertain future.

What caused these levels of abandonment and wet-nursing? There is considerable evidence that they were associated with poverty. In northern Italy in the sixteenth and early seventeenth centuries there is a close correlation between years of economic crisis and the number of babies abandoned. The same conclusion emerges from studies of the Inclusa in Madrid in both the seventeenth and eighteenth centuries; in Joan Sherwood's words, 'Infants flooded the Inclusa every time the price of grain went up.' In London, where abandonment was dealt with by the parish, the level 'increased in line with bread prices in the late-seventeenth and early-eighteenth centuries'.[32] Similarly in Limoges in France where the number of children abandoned tripled between the 1740s and the 1780s there was a close correlation between the increase and grain prices. Looking at France as a whole, Olwen Hufton finds that 'the strong upward movement of numbers of *enfants trouvés* roughly coincides with the onset in each province of long-term deteriorating economic conditions'.[33]

There is no doubt also that the increase in abandonment was associated with an increase in illegitimacy. One of the arguments in favour of foundling hospitals was that they allowed a woman who had conceived an illegitimate baby to preserve her honour; the abandonment could be done in secret, anonymously. Equally, one of the arguments against them was that they took away the shame of illegitimacy. There was an undoubted rise in the illegitimacy rate in the late eighteenth century, and this shows up in the admission figures for foundling hospitals. In Paris in the eighteenth century 70–80 per cent of the abandoned were illegitimate, a proportion rising to 80–95 per cent in the nineteenth century. In most large French towns probably over 60 per cent of those abandoned were illegitimate.[34] In Italy, with the important exceptions of Tuscany and Milan, nearly all babies abandoned were illegitimate. It is, of course, true that the mothers of illegitimate babies were likely to be in poverty, and it may have been poverty quite as much as shame which led to abandonment. In Bologna it is difficult to see how honour was preserved for those women who were too poor to pay a fee to the foundling hospital, and had to act as unpaid wet-nurses for a year. In Corsica women seem to have tried to preserve their honour by killing their illegitimate children, abandonment being resorted to by the poor who were not greatly concerned about honour.[35]

Do poverty and illegitimacy between them account for the levels of abandonment? Not entirely. We need to recall that in many towns a half or more of those abandoned were legitimate. In Limoges where, as we have seen, the number of children abandoned tripled between the 1740s and the 1780s, a majority were almost certainly legitimate. In Madrid about half of the babies abandoned were legitimate, in Moscow and St Petersburg between one-third and a half, in London in the 1740s and 1750s about one-third. In Milan in the 1840s a majority of those abandoned were legitimate; put another way, about one-third of all legitimate children born in Milan were being left at the foundling hospital.[36]

There is a close connection between the abandonment of the legitimate and wet-nursing; abandonment was wet-nursing at public expense, for the intention and sometimes the practice was to reclaim the child. In Milan in the 1840s and 1850s more than 13,000 children were reclaimed, nearly three-quarters of whom had spent more than two years in the foundling hospital.[37] This seems to have been less a response to changing economic conditions, than to an ongoing necessity for mothers to earn, and the difficulties of doing so if there were more than two children to look after at home at any one time; the foundling hospital was the resource which enabled this strategy to be put into practice. The norm, as in wet-nursing, was to reclaim the child, though often it had died.[38] Foundling hospitals were often dependent on the poorest wet-nurses. Those who were willing to pay for a wet-nurse would have more chance of seeing their child alive at weaning. Outside the upper and middle classes, the families which were likely to use wet-nurses were those in which there was artisanal or shop work for women in towns. For example, in Lyons in France in the eighteenth century women who worked in the food trades or in silk manu-facturing, sometimes away from home, were likely to place their children out to rural wet-nurses. The nurses themselves came from the poorer rural families, the pay from wet-nursing being a key contribution in an 'eco-nomy of makeshifts'.[39] This system grew and flourished in the nineteenth century, only coming to an end at the time of the First World War, perhaps coinciding with the withdrawal of women from those forms of employ-ment in which wet-nursing had seemed an obvious strategy.[40] Wet-nursing was probably most prevalent in France. There is evidence of its existence in villages surrounding London in the seventeenth and early eighteenth centuries but not thereafter, and in any case it seems to have largely met the needs of the well-to-do.[41] But wet-nursing depended as much on a supply of wet-nurses as on the demand for their services; in Stockholm it survived, into the twentieth century, until there was alternative state support for unmarried mothers.[42] It is possible that it existed in most centres of old industry in Europe, as it certainly did in Milan, and it would be wrong, therefore, to see it as exclusively French.[43]

Jean Meyer has argued that the French evidence on abandonment 'seems to indicate a growing indifference both to children and to the traditional family pattern in French towns in the eighteenth century'.[44] Others have put the opposite case, that in times of extreme poverty abandonment might at least appear to offer the greatest hope of survival both to the infant abandoned and to the rest of the family – for the mother might be able to make a greater contribution to the family economy if relieved of the baby.[45] Similarly, the practice of putting children out to rural wet-nurses may be seen as part of a rational family strategy aiming to maximise income and therefore well-being through enabling the mother to be engaged in the labour market. Such strategies need to be put in the context of the high infant and child mortality rates for children who were neither abandoned nor put out to wet-nurses. They may plausibly suggest an acceptance of the likelihood of infant mortality, and to a lesser extent child mortality, an acceptance which by no means precluded grief when it actually happened.

The police documents of Paris have enabled Arlette Farge to put a human face on these more or less plausible generalisations in considering parental attitudes to children. We know, for example, how Louise Brulé, the wife of a servant, who had put her son out to nurse in 1765, wanted to have him back when he was one, and how the child died on the journey, leaving the mother distraught and 'all in tears'. And we know of the distress of both parents and children when the Parisian authorities periodically tried to round up teenagers to send them off to populate Louisiana or Mississippi, and of the prompt action taken by many parents to secure the release of their children.[46]

Although they died in such numbers, children constituted a much higher proportion of the population than they do in modern society. Somewhere between one-third and one-half of the total population was likely to be under fifteen.[47] In any society before the twentieth century there were, as Peter Laslett expressed it, 'crowds and crowds of little children'.[48] This demographic fact alone made it almost inevitable that children would be expected to contribute to the family economy at an early age; it would have been impossible to support this proportion of children if they had remained wholly dependent.

A third feature of the demographic structure of these centuries which distinguishes them sharply from the twentieth and twenty-first centuries is that many children could expect one or both of their parents to die before they themselves reached adulthood. For English children born in the mid-eighteenth century, around 14 per cent would have lost one parent by the age of ten, and around 20 per cent would have lost one by the age of fifteen; on the other hand orphanage was not that common; only 2 per cent would have lost both parents by the age of ten, and 4 per cent by the age of fifteen.[49] If one parent died, the survivor would almost certainly remarry. Remarriages might constitute between one-quarter and one-third of all marriages. In cities like London where mortality rates were exceptionally high, it was quite likely that children would at some point have to accommodate themselves to a stepmother or stepfather, and to stepbrothers and stepsisters.[50] In the twentieth and twenty-first centuries family break-up by divorce has replaced family break-up by death.

A fourth distinguishing demographic characteristic is that siblings were much more spaced out by age than has become the norm in the twentieth and twenty-first centuries. Mothers might expect at least fifteen years of childbearing, with roughly one child every two years. The eldest child might well have left the family home by the time the youngest was born. One consequence of this, combined with high mortality rates, was that children did not grow up surrounded by a multiplicity of siblings. Where urban populations were in decline, as in Rheims in the fifteenth century or Coventry in the sixteenth century, three-quarters of households with children had only one or two children. As a general rule a majority of households with children would at any one time have had no more than three.[51]

At what age did children leave home? Stone reckoned that at the lower end of the social scale children 'left home at between seven and fourteen to begin work as domestic servants, labourers or apprentices, but in all cases living in their masters' houses rather than at home or in lodgings'.[52] More detailed work on census materials has shown this to be wrong. It was in fact rare to leave before the age of ten, the peak ages being between thirteen and sixteen. And by no means every child left. In England, where the practice of leaving home for service was probably more prevalent than elsewhere, and where about 60 per cent of the population aged between fifteen and twenty-four were servants, around one-third of children were still living in the parental home at the age of fifteen or over. Elsewhere one half or more of twenty- to twenty-four-year-olds lived at home.[53] The reason for this difference can be found in labour requirements and inheritance practices. It was in the families of landless labourers that children were likely to leave home earliest; there was no way they could contribute usefully to the family economy. In the western counties of England it was the practice for children of poor parents to be bound out to farmers at the age of nine, and to remain with them until they were twenty-one. But where the family had some craft by-employment, or a holding of some substance, and particularly where the oldest child could expect to inherit, there was less reason to leave home. Middle children were likely to leave at an earlier age than the eldest or the youngest.[54]

The most common exit from childhood was to become a servant, employed on a yearly basis, and provided with board and lodging in the employer's house. Next to it in importance was apprenticeship, and the age at which people were engaged as apprentices is very similar to that at which they became servants. It may have been as low as twelve in sixteenth-century France, but by the eighteenth and nineteenth centuries in middle Europe it was most frequently at fourteen. The same was true of England in the eighteenth century.[55]

Under the impact of industrialisation, where the family became less a unit of production than a unit of wage-earners, there was much less incentive on the part of parents to persuade teenagers to leave home. It is true that there might be problems of space within the home if there was a large number of children, but in other respects the parents had every incentive to keep wage-earning adolescents at home, and contributing to the family budget. There was thus a gradual change to the system whereby adolescents left home at around the age of fourteen. Nevertheless, such information as we have suggests that boys at any rate did normally leave home prior to marriage; in England and Wales in 1851 about one-quarter of all boys aged fifteen, and over 40 per cent of those aged eighteen, were living outside the parental home.[56] Given the continued prevalence of domestic service as an occupation for girls, it seems likely that they too would often leave home prior to marriage; the English evidence points to a falling age of leaving home for girls between 1700 and 1860.[57]

Community

It was undoubtedly chiefly within the family that children learned about the world into which they had been born, and about the roles which they could expect to play. But the family was not the only means of socialisation. The community in which he or she lived played an important part in the life of the child. Just how important it is very difficult to say. We know more about the role played by the community at the very beginning of childhood, and at its end, than we do for its duration. Childbirth was in many ways a communal activity, though an almost exclusively female one.[58] And adolescents often formed groupings with political and social significance. What was the relationship between the community and children from birth to the early teenage years? In cities and towns at any rate there seems to have been provision, not only, as we shall see in the next chapter, for the destitute, but also to help others who fell into difficulties. Thus in Norwich there was a system of public provision for sick children. In the same city a child was removed from its mother who had been beating it excessively. But most important of all, at the point where childhood was coming to an end, there was a degree of public supervision of apprenticeship which served to integrate the child into the larger society and strongly suggests a communal concern for the child's welfare.[59]

What about less formal approaches to child-rearing within the community? At least until the later nineteenth century,[60] we know little about how far the early stages of child-rearing may have been shared between families. Some form of communal child-rearing probably became inevitable in urban conditions, for the street was more attractive than the crowded home. It is possible that in rural areas children may have been more home-based, though they would certainly be present in the fields at moments of maximum pressure in the agricultural year.

In so far as we do know about the social life of children, it is mainly through the complaints of their social superiors who frequently deplored the activities of gangs of children disturbing the peace of neighbourhoods. In Bristol in the late seventeenth century, children were said to be 'lousing like swarms of locusts in every corner of the street'. In the smaller town of Olney in Buckinghamshire, the poet William Cowper complained that 'children of seven years of age infest the streets every evening with curses and with songs'. Children showed no respect for churches; in 1681 they were found playing cards on the communion table in Durham Cathedral. A certain amount of unruliness was licensed in the numerous occasions for misrule which punctuated the calendar.[61] Children, we need to remember, constituted a much larger proportion of the population than they do now, and would have been correspondingly visible – and audible. Sometimes there was a touching recognition of their frailties; in Elizabethan Winchester children up to the age of twelve who relieved themselves out of doors did not commit an offence.[62]

Keith Thomas has argued that children in early modern England lived in a subculture whose values differed markedly from those of the adult world. They had, he notes, 'a casual attitude to private property, an addiction to mischief, and a predilection for what most adults regarded as noise and dirt'. They placed a high valuation on what adults regarded (and often disparaged) as play; they were adept at making toys out of natural objects; and their activities were regulated by elaborate codes and rituals, including their own language. In this they sound like modern children, for example those studied in the north-east of England where 'children construct their own ordered system of rules by reinterpreting the social models given to them by adults'. There may be, as the Opies argued, a remarkable continuity in children's cultural forms.[63]

Schooling

The community was one source of extra-family socialisation. Schooling was another. We are concerned here to see schooling from the bottom upwards rather than, as in the next chapter, from the top downwards. That is to say, the focus will be on the level of demand for schooling. It must be said at once that it is not easy to separate out demand from supply, and that the sources encourage a perspective from the point of view of supply. Thus both in the sixteenth century, under the influence of religion, and in the eighteenth century, with secular influences dominant, there were enormous and often successful efforts to increase the supply of schools, and to try to enforce attendance. In what senses did children who attended these schools do so willingly? And how far did the supply of schools match the demand?

There were certainly vast disparities in supply. As a general rule, towns, Protestant areas, lowland rather than highland agricultural areas, and boys rather than girls, were favoured. Thus in Scandinavia there were hardly any schools in rural areas. The gender difference is perhaps the most striking one; in the German duchy of Brandenburg in the early sixteenth century, there were fifty-five boys' schools and only four girls' schools. In the French diocese of Tarbes in the late eighteenth century some two-thirds of the eligible boys attended school as against only one in fifty of the eligible girls.[64]

What could schooling offer to the lower classes of Europe in the early modern period? First, religious education. This was the main motivation for the foundation of schools in the sixteenth century, and there is no reason to suppose that there was not a corresponding demand. In Catholic areas there were catechism schools whose main function was to instruct children about to receive first communion.[65] Within Protestantism, the reading of the Bible and the learning of catechisms were fundamental to a child's religious education, and the huge output of literature may have been as much the response to as the creation of a demand. In England between the mid-sixteenth and mid-seventeenth centuries, no less than 350 different catechisms were published.[66] We can gauge something of the demand for this kind of education from the response in the late eighteenth and early nineteenth centuries to the English Sunday schools; it is estimated that a very high proportion of English working-class children attended.[67]

A second reason why parents may have encouraged or forced their children to attend school may be described as secular. Schools taught reading, a skill which, as we have seen, was of vital importance within Protestantism, but one which was also increasingly valued for secular reasons. An education beyond the elementary level was crucial for social advancement, and there was a growing number of opportunities for such advancement as the bureaucracies of the state grew. But even at a rudimentary level, a basic level of literacy was valued for two reasons. First, it enabled people to make some sense of the demands made upon them by the printed rules and ordinances which flowed in copious abundance from the state. And secondly, it gave them access to the popular literature of ballads, chapbooks and almanacs which flourished in this period.

A third reason why parents may have sent their children to school is that the school could provide a convenient childminding service. Some schools, though we have no means of knowing how many, took in children from the age of three. There is evidence for such schools in Spain, and in nineteenth-century England, where some 40 per cent of those in the dame schools were under the age of five. In Antwerp there was immediate demand for the four nursery schools set up in the 1840s by the Société d'Ecoles gardiennes, and looking after 1,160 infants of paupers aged two to six from 7 a.m. to 7 p.m. daily.[68] At an age when the child clearly interfered with the productivity of the parents, particularly if the mother had to try to find work outside the home, it might be worth paying out a small weekly fee to have the child looked after, and the opportunity would be all the more attractive if, as in Antwerp, the service was free.

Payment of fees was of course the downside of schooling for the family economy. Although there was some free schooling through charitable endowments of one kind or another, the vast majority of parents whose children attended school had to pay.[69] For the poor, perhaps some 20 per cent of the population, payment of fees was out of the question; they were often the target population for work schools which aimed to finance themselves out of the industrial labour of the children. Slightly more prosperous parents would be aware not only of the outgoing of the fee, but also of the possibility of the loss of the child's earning capacity through attendance at school. It is not surprising to find that attendance at school was normally intermittent and irregular. In rural areas schooling might well be confined to the winter months or less; in the Low Countries in the seventeenth century and in Norway in the eighteenth century, the school year did not extend beyond ten weeks. From Liguria in Italy in the 1870s and 1880s it was reported that 'there is no dislike of schooling on the part of the peasantry, but the schools are up to now ill-adapted to the needs and requirements of rural life. Every year at the time of the harvest, the schools are all deserted.' In towns, the school year might be more continuous, but overall attendance might be no greater. Moreover, few children attended school for more than three years, and many for less.[70]

Temporary hardship or opportunities for child labour reduced school attendance. In France there was a 'marked contraction in the number attending elementary schools' in years of bad harvest and high food prices such as 1589–94, 1693–5 and 1711–13. In Bremen in Germany the number of petty schools fell from around one hundred in 1788 to sixty in 1810 as opportunities opened up for children to work in tobacco processing. There was a decline in literacy levels in Lancashire in the peak period of the industrial revolution when child labour opportunities were at their greatest.[71]

It is not difficult to produce figures indicating high levels of schooling and of literacy in parts of early modern Europe.[72] But to see this in proportion we need to look at it from the point of view of the family economy and of the socialisation of the child. It is here that the contrast with the late nineteenth- and twentieth-century period of compulsory and regular schooling becomes marked. In northern and central Europe, though not in the east and south, the vast majority of boys, and a much lower proportion of girls, had some schooling in the early modern centuries, but that schooling took up a significantly lower amount of their time than was to be the case later; it was fitted around the much more central part of their education which consisted of an initiation into work within the family. A study of working-class autobiographies in nineteenth-century England revealed on the part of the writers (who might be assumed to be a section of the working class peculiarly alive to the importance of schooling), a 'general recognition of the subordination of education to the demands of the family economy'.[73]

Nevertheless there is clear evidence of a demand for schooling. As David Vincent writes, 'Education was far from being a commodity that was forced upon the working class community by outside agencies.'[74] Much of it, probably between 70 and 80 per cent in mid-eighteenth century England, and still as much as one-quarter in 1875, was provided by private enterprise.[75] Some schools were set up in direct response to parental demand. David Love described how he

was persuaded by some people in a large village to keep a school to teach their children: they found me a large empty place, somewhat like a barn,

with a fire place at the end: they soon furnished it with forms and tables,
and the first week I got more than twenty scholars, increasing each week,
till I had above forty; but I got no more than a penny each week for
readers, and three halfpence for writers, so that my wages were but very
small and ill paid.[76]

The schooling demanded was limited to the acquisition of skills, and parents paid accordingly, more for writing than for reading. Equally parents
had some control. They could and did move their children from school to
school, and they preferred the private schools to those set up by authority,
whether church or state.[77]

It is possible, of course, that the demand for schooling came more
from parents than from children. Schooling was hardly so organised as
to appeal to children; rather there was likely to be, as Keith Thomas has
expressed it with regard to early modern England, 'a repressive regime,
governed autocratically, sustained by corporal punishment and tempered
only by the master's mildness, incapacity, or financial dependence upon
his pupils'. Children were likely to look for any means of subverting
or escaping from such regimes, perhaps as in Wales in the late eighteenth century trying to squeeze a few extra days' holiday by telling their
parents that the holidays lasted for five weeks rather than a month.[78]
A more violent opposition to school is indicated by the situation in
Central, New Mexico in the nineteenth century where the teacher had a
six-shooter strapped under his swallowtail coat, a form of defence which
did not prevent him from being knocked senseless by an older boy with
a large chain.[79] That, doubtless, was exceptional, but we certainly cannot
discount Shakespeare's assumption that children went 'unwillingly to
school'.

So far as parents are concerned, however, it was only when the authorities of church and state began to enforce school that signs of opposition
to it come to the surface. Much of this opposition was not to education
in itself, but to the syllabus, the system of control, the regulations, and
the fines for non-attendance. From the Orléanais it was reported in 1881
that 'our peasants are very irritated about the new laws of compulsory
primary education . . . They say, "The government can build the prisons,
they will never be large enough to take us all." ' In London, where in 1889
there were nearly 13,000 summonses issued against parents for the non-
attendance of their children at school, parents and children clearly resented
the new powers granted to enforce school attendance – and they found
much sympathy among magistrates.[80]

Interest and emotion

In these four centuries home, work and school set the contexts in which children lived. Until the nineteenth century work for most children took place within the family. It is therefore to the family we need to return to ask the most difficult of all questions: what was the quality of relationships within the family? Were boys preferred to girls? How did siblings relate to one another?

There is an often unspoken assumption which governs responses to these questions. In the modern world children have no economic value, and it is easy to assume that it is this fact which alone makes possible the flourishing of love of children by parents. In other contexts, 'interest' (the parents' need of the child's labour) will interfere with 'emotion'. Indeed interest and emotion are often thought of as residing at opposite ends of a pole, in conflict with one another. Such an assumption seems to underlie Michael Anderson's analysis in *Family Structure in Nineteenth-Century Lancashire*. Studying the textile town of Preston, Anderson emphasised the importance of the family to workers in this expanding town; it was through family connections that people found jobs, and it was to the family that they turned as a resource in times of hardship. But Anderson saw these family ties as more instrumental than affective, and concluded 'that a really strong affective and non-calculative commitment to the kinship net could develop' only with industrial prosperity and the welfare state.[81] A similar, though more extreme version of this theory, can be found in a study of the family in nineteenth-century Bavaria. Robert Lee argues that 'By and large parental attitudes towards children continued to be determined by the economic utility which could be gained from additional family members. Until the child had received some training in a particular, if rudimentary, skill, or had proved its economic usefulness for the domestic household economy, it was seldom accepted either economically or emotionally as a full family member.' Once the child had acquired some economic usefulness, 'parental attitudes noticeably changed', but even so 'the treatment of children and their socialisation within the family was dictated by economic considerations', and if they were surplus to family labour needs, they would be employed outside the family holding as servants.[82] Thus, whether we are considering peasant communities or industrial societies, the argument is that cold economic considerations outweighed warm emotional attachment, indeed prevented any expression being given to the latter.

We need to separate out attitudes to infants and to those who survived beyond their first birthdays. Edward Shorter suggested that indifference to the fate of infants was the cause of infant mortality rather than that high infant mortality rates forced mothers to protect themselves against psychological stress by donning the armour of indifference.[83] There is certainly evidence that some mothers viewed the death of infants as something outside their control (as in many cases it was), but while they might be, as was reported of Irish and black New York mothers in the early twentieth century, 'horribly fatalistic' about the mortality of children, they were not 'callous'; and an apparent element of boastfulness about the number of children born and the number lost was not incompatible with feelings of grief and bereavement.[84] Economic circumstances gave many mothers little option but to give less than optimum care to their babies. This was true not only of those who abandoned their children, or who put them out to wet-nurses, but also of those who worked in seasonal trades. Thus in the Montpellier region in the season of silkworm growing, 'the women are constantly busy with gathering mulberry leaves or with the worms themselves. The children are neglected, suffer, and die. The habit of seeing such a great number perish in this season has given rise to a proverb which says that "in the time you see the silkworm rise, the most kids go to paradise".'[85] The problem with all statements of this kind is that they come from outside observers; if grief was felt in the case of death, it was unlikely to be expressed to someone of another class.

There is some evidence to suggest that boys received better treatment than girls. What do we make of the fifteenth-century Bohemian traveller who recorded that 'In the country of Portugal there are many strange customs. When girls are born they see to it that the children seldom die', as if the opposite was the case elsewhere?[86] When the legitimate composed a large proportion of those abandoned, girls were more likely to be abandoned than boys, in the ratio of 76 boys to every 100 girls in sixteenth-century Siena, and 58 boys to every 100 girls in mid-seventeenth-century Naples.[87] In the Pyrenees in the nineteenth century the birth of a boy was greeted with gunfire, that of a girl with 'cruel disappointment', while in the Limousin mothers without sons would say that they had no 'children' even if they had several daughters.[88] Different rates of survival by gender have also suggested that parents in nineteenth-century North America may have invested more care in the gender likely to be of economic value, but the evidence on this is hard to assess.[89]

We are equally hard-pressed to find good evidence of attitudes to older children. Only in the nineteenth and early twentieth centuries with the increasing availability of working-class autobiographies and of oral history transcripts can we begin to build up a picture of the emotional life of the family; and even in these sources writers and speakers often find it difficult to go beyond formulaic expressions, normally indicating parental, or at least maternal love. But one thing can be said with some confidence: children identified with the needs of the family. They might resent the fact that they had been born into a particular class of society, but they identified closely with their own families, knowing that they would be expected at an early age to contribute as they could. In Germany, where schooling was enforced relatively early, autobiographers saw it 'as an obligation that interfered with the child's work'.[90] Pride frequently marks the child's first contribution to the family budget, something which could not have happened if they had been treated with brutality in early childhood. Economic considerations did, as Lee claims, largely determine a child's 'position and function', but that need not have been at the expense of affection between child and parent. The two were intertwined. Similarly, although birth order might hold out different prospects for one child as against another, there is no evidence of acute sibling rivalry. The eldest child might well be expected to enter the labour market or in other ways contribute to the family economy at an earlier age than later children, and younger children in economies where there was no family labour available for them, and where there was no wage labour near the family home, might have to leave home, but these fates seem to have been accepted.[91]

Some autobiographers wax lyrical about their early childhood memories. William Thom in his *Rhymes and Recollections of a Hand-Loom Weaver* (1844) addressed his readers in these words:

Oh the days of childhood! Voyage thereafter as we may on smooth or on broken water, these are the landmarks that will never fade. The blue of our native hills may be lost to the eye for long, long years, yet once again we press their heathery bells; but you ye sunny scenes of infancy, though ye glimmer through every darkness, and at every distance, we never meet again.

Others, particularly it seems in Germany, regretted that their childhood years were not, as they should have been, the happiest of their lives. Adelheid Popp, born in 1869 in a family of village weavers in Austria, lamented that 'No bright moment, no sunbeam, no hint of a comfortable home where motherly love and care could shape my childhood was ever known to me.'[92] Clearly for these writers a romantic conception of childhood had taken some root. But, as writers of autobiography, they were of course exceptional. Were such attitudes widespread? We simply do not know, though there is some evidence in the response to the condition of children working in factories that working people found those conditions so horrendous that they began to formulate ideas of what childhood ought to be in a better world. It was only in the twentieth century, however, that such ideas became at all widespread.

Notes

1 M. Mitterauer and R. Sieder, *The European Family: Patriarchy to Partnership from the Middle Ages to the Present* (Oxford, 1982), pp. 29–32.

2 A. Macfarlane, *The Origins of English Individualism: The Family, Property and Social Transition* (Oxford, 1978); J. Goody, *The Development of the Family and Marriage in Europe* (Cambridge, 1983); D. Herlihy, *Medieval Households* (Cambridge, Mass. and London, 1985).

3 Mitterauer and Sieder, *European Family*, pp. 32–5.

4 D.E. Vassberg, 'Juveniles in the rural work force of sixteenth-century Castile', *Journal of Peasant Studies*, 11 (1983), pp. 62–75; I.K. Ben-Amos, *Adolescence and Youth in Early Modern England* (New Haven and London, 1994), pp. 40–7.

5 H. Cunningham, 'The employment and unemployment of children in England c. 1680–1851', *Past and Present*, 126 (1990), pp. 115–50.

6 R.M. Smith, 'Some issues concerning families and their property in rural England 1250–1800' in R.M. Smith (ed.), *Land, Kinship and Life-Cycle* (Cambridge, 1984), pp. 68–71.

7 Mitterauer and Sieder, *European Family*, pp. 42–3.

8 R.L. Rudolph, 'The European peasant family and economy: central themes and issues', *Journal of Family History*, 17 (1992), pp. 132–3.

9 Ibid., p. 133.

10 H. Medick, 'The proto-industrial family economy: the structural function of household and family during the transition from peasant society to industrial capitalism', *Social History*, No. 3 (1976), pp. 304–5.

11 J.M. Baart, 'Ceramic consumption and supply in early modern Amsterdam: local production and long-distance trade', in P.J. Corfield and D. Keene (eds), *Work in Towns 850–1850* (Leicester, 1990), p. 77.

12 M. Spufford, 'First steps in literacy: the reading and writing experiences of the humblest seventeenth-century autobiographers', *Social History*, IV (1979), pp. 412–14; G.L. Gullickson, *Spinners and Weavers of Auffay: Rural Industry and the Sexual Division of Labor in a French Village, 1750–1850* (Cambridge, 1986), p. 75.

13 Rudolph, 'European peasant family', pp. 128–9.

14 U. Pfister, 'The protoindustrial household economy: toward a formal analysis,
    Journal of Family History, 17 (1992), pp. 210–14; Gullickson, *Spinners and
    Weavers of Auffay*.

15 U. Pfister, 'Work roles and family structure in proto-industrial Zurich',
    Journal of Interdisciplinary History, XX (1989), pp. 83–105.

16 R. Wall, 'Work, welfare and the family: an illustration of the adaptive family
    economy', in L. Bonfield, R.M. Smith and K. Wrightson (eds), *The World We
    Have Gained: Histories of Population and Social Structure* (Oxford, 1986),
    pp. 261–94, esp. p. 278.

17 Cunningham 'Employment and unemployment', 126–31; Gullickson,
    Spinners and Weavers of Auffay, p. 75.

18 See e.g. S.L. Engerman, 'Expanding protoindustrialization', *Journal of Family
    History*, 17 (1992), pp. 244–5.

19 S. Horrell and J. Humphries, ' "The exploitation of little children": child labor
    and the family economy in the industrial revolution', *Explorations in
    Economic History*, 32 (1995), pp. 485–516.

20 G. Alter, 'Work and income in the family economy: Belgium, 1853
    and 1891', *Journal of Interdisciplinary History*, XV (1984), pp. 255–76;
    M.R. Haines, 'Industrial work and the family life cycle, 1889–1890', *Research
    in Economic History*, 4 (1979), pp. 325, 328; C. Goldin, 'Family strategies
    and the family economy in the late nineteenth century: the role of secondary
    workers', in T. Hershberg (ed.), *Philadelphia: Work, Space, Family and Group
    Experience in the Nineteenth Century* (New York and Oxford, 1981), p. 284;
    E. Camps I Cura, 'Family strategies and children's work patterns: some
    insights from industrializing Catalonia, 1850–1920', in H. Cunningham
    and P.P. Viazzo (eds), *Child Labour in Historical Perspective, 1800–1985:
    Case Studies from Europe, Japan and Colombia* (Florence, 1996), p. 67; L.A.
    Tilly and J.W. Scott, *Women, Work, and Family* (New York, 1978), quoting
    p. 134.

21 P. Razzell, 'The growth of population in eighteenth-century England: a critical
    reappraisal', *Journal of Economic History*, 53 (1993), pp. 757–8, revising
    the figures in E.A. Wrigley and R.S. Schofield, *The Population History of
    England 1541–1871: A Reconstruction* (London, 1981), p. 249; H. Kamen,
    European Society 1500–1700 (London, 1984), p. 25; J-L. Flandrin, *Families
    in Former Times: Kinship, Household and Sexuality* (Cambridge, 1979),
    pp. 199–201.

22 Calculated from B.R. Mitchell, *European Historical Statistics 1750–1975*
    (2nd revised edn, London, 1981), pp. 137–44.

23 P.J. Greven, *Four Generations: Population, Land, and Family in Colonial
    Andover, Massachusetts* (Ithaca and London, 1970), p. 191; J. Demos, *A*

Little Commonwealth: Family Life in Plymouth Colony (New York, 1970), p. 66. Demographic conditions were much less favourable in Virginia and Maryland; see R.W. Beales, 'The child in seventeenth-century America', in J.M. Hawes and N.R. Hiner (eds), *American Childhood: A Research Guide and Historical Handbook* (Westport, Conn. and London, 1985), pp. 18–23.

24 R. Mols, 'Population in Europe 1500–1700', in C.M. Cipolla (ed.), *The Fontana Economic History of Europe: The Sixteenth and Seventeenth Centuries* (London, 1974), pp. 69–70.

25 E.A. Wrigley, *Population and History* (London, 1969), pp. 166–7; S.H. Preston and M.R. Haines, *Fatal Years: Child Mortality in Late Nineteenth-Century America* (Princeton, 1991), p. xviii.

26 D.I. Kertzer, *Sacrificed for Honor: Italian Infant Abandonment and the Politics of Reproductive Control* (Boston, 1993), pp. 72–3.

27 V. Hunecke, 'Les enfants trouvés: contexte Européen et cas milanais (XVIII-XIX siècles)', *Revue d'histoire moderne et contemporaine*, XXXII (1985), p. 4; J. Boswell, *The Kindness of Strangers: The Abandonment of Children in Western Europe from Late Antiquity to the Renaissance* (London, 1989), pp. 15–16.

28 Kertzer, *Sacrificed for Honor*, p. 10.

29 Hunecke, 'Les enfants trouvés', p. 4; P. Gavitt, *Charity and Children in Renaissance Florence: The Ospedale degli Innocenti, 1410–1536* (Ann Arbor, 1990), p. 21; E. Sonnino, 'Between the home and the hospice: the plight and fate of girl orphans in seventeenth- and eighteenth-century Rome', in J. Henderson and R. Wall (eds), *Poor Women and Children in the European Past* (London, 1994), pp. 94–116.

30 G.D. Sussman, *Selling Mothers' Milk: The Wet-Nursing Business in France 1715–1914* (Urbana, Chicago and London, 1982), pp. 110–12.

31 P.P. Viazzo, M. Bortolotto and A. Zanotto, 'Five centuries of foundling history in Florence: changing patterns of abandonment, care and mortality', and D.I. Kertzer, 'The lives of foundlings in nineteenth-century Italy', in C. Panter-Brick and M.T. Smith (eds), *Abandoned Children* (Cambridge, 2000), pp. 70–91 and 41–55.

32 Kertzer, *Sacrificed for Honor*, p. 73; C. Larquié, 'La mise en nourrice des enfants madrilènes au XVII siècle', *Revue d'histoire moderne et contemporaine*, XXXII (1985), p. 129; J. Sherwood, *Poverty in Eighteenth-Century Spain: The Women and Children of the Inclusa* (Toronto, 1988), p. 5; V. Fildes, 'Maternal feelings re-assessed: child abandonment and neglect in London and Westminster, 1550–1800', in V. Fildes (ed.), *Women as Mothers in Pre-Industrial England* (London, 1990), pp. 155–6.

33 J-C. Peyronnet, 'Les enfants abandonnés et leurs nourrices à Limoges au
    XVIII siècle', *Revue d'histoire moderne et contemporaine*, XXIII (1976), pp.
    418–30; O.H. Hufton, *The Poor of Eighteenth-Century France 1750–1789*
    (Oxford, 1974), pp. 332–3; see also C. Delasselle, 'Abandoned children in
    eighteenth century Paris', in R. Forster and O. Ranum (eds), *Deviants and the
    Abandoned in French Society* (Baltimore and London, 1978), pp. 70–2. For
    a counter-example, consider Ravenna where between 1720 and 1790 the level
    of abandonment was falling or constant while grain prices were rising
    (Kertzer, *Sacrificed for Honor*, p. 210).

34 Delasselle, 'Abandoned children in eighteenth century Paris', p. 62;
    R.G. Fuchs, *Abandoned Children: Foundlings and Child Welfare in
    Nineteenth-Century France* (Albany, 1984), pp. 66–9; J. Meyer, 'Illegitimates
    and foundlings in pre-industrial France', in P. Laslett et al. (eds), *Bastardy
    and its Comparative History* (London, 1980), p. 25; see also L. Valverde,
    'Illegitimacy and the abandonment of children in the Basque Country,
    1550–1800', in Henderson and Wall (eds), *Poor Women and Children*,
    pp. 51–64, which explains a correlation of rising abandonment and falling
    illegitimacy by the shift of responsibility for the illegitimate child from fathers
    (who had resources) to mothers (who did not).

35 Kertzer, *Sacrificed for Honor*, pp. 42–3, 102; S. Wilson, 'Infanticide, child
    abandonment, and female honour in nineteenth-century Corsica',
    Comparative Studies in Society and History, 30 (1988), pp. 762–83.

36 Peyronnet, 'Les enfants abandonnés', pp. 418–30; L.A. Tilly, R.G. Fuchs,
    D.I. Kertzer and D.L. Ransel, 'Child abandonment in European history:
    a symposium', *Journal of Family History*, 17 (1992), pp. 7–10; A. Levene,
    'The origins of the children of the London Foundling Hospital, 1741–1760:
    a reconsideration', *Continuity and Change*, 18 (2003), pp. 201–36; Hunecke,
    'Enfants trouvés', p. 19; Kertzer, *Sacrificed for Honor*, p. 80.

37 Hunecke, 'Enfants trouvés', p. 14; Kertzer, *Sacrificed for Honor*, p. 79.

38 Hunecke, 'Enfants trouvés', pp. 19–26.

39 J.R. Lehning, 'Family life and wetnursing in a French village', *Journal of
    Interdisciplinary History*, XII (1982), p. 655; Sussman, *Selling Mothers' Milk*.
    Olwen Hufton explores 'an economy of makeshifts' in *The Poor of
    Eighteenth-Century France*.

40 Sussman, *Selling Mothers' Milk*, pp. 161–88.

41 F. Newall, 'Wet nursing and child care in Aldenham, Hertfordshire,
    1595–1726', in Fildes, *Women as Mothers*, pp. 122–38.

42 S. Hedenborg, 'To breastfeed another woman's child: wet-nursing in
    Stockholm, 1777–1937', *Continuity and Change*, 16 (2001), pp. 399–422.

43 Hunecke, 'Enfants trouvés', pp. 15–17.

44 Meyer, 'Illegitimates and foundlings', p. 258.

45 Peyronnet, 'Les enfants abandonnés', pp. 440–1.

46 A. Farge, *Fragile Lives: Violence, Power and Solidarity in Eighteenth-Century Paris* (Cambridge, 1993), pp. 51–62.

47 Kamen, *European Society*, p. 26; Wrigley and Schofield, *Population History of England*, pp. 216, 443–50.

48 P. Laslett, *The World We Have Lost* (2nd edn, London, 1971), pp. 109–10.

49 M. Anderson, 'The social implications of demographic change', in F.M.L. Thompson (ed.), *The Cambridge Social History of Britain*, 3 vols (Cambridge, 1990), Vol. 2, pp. 48–50.

50 Kamen, *European Society*, p. 28; V. Brodsky, 'Widows in late Elizabethan London: remarriage, economic opportunity and family orientations', in Bonfield, Smith and Wrightson, *The World We Have Gained*, pp. 136–40.

51 C. Phythian-Adams, *Desolation of a City: Coventry and the Urban Crisis of the Late Middle Ages* (Cambridge, 1979), pp. 224, 233–4.

52 L. Stone, *The Family, Sex and Marriage in England 1500–1800* (London, 1977), p. 107; J. Gillis makes the same point, quoted in M. Mitterauer, *A History of Youth* (Oxford, 1992), p. 72.

53 R. Wall, 'The age at leaving home', *Journal of Family History*, 3 (1978), pp. 189–90; A. Kussmaul, *Servants in Husbandry in Early Modern England* (Cambridge, 1981), pp. 3, 72; Mitterauer, *History of Youth*, pp. 73–4.

54 Wall, 'Age at leaving home', pp. 192, 197–8; id., 'Leaving home and the process of household formation in pre-industrial England', *Continuity and Change*, 2 (1987), pp. 91–2; Cunningham, 'Employment and unemployment', 132–3; Mitterauer, *History of Youth*, pp. 72–4, 89–92; see also K.D.M. Snell, *Annals of the Labouring Poor: Social Change and Agrarian England, 1660–1900* (Cambridge, 1985), pp. 323–32.

55 Mitterauer, *History of Youth*, pp. 69–70; Snell, *Annals of the Labouring Poor*, p. 236.

56 Anderson, 'Social implications of demographic change', p. 69.

57 Snell, *Annals of the Labouring Poor*, pp. 325–6.

58 A. Wilson, 'The ceremony of childbirth and its interpretation', in Fildes (ed.), *Women as Mothers*, pp. 68–107.

59 M. Pelling, 'Child health as a social value in early modern England', *Social History of Medicine*, I (1988), pp. 135–64; id., 'Apprenticeship, health and social cohesion in early modern London', *History Workshop*, 37 (1994), pp. 33–56.

60 See E. Ross, 'Survival networks: women's neighbourhood sharing in London before World War I', *History Workshop*, 15 (Spring 1983), pp. 12–13.

61 H. Cunningham, *The Children of the Poor: Representations of Childhood since the Seventeenth Century* (Oxford, 1991), pp. 22–3; K. Thomas, 'Children in early modern England', in G. Avery and J. Briggs (eds), *Children and Their Books* (Oxford, 1989), pp. 51–5.

62 Pelling, 'Child health as a social value', p. 140.

63 Thomas, 'Children in early modern England', pp. 57–63; A. James, 'Confections, concoctions and conceptions', in B. Waites et al. (eds), *Popular Culture* (London, 1982), pp. 294–307; I. and P. Opie, *The Lore and Language of Schoolchildren* (1959; St Albans, 1977).

64 R.A. Houston, *Literacy in Early Modern England: Culture and Education 1500–1800* (Harlow, 1988), pp. 33–8, 50.

65 Ibid., p. 15.

66 I. Green, ' "For Children in Yeers and Children in Understanding": the emergence of the Elizabethan catechism under Elizabeth and the early Stuarts', *Journal of Ecclesiastical History*, 36 (1986), pp. 400–1; cf. R.B. Bottigheimer, 'Bible reading, "Bibles" and the Bible for children in early modern Germany', *Past and Present*, 139 (1993), pp. 66–89.

67 T.W. Laqueur, *Religion and Respectability: Sunday Schools and Working Class Culture 1780–1850* (New Haven and London, 1976).

68 Houston, *Literacy*, p, 11; P. Gardner, *The Lost Elementary Schools of Victorian England: The People's Education* (London, 1984), p. 24; C. Lis, *Social Change and the Labouring Poor: Antwerp, 1770–1860* (New Haven and London, 1986), p. 122.

69 Houston, *Literacy*, pp. 48, 51–2.

70 Ibid., p. 54; C.M. Cipolla, *Literacy and Development in the West* (Harmondsworth, 1969), pp. 32–4, quoting p. 33.

71 Houston, *Literacy*, pp. 39, 53; M. Sanderson, 'Education and social mobility in the industrial revolution in England', *Past and Present*, 56 (1972), pp. 75–104.

72 Houston, *Literacy*, pp. 49–50.

73 D. Vincent, *Bread, Knowledge and Freedom: A Study of Nineteenth-Century Working Class Autobiography* (London, 1981), p. 94.

74 Ibid., p. 102.

75 T.W. Laqueur, 'Working-class demand and the growth of English elementary education, 1750–1850', in L. Stone (ed.), *Schooling and Society* (Baltimore and London, 1976), pp. 192, 202–3; Gardner, *Lost Schools*, p. 76.

76 Vincent, *Bread, Knowledge and Freedom*, p. 103.

77 Laqueur, 'Working-class demand', pp. 195–201; Vincent, *Bread, Knowledge and Freedom*, pp. 100–3; P. McCann, 'Popular education, socialization and social control: Spitalfields 1812–24', in P. McCann (ed.), *Popular Education and Socialization in the Nineteenth Century* (London, 1977), pp. 28–30; Gardner, *Lost Schools*.

78 K. Thomas, *Rule and Misrule in the Schools of Early Modern England* (Reading, 1976), quoting p. 14; id., 'Children in early modern England', pp. 66–7.

79 E. West, 'Heathens and angels: childhood in the Rocky Mountain mining towns', in H.J. Graff (ed.), *Growing Up in America: Historical Experiences* (Detroit, 1987), p. 373.

80 G. Dallas, *The Imperfect Peasant Economy: The Loire Country, 1800–1914* (Cambridge, 1982), quoting p. 91; D. Rubinstein, 'Socialization and the London School Board 1870–1914: aims, methods and public opinion', in McCann, *Popular Education and Socialization*, pp. 231–64; J. Davis, 'A poor man's system of justice: the London Police Courts in the second half of the nineteenth century', *Historical Journal*, 27 (1984), pp. 329–30.

81 M. Anderson, *Family Structure in Nineteenth-Century Lancashire* (Cambridge, 1971), p. 178.

82 R. Lee, 'Family and "Modernisation": the peasant family and social change in nineteenth-century Bavaria', in R.J. Evans and W.R. Lee (eds), *The German Family: Essays on the Social History of the Family in Nineteenth- and Twentieth-Century Germany* (London, 1981), pp. 96–7.

83 E. Shorter, *The Making of the Modern Family* (London, 1976), pp. 202–3.

84 R.H. Bremner (ed.), *Children and Youth in America: A Documentary History*, 2 vols (Cambridge, Mass., 1971), Vol. 2, p. 17; Lady Bell, *At the Works: A Study of a Manufacturing Town* (1907; London, 1911), pp. 269–70; M.E. Loane, *From Their Point of View* (London, 1908), p. 124.

85 Shorter, *Making of Modern Family*, p. 172.

86 Quoted in Wilson, 'Infanticide, child abandonment, and female honour in nineteenth-century Corsica', p. 778.

87 Kertzer, *Sacrificed for Honor*, pp. 111–12; see also D.L. Ransel, *Mothers of Misery: Child Abandonment in Russia* (Princeton, 1988), pp. 130–49.

88 C. Heywood, 'On learning gender roles during childhood in nineteenth-century France', *French History*, 5 (1991), p. 451; Boswell, *Kindness of Strangers*, p. 35.

89 E.A. Hammel, S.R. Johansson and C.A. Ginsberg, 'The value of children during industrialization: sex ratios in childhood in nineteenth-century America', *Journal of Family History*, 8 (1983), pp. 346–66; D.T.

Courtwright, 'The neglect of female children and childhood sex ratios in nineteenth-century America: a review of the evidence', *Journal of Family History*, 15 (1990), pp. 313–23. B.A. Hanawalt suggests that there may have been a relative neglect of female children in medieval London: see her *Growing Up in Medieval London: The Experience of Childhood in History* (Oxford, 1993), p. 58.

90 M.J. Maynes, 'The contours of childhood: demography, strategy, and mythology of childhood in French and German lower-class autobiographies', in J.R. Gillis, L.A. Tilly and D. Levine (eds), *The European Experience of Declining Fertility: A Quiet Revolution, 1850–1970* (Oxford, 1992), p. 117.

91 L.A. Tilly, 'Linen was their life: family survival strategies and parent–child relations in nineteenth-century France', in H. Medick and D.W. Sabean (eds), *Interest and Emotion: Essays on the Study of Family and Kinship* (Cambridge, 1984), pp. 300–16. 'Dimensions of inequalities among siblings' are considered in a special number of *Continuity and Change*, 7, Part 3 (1992).

92 Vincent, *Bread, Knowledge and Freedom*, pp. 91–2; Maynes, 'The contours of childhood', pp. 101–124, quoting p. 101.

CHAPTER 5

Children, philanthropy and the state in Europe, 1500–1860

Policies towards children in this period may be divided into two broad time-spans: 1500–1750 and 1750–1860. What marks out the second of these is the scale of the involvement of central governments. But in both periods there were two common underlying issues which forced voluntary organisations and governments into formulating and operating policies towards children. The first of these was that children were being born whom parents were unwilling or unable to rear. They might be illegitimate or orphans, but they might quite as likely be the children of married couples. The second issue was that of schooling, and the increasing sense that it might be desirable to extend it to entire populations.

Children and poverty

Throughout Europe the evidence is that for a large part of the life cycle children contributed to rather than relieved the problem of poverty, and that this was recognised to be the case. Its most dramatic expression was the abandonment of babies. But it also confronted local officials and philanthropists whenever they had to deal with poverty. Children constituted a large percentage of the poor. Listings of the poor in various English parishes in the sixteenth and seventeenth centuries indicate that children made up between 42 per cent and 53 per cent of all the poor, some 25 per cent of the total being under ten. It is true that these percentages are only a little higher than the percentage of children in the population as a whole, but to the administrators of the Poor Law children loomed large.[1] In England and Wales in the early nineteenth century 195,000 children of paupers were being permanently relieved by parishes.[2] Nor was England exceptional in this. In a parish in Louvain in the Netherlands in 1541 over half of the 765 people qualifying for relief were children. In Montpellier in the eighteenth century, two-thirds of admissions to the Hôpital Général were children, the vast majority of them under the age of ten.[3]

The majority of children in poverty were being brought up in families. In Lyons the ordinances of the Aumône-Générale, established in the 1530s, recognised that there was poverty deserving relief among 'poor house-holders and artisans heavily burdened with children', the number of children generally being three. In a survey of 400 poor families in London in 1552, 350 consisted of 'poor men overburdened with their children'. In Harlow in Essex towards the end of the sixteenth century some employed men needed relief because they were 'greatly charged with young children'.[4] In seventeenth-century Norfolk, 'the more children one had, the worse off one became'. John Locke at the end of the seventeenth century did not think that a man and his wife 'by their ordinary labour' would be able to support more than two children.[5] In Aix-en-Provence in the seventeenth and eighteenth centuries 'the normal salary of a man and wife could comfortably support only one child', and the Charité admitted one child in families which had four children under fourteen. As Olwen Hufton has expressed it, 'for any poor family the mere existence of children spelt economic disaster'.[6]

What marked out the two and a half centuries from 1500 to 1750 in the response to this problem was a decisive shift from charitable action initiated and controlled by the Church to one where laymen were the dominant force. The Church in the middle ages had not only established and controlled charitable institutions, such as hospitals, which served the needs of the whole population, but had also begun in the fourteenth century to run foundling hospitals for abandoned babies and children. In legend at any rate the origins of this movement can be traced to the moment when fishermen in Rome brought before Pope Innocent III (1198–1216) the bodies of babies who had been drowned in the Tiber. Foundling hospitals took root in Italian cities in the thirteenth and fourteenth centuries, and spread to Spain in the fifteenth and sixteenth centuries, and to Portugal and France in the seventeenth century.[7] In sixteenth-century Spain, for example, Seville, Madrid, Toledo, Valladolid, Salamanca, Córdoba and Santiago de Compostela all had foundling hospitals.[8] In many of these foundations in southern Europe civic organisations were more prominent than religious orders, and they were generally run by lay boards in consultation with the Church.[9] Sometimes there was a deliberate wish on the part of a founder to distance himself from the Church. In Italy Francesco Datini, without legitimate children himself, saw in a legacy to set up a foundling hospital a way of perpetuating himself and of glorifying his city; and he was determined that it was the Prato Council and not the Church which should have the responsibility for administering his legacy. As it happened it was in neighbouring Florence that Datini's will was put into effect in the Ospedale degli Innocenti, a foundling hospital which was a testimony to civic humanism, rather than to the Church.[10] This desire for personal immortality and for the future of the state inspired many donations and foundations over the next centuries. It was common for the wealthy to leave money to set up schools, to provide dowries for poor girls, or to fund apprenticeships for poor boys.[11]

Economic crisis and the disorder it engendered was sometimes the occasion for the laicisation of charity, as in Lyons in the 1530s, but it did not depend on such crises. As Cissie Fairchilds has noted, 'the merchants of almost every major town in Western Europe began in the late fifteenth and early sixteenth centuries to establish new charities, which they, and not the Church, would control'. Natalie Davis detects in this 'an international movement for welfare reform in Europe during the decades after 1520'.[12] Between 1522 and 1545 some sixty towns in Germany, the Low Countries, France and Switzerland reshaped their social policies, and central authorities were equally active in the Netherlands, France, England, Scotland and Spain.[13] In part this was a matter of public order, for children were prominent amongst the vagrants and beggars whom the authorities from the sixteenth century onwards were determined to control. The Spanish humanist Juan Luis Vives, whose enormously influential *De Subventione Pauperum*, written in the 1520s, was addressed to the Consuls and Senate of Bruges, described how 'The young children of the poor are villainously brought up, they [mothers] and their sons lying outside the churches or wandering round begging.'[14] In Lyons in the sixteenth century townsmen complained of 'the great number of little children crying and hooting with hunger and cold day and night through the town, making a marvellous racket in the churches'. In Venice in the mid-sixteenth century there were anxieties about 'the enormous increase in the number of child rogues and beggars, who wander round the squares of San Marco and Rialto, and sleep at night in the doorways . . .'[15] The streets of Stockholm in the seventeenth century were infested with begging and vagrant children. In the 1650s in preparation for the coronation of Queen

PLATE 1 *Child Holding An Apple* by Caesar van Everingden. The National Loans Collection Trust at Canon Hall Museum (Barnsley Metropolitan Borough Council).

PLATE 2 *The Age of Innocence* by Joshua Reynolds. Plymouth City Museum and Art Gallery.

PLATE 3 *The Child Enthroned*, c.1894, by Thomas Cooper Gotch (1854–1931). Private Collection/www.bridgeman.co.uk.

PLATE 4 Illustration from 'The Royal Commission on the Condition and Treatment of Children Employed in the Mines of the United Kingdom' (1842). Mary Evans Picture Library.

LANT ST. BOARD SCHOOL (SOUTHWARK), 1875.
Lowest type.

LANT ST. BOARD SCHOOL (SOUTHWARK), 1878.
Slight improvement.

LANT ST. BOARD SCHOOL (SOUTHWARK), 1902.
Great Improvement.

PLATE 5 Interdepartmental Committee on Physical Deterioration, British Parliamentary Papers, 1904, Vol. XXXII. British Library shelfmark BS. REF. 1. Copyright © The British Library.

PLATE 6 From *The Twentieth-Century Child* by Edward H. Cooper, 1905 (frontispiece). British Library shelfmark 012630.dd.5. Copyright © The British Libary.

Christina several hundred of them were interned, and released outside the city after the event, and in 1682 the governor of Stockholm appointed special guards to stop street children stealing into church during sermons – for the children the churches presumably offered some shelter and warmth.[16] In southern France in the eighteenth century 'often whole gangs of homeless children roamed the roads, finding protection and fellowship in numbers'. In Prussia over one-third of the mendicant population were said to be children.[17]

The solution was to place these children in institutions of some kind, where they might be reared to become model subjects. In Bruges, Vives recommended that the quicker boys might teach others and then proceed to 'a seminary of priests. Let the others move on into workshops, according to their individual bents.' Girls who showed an inclination for learning might be allowed to continue with it, providing 'everything tend[ed] to better conduct'. Two censors should be appointed, 'men of weight and of conspicuous integrity', amongst whose duties would be to check 'what the children are doing, what progress they are making, what are their behaviour, natural gifts, and promise, and if there are any who are doing wrong'.[18] A typical programme consisted of setting up or taking over hospitals for poor or abandoned children, providing some form of education for such of these children as survived infancy, and funding apprenticeships for boys and dowries for girls.[19] More adventurously, in Venice the solution was to apprentice beggar children as cabin-boys, thus solving the problem of child beggary and meeting the needs of the state for sailors.[20] Children were in many ways at the centre of these programmes of reform, offering hope for the future; in Aix 'Charity for children was perhaps the most widespread and popular type of charity'. Christian humanism provided the philosophic underpinning for these initiatives, and in its name the streets were cleared of beggars and the poor were placed in institutions, allowing for what Fairchilds calls a 'surveillance of their moral condition', and a sharpened distinction between the worthy and the unworthy; but also, perhaps, as Vives' writing suggests, opening up opportunities for brighter boys.[21] And although laymen were in control of these programmes, they were suffused with a religious ethos in both Catholic and Protestant areas of Europe.[22]

Although all historians of the early modern period draw attention to this process of the laicisation of charity, this did not mean that social policies were devised and implemented entirely independently of either ecclesiastical or state authorities. On the contrary. Outside England, where the state-imposed Poor Law ensured that there was coverage in rural as

much as in urban areas, many of them are best seen as municipal enter-
prises, closely integrated into the political, ecclesiastical, social and economic structures of each town, and receiving their funding from a variety
of sources, partly charitable, partly from tax. In Portugal, for example,
institutions for foundlings were run directly by the town councils or the
responsibility was contracted out to *misericórdias*, lay confraternities
established under royal patronage, each branch being well integrated into
the power structure of the local community.[23]

In addition, central governments were increasingly taking the lead in
issues to do with childhood, indicating a growing moralisation of the poor
– and a sharp awareness of the economic consequences of immorality.
Throughout Europe there was a new harsher attitude to infanticide. In the
Holy Roman Empire in a law of 1532 the mother of an illegitimate child
found dead was presumed to be guilty unless she could prove it to have
been stillborn or to have died naturally; the penalty was death by burial
alive or by a stake through the chest. In France in 1556 unmarried girls or
widows who were pregnant had to make a declaration of pregnancy before
a magistrate, partly to prevent infanticide, and partly to find out who the
father was and to enforce financial support; a woman who concealed pregnancy and birth was herself liable to the death penalty. The Ordinance of
Moulins of 1586 more positively sought to make provision for abandoned
and destitute illegitimate children, though it was at best unevenly enforced.
In England, too, it was from the mid-sixteenth century that there were
increasing attempts to end infanticide by harsh punishment, culminating in
an Act of 1624 which imposed the death penalty. There were similar laws
in Sweden (1627), Württemberg (1658), Denmark (1683), Scotland
(1690) and Bavaria (1751).[24] In Germany under these laws at least 30,000
women were executed for infanticide in the period 1500 to 1800.[25]

The children who benefited from state, ecclesiastical, municipal and
philanthropic enterprise were frequently displayed in public rituals. On
feast days in northern Italy orphans processed in the public squares.[26] No
important funeral was complete without a delegation of children from
the foundling hospitals. In Paris, writes Philippe Ariès, the children of le
Saint-Esprit, of la Trinité and of les Enfants Rouges 'became specialists
in death'.[27] Both in Lyons and in Aix-en-Provence, orphan boys took part
in civic and religious processions.[28] Throughout Castile the Colleges of
the Niños de la Doctrina, which took in poor boys, feeding, clothing and
housing them, teaching them reading and writing, and instructing them
in Christianity, required the boys to accompany funeral processions.[29]
These were, from the point of view of the foundling hospitals and other

charitable foundations, fund-raising opportunities. In Stockholm in the seventeenth century schoolchildren were attending up to 300 funerals a year, a system which allowed both the schools and the children to survive, but which in effect operated as a death tax on the wealthy, one widow having to wait years to bury her husband while she accumulated the funds necessary for the funeral. In Stockholm this system was eventually suppressed, but at its height, there and elsewhere, it pointed to the key symbolic role children played in representing the community, and in testifying to the benefactions of the wealthy.[30]

Schooling

The churches also began to lose their exclusive role in providing schooling, but again without any diminution of the importance of the teaching of religious doctrine which remained the prime motive for the founding and running of schools. But schooling was also seen as a means of bringing order and discipline to a population and of training it in useful work skills. In both its religious and secular aims it was likely to be of concern to governments which were bound to look askance at the impact of religious heterodoxy or ignorance on good order. Nevertheless it was not until the eighteenth century that governments began to play a major role in the provision of schooling; in the sixteenth and seventeenth centuries the initiative rested with laypeople and with the churches. The outcome was an enormous increase in the number of such schools. Thus in England the period 1480 to 1660 may have seen the opening of some 800 new schools of all types, and the rate of growth of non-classical endowed schools was faster after 1660, and especially in the early eighteenth century, than it had been in the preceding period.[31]

In Protestant countries the household was seen as the ideal location for education, but the experience of civil war in Germany in the 1520s convinced Luther that the emphasis must be shifted from the household to the public provision of schooling; for the mass of the population households could not be relied upon. In 1530 Luther set out the argument for state compulsion, claiming that if parents did not attend to education, 'children cease to belong to their parents and fall to the care of God and community'. Sometimes this was put even more forcefully, reformers arguing before the Strassburg council in 1547 that 'children belong more to God and the community – we mean both the religious and the political community – than to their parents', and that 'a Christian reformation requires above all other things a government willing to hold parents to their duty to raise children to serve the common purpose of the community'. There was no disguising here the political as well as religious function of schooling, but the one was seen as working in harmony with the other. The outcome was a stream of ordinances encouraging the setting up of schools, for example in Nordhausen in 1583: 'Although no decree ought to be necessary to compel parents to do their duty to their own children, we are aware of a great failing on their part, because so many of them do not know what it means to instruct children. Parents and guardians shall therefore send their children to school so that in their early childhood they may learn to pray, know God, and acquire discipline, decency, and sound skills.' The religious and the secular interpenetrated, but the religious came first. Nothing makes this clearer than the elevation to prime importance of the catechism as a teaching tool; its question and answer technique was designed to imprint on the young mind the fundamentals of the Christian faith.[32]

In Germany, writes Gerald Strauss, 'Nearly everywhere school attendance was demanded (made obligatory is too strong a word, though this was the intention) and assiduously promoted.' Most children, even in rural areas, seem to have had access to some kind of school, though not all attended. Most of them probably acquired some level of literacy, though they had a pronounced tendency to forget their catechisms as they grew older.[33]

In Scotland, where the Calvinist Reformation aimed to raise a nation of believers familiar with the Bible, there was, as in Germany, co-operation between church and state, which led in 1616 to an Act of the Scottish Parliament specifying that every parish should have a school and a teacher. Gradually through the seventeenth century this was enforced, leading to widespread, if not quite universal literacy in the well-populated central lowlands. In Sweden, similar levels of literacy were achieved not so much through the provision of schools as by the Lutheran Church's combination of encouragement of catechitical instruction in the home reinforced by public interrogation on Sundays, and a close link between church and state. The population was under a degree of surveillance by both church and state, with the local ministers charged with a key responsibility in education.[34]

This thorough politicising of schooling was apparent in a rather different form in England. Literacy levels were much lower than in Germany, Scotland or Sweden, mainly because there was much less pressure from either church or state to place a responsibility for schooling on each parish. The result was that much was left to local initiative. Individual efforts to provide schooling were joined in the late seventeenth and early eighteenth centuries by what was called associated philanthropy, or the formation of a society to meet some need. The Society for the Propagation of Christian Knowledge (SPCK) was founded by Anglican laymen to set up 'Charity Schools' for the children of the poor, with the usual blend of religion, reading and writing. They were an immediate success, 'the charitable provision of elementary education for poor children [becoming] the greatest philanthropic passion of the day'. By 1729 there were 1,419 such schools with 22,303 pupils.[35] It would be quite wrong to see this movement as apolitical. The aim of the SPCK was to reinforce the Anglican Church against its enemies whether Catholic or dissenting, and it was inevitably closely involved in politics. In the early 1700s the movement became infected with support for the exiled Stuart kings, something which was firmly quashed by the Whigs after the Hanoverian succession so that the schools could become pillars of the social order.[36]

Protestantism was undoubtedly a stimulus to schooling, but so also was Catholicism, sometimes in response to the Protestant threat, as in Bavaria,[37] but sometimes of its own accord. In northern Italy the Schools of Christian Doctrine, run by a lay confraternity, established themselves in the 1530s, teaching religion, reading and writing on Sundays and on religious holidays. Endorsed by the Council of Trent, the schools expanded to the point where in Milan, for example, in 1591 7,000 boys and 5,750 girls were attending.[38] In Antwerp craftsmen first taught the poor children in the town, and then, in bands of ten, they went out to the countryside every Sunday morning, teaching reading, writing, arithmetic and religion, and eventually bringing the children to the town where the priests prepared them for first communion.[39]

The provision of a rudimentary schooling for the poor was a feature of both Catholic and Protestant education policy, but it was not the most important aspect of it. Secondary schooling and university education occupied most of them much more, and were the focus of their attention. The Jesuits, whose influence on education in this period can hardly be overstated, concentrated almost exclusively on secondary education. The key factor which distinguished elementary from secondary education was that the former was entirely vernacular, whereas in the latter the emphasis was on learning Latin. Along with this went a clear sense that secondary education should be exclusive, catering for boys from well-to-do families and preparing them for prestige occupations. There were some opportunities for bright boys from poor families to rise into secondary school, but they were very limited, and counterbalanced by an almost universal sense that, as Spanish intellectuals argued, access to the grammar schools should be restricted to the 'naturally superior' classes. Sometimes the social prejudices underlying this broke to the surface. 'It is repugnant to the rules of propriety', wrote an anonymous citizen of Montpellier in 1768, 'that a sedan-chair bearer, a street porter, a vile and abject man, should have the right to send his son to a secondary school . . . and that children of the common people, who have neither upbringing nor sentiments, should mix with sons of good families, providing bad examples and a contagious source of bad behavior.'[40] The prejudice against girls continuing into secondary schooling of the same kind as that for boys was equally strong. There were schools for daughters of the wealthy beyond elementary level, but they were of a finishing school character. The classical curriculum, the passport to success in early modern Europe, was denied to them, sometimes by a specific ban, as in Banbury in England in 1594, and in Braunschweig in the seventeenth century.[41]

1750–1860

The defining feature of the period from 1750 to 1860 was an increase in central government involvement in programmes for children. Some countries, for example Great Britain, were largely unaffected by this, but it was a marked feature of countries with pretensions to enlightened absolutism. Connected with this was a huge increase in the number of children who needed assistance; central government's larger role was sometimes as much reactive as proactive. But it was not wholly so; in the promotion of education in particular, enlightened absolutists and their advisers began to nurse an ambition of instituting national systems of education. Often they started at the top of the educational hierarchy with universities and elite secondary schools the functions of which became increasingly to produce servants of the state rather than of the Church. In 1763 the Breton magistrate La Chalotais published *Essai d'éducation nationale*, a short book with almost as much impact inside and outside France as Rousseau's *Émile*, published in the same year. Its theme was the massive power of education to change the character of a whole people, even though, in La Chalotais' view, it was a mistake to educate the mass of the people.[42] In Poland, where its influence was strong, the view was expressed that 'The public good requires that in one nation, ruled by one government, there should be one manner of teaching, one kind of learning, and one sort of books used by students, as also the same laws and regulations; this cannot be achieved if schools are not under common supervision, and who can better accomplish this than the King?'[43] Schools were becoming seen as instruments for achieving national identity. 'Schools', pronounced Maria Theresa in 1770, 'are and always will be a *politicum* [i.e., a matter of the state].' One of her influential advisers, Joseph von Sonnenfels, wrote: 'Observe the major goal of public education, the true source of love for the fatherland: to instil into the hearts of children the certainty that their welfare is inseparably joined to the welfare of the state and that the laws are wise, the trespassers unfortunate and foolish people.'[44]

This did not imply that Christianity was excluded from the curriculum, far from it; it remained at its centre, and was the inspiration for many of the new initiatives.[45] In Prussia in the early eighteenth century Pietist influence was enormously influential on Frederick William I. In Austria Catholic reformism was equally important.[46] A commitment to a reformed and active Christianity underlay the Netherlands Society for the General Good, founded in 1784, and the inspiration for the spread of elementary schooling in that country. Laws embodied the belief that Christianity should provide the foundation for education. In Poland in 1783 the law regulating elementary schools declared their purpose to be 'instructing the people in religion, informing them about the duties of their estate, about labour and craft appropriate for that estate'. And the Danish law of 1814, establishing compulsory schooling in rural areas, stated 'the aim of the children's education' to be 'to form them into good, law-abiding people, in accordance with the teachings of the evangelical Christian religion, as well as to bring them the skills and proficiencies which are necessary for them to be useful citizens of the state'.[47] But the Christianity thus promoted was often in opposition to other forms of that religion. In Catholic countries in particular the suppression and often expulsion of the Jesuits from the late 1750s necessitated a search for new structures and teachers, sometimes aided, as in Austria, by the expropriation of Jesuit property which was used to establish a network of primary schools.[48] But in most Protestant countries also the proponents of advances in education stood on the reforming wing of Protestantism, and they were anxious to work alongside enlightened governments. In the Netherlands, where primary schools won admiration throughout Europe in the early nineteenth century, the Society for the General Good provided much of the input for setting up systems of training for teachers, the production of textbooks, and for an inspectorate, all of them crucial to a success which derived from 'a harmonious coalition of voluntary and state agencies'.[49]

A significant number of countries tried to institute a system of compulsory schooling in the eighteenth or early nineteenth century. There were hesitations and exceptions,[50] but the trend could not be doubted. In Prussia it stemmed from 1717, to be reiterated by Frederick the Great in 1763. In Austria the principle was established in 1774, with five days' schooling a week for at least part of the year for those aged six to twelve, and with fines for parents whose children did not attend. This was extended to Hungary in 1777. In revolutionary France the Convention in 1793 voted to establish state-run primary schools with attendance compulsory in principle, a provision which was watered down in 1795 when attendance was left to voluntary parental choice. In the Netherlands the national government's responsibility for the education of all children from the age of six to twelve was set out in a law of 1806. The Danish law of 1814 made schooling compulsory from the age of six or seven up to confirmation, which usually happened at fourteen; there was to be four weeks' holiday at harvest time, and those over ten could have partial remission to work on the land.[51] These laws suggest a degree of state control over education of the kind which is more commonly associated with the period from the 1880s to the 1920s. In practice it was very difficult for states to enforce them. The clergy remained the main teachers everywhere, and the state had no option but to rely upon them even though for many of the reformers they represented the force of darkness. Funding for schooling was equally difficult. In Portugal taxes intended for the support of 479 elementary schools were siphoned off to more prestigious educational ventures.[52] In Prussia, often held up as a beacon of success, 'The attempts that the centre did make to improve primary education almost invariably foundered on resistance in the localities.'[53] The edict of 1717 was 'little more than an exercise in wishful thinking' and 'was simply never enforced', and the General-Landschul-Reglement of 1763 was also not well enforced. There was rather greater success in Austria where Jesuit and other money took off some of the financial burden which otherwise fell on localities and parents. But as Derek Beales has concluded 'It was virtually impossible in the eighteenth century to imagine a society capable of establishing, let alone affording, any kind of secularised system of universal education.'[54] The will was sometimes there, but not the means.

States were also increasingly involved in attempts to cope with the number of abandoned and otherwise impoverished children. Perhaps a crucial moment in this process was the French crown's involvement from the 1670s onwards in financial support for the Hôpital des Enfants Trouvés in Paris which had been set up by Vincent de Paul in 1638. This hospital had a reputation throughout Europe, and other absolutist or would-be absolutist rulers were likely to copy the French crown's initiative.[55]

In part the increasing assertion of royal control was due to the failures of charity. De-Christianisation, indicated by a marked decline in legacies, an increasing level of poverty, and maladministration, meant that the charities were manifestly failing to meet needs. In France from about 1760 they were subject to fierce criticism from Enlightenment thinkers who urged a more positive role on the part of the state. The decline in charitable donations was crucial. In Montpellier 44.9 per cent of wills in 1740–1 contained charitable provisions compared with only 24.3 per cent in 1785–6. And where charity was forthcoming it was often misdirected towards those who seemed the most deserving rather than to those most in need; Jean Rouzière of Clermont left 10,000 livres for establishing in his home town an institution for the upbringing of twelve orphan girls, but when the orphanage was opened in 1782 only two such girls could be found. In France the years after 1760 saw 'the destruction of the traditional municipal charity as a viable institution'. Central governments stepped into the vacancy left by this failure of private charity.[56]

The situation was all the more desperate because of the rapid increase in the level of abandonment, described in Chapter 4. It may well be that state policies contributed to that level; that is to say, people took advantage of facilities for abandoning their children where they were available, and where the practice of abandonment was sanctioned. The point is perhaps most graphically made by looking at the London Foundling Hospital, which opened in 1739, but was selective in those it admitted, taking in about 150 per year in the first half of the 1750s. In 1756 the Hospital opened its doors in return for state funding and was immediately swamped with babies, some 3,000 per year over the next five years, over two-thirds of whom died. In 1760 state funding ended and the Foundling Hospital thereafter reverted to a restrictive entry policy, confining entry to the illegitimate from 1801.[57] What the London figures show, and they are amply confirmed by those for the rest of Europe, is that there was a colossal demand for the services which the foundling hospitals offered from those who were married as well as from the mothers of the illegitimate. The history of abandonment points up the fact that there were constantly being born large numbers of children whom parents were unable or unwilling to rear, and that families would hand over these children to other agencies where they were available.

Despite the flirtation of Protestant governments with the foundling system in the eighteenth century, it was for the most part a phenomenon specific to Catholic countries, where policies had facilitated abandonment on the scale on which it existed in the eighteenth and nineteenth centuries.

It was not, of course, that Protestant countries were immune from either poverty or illegitimacy, but their response to them differed from that in Catholic countries, and abandonment figures were very much lower. Such evidence as we have of abandonment levels in England suggests that in seven London parishes foundling baptisms as a percentage of total baptisms rose from about 1 per cent in the 1590s to over 6 per cent in the early eighteenth century, dropping off from the 1720s. This puts the level considerably below that in Catholic countries, and the trend downwards from the 1720s was at odds with that elsewhere. It may be that there is a larger amount of abandonment concealed in Poor Law records, for it was through the 15,000 parishes, each of which had responsibility for the implementation of the Law, that the English coped with the problem of unwanted children, and in particular of bastards. What is unusual about the English evidence is that there are no obvious signs that babies were being abandoned at birth.[58] Some historians of the foundling system, when they look at England, wonder whether the English equivalents of the foundling hospitals were the privately-run baby farms, concerning which there were, in the nineteenth century, a series of scandals, the entrepreneurs who ran these farms having killed the children in their care. But there is no evidence to suggest that baby farms were at all widespread. Supporters of foundling hospitals would have argued that the lack of facilities for abandonment would have led to a higher infanticide rate in England than elsewhere, but as we have seen in Chapter 4, the circumstances which led to infanticide need to be distinguished from those which led to abandonment. It is possible that the unmarried domestic servants who were those most likely to be convicted of infanticide in the eighteenth century would have disposed of their children in foundling hospitals had these been available, but their primary aim was to conceal all evidence of a birth having happened, and in small-scale communities at any rate infanticide achieved that more effectively than abandonment. And there is nothing to suggest an exceptionally high rate of infanticide in England. The truth seems to be that English families and mothers supported their babies at birth, and that it was later that they became visible as a burden on the Poor Law.[59] Outside England, in Germany for example, the typical institution for children was not a foundling hospital but an orphanage, and it may be, though we do not know, that a proportion of those who passed as 'orphans' had in fact been abandoned. A clue to this possibility may lie in a proposal considered by the governors of the London Foundling Hospital to change the name to Orphan Hospital because of 'the general notions of the common people that the name Foundling carrys with it the

Idea of contempt, and that of Orphan of compassion'.[60] One may suspect that in considering this they were quite as much concerned with the notions of their financial supporters as with those of 'the common people'.

No eighteenth-century rulers were entirely immune from the prestige which lay in association with initiatives in the care of children. Both in Moscow and in St Petersburg the foundling hospitals were built on royal initiative under Catherine II, the Moscow one rivalling the Kremlin 'for dominance of the central Moscow skyline'.[61] For a time it seemed as if foundling hospitals, under the impact of Enlightenment ideas, might break decisively from their association with Catholicism. They spread into Germany and Scandinavia.[62] The British government opened two in Ireland, in Dublin in 1730 and in Cork in 1747, each part of a larger strategy designed to convert Ireland to Protestantism.[63] But it was above all secular arguments in favour of foundling hospitals which began to appeal to princes and patriots. They would prevent the crime of infanticide, they would remove from the streets the scandal of seeing abandoned babies and riotous children, above all they would produce a rise in population, a population moreover trained from youth for the service of the state – as soldiers and sailors, as servants, or simply as adults inured to hard labour. As early as 1670 Louis XIV had seen foundlings as potential soldiers. They were, argued a German in the 1760s, 'young plants the state can make good use of for its future population'.[64] Without family attachments, claimed a French publicist in the 1780s, foundlings could be trained to 'look upon death and danger with indifference, [and] will be equally well suited to serve as sailors, to supplement the militia, or to populate colonies'.[65] In Russia Ivan Betskoi, the key figure in the founding of the Moscow and St Petersburg foundling hospitals, had even greater ambitions, hoping to build a middle class on western lines out of the children raised by the state.[66] The Decree of 1811 in France which set up a national system for dealing with abandoned children envisaged male children being at the disposal of the navy at the age of twelve. More generally, it was hoped that a well-organised system of care and control of abandoned children would replenish populations and add to national strength. It was, appropriately, in the French Revolution that these ambitious policies of state care for children reached their apogee. With the abolition of seigneurial jurisdiction in 1790, the responsibility for foundlings reverted to the state, or rather to local authorities who were encouraged to see them as 'les enfants naturels de la patrie'.[67] Allowing for a difference of language, the sentiments are similar to those voiced in the late nineteenth and early twentieth centuries when children were again seen as important in the assertion of national strength. As Otto Ulbricht has suggested, 'the organisation of foundling hospitals . . . was . . . a measure of childcare of considerable scale, potentially embracing all poor children'. Or in Jacques Donzelot's words, the foundling hospitals and other institutions can be seen as 'a laboratory for observing working-class behavior, as a launching ramp for tactics designed to counter the socially negative effects of this behavior and to reorganize the working-class family in terms of socio-economic urgencies'.[68]

The hope that foundlings might be reared to state service was paralleled by a more widespread belief that conditioning poor children to labour might have an immediate as well as long-term benefit. Children came to be thought of as vital to the flourishing of certain industries. It is true that this was not a novelty. From the end of the sixteenth century the Leyden cloth-makers had recruited dozens of boys from orphanages and poorhouses, a system which became thoroughly organised in the later seventeenth century; between 1638 and 1671 some 8,000 young workers were imported into Leyden for the work.[69] And in England in the sixteenth and seventeenth centuries there were numerous attempts to set up working schools to relieve the poorhouses and, so it was hoped, to make a profit. The charity schools, the most significant educational initiative in England in the early eighteenth century, were originally designed, as we have seen, to strengthen the Anglican Church by catechitical instruction, but soon came to see the need for incorporating work into the curriculum; by the 1720s it was acknowledged that 'a working school is in all respects preferable to one without labour and more in keeping with the present trend of public opinion'.[70] That trend continued. In the second half of the eighteenth century Houses of Industry were set up to put the poor to work, many of them being children. In Dublin, for example, the House of Industry founded in 1773 rapidly filled up with children, who eventually had to be segregated into separate buildings. This takeover of the Houses of Industry by children was implicitly acknowledged when, from the 1780s, they began to be called Schools of Industry. England and Ireland were by no means alone in these developments. Work schools were set up in France in the 1760s, and by 1789 Lyons alone had six such schools. In Germany, too, there was support for them. William Pitt, the British prime minister, was confident in 1796 that 'Experience had already shown how much could be done by the industry of children and the advantages of early employing them in such branches of manufactures as they are capable to execute.'[71]

The advantages were partly to the children (it habituated them to regular work), partly to the Poor Law authorities (expenses would be reduced), and partly to the industries (who increasingly relied on the labour of children). In Antwerp in 1781 textile manufacturers called the local orphanages for boys a 'training school for the factories'. From Germany it was reported in 1824 that 'There is scarcely a single manufacturer who has set up in Potsdam or Berlin since the mid eighteenth century without claiming children from the orphanage for his enterprise. The conditions stipulated are always alike and boil down to the orphanage's provision for the children on its own cost joined to the manufacturers' endeavouring to train the children – out of patriotism – in the required skill, without wages, save for lodging and fuel.' In Potsdam the girls' orphanage had contracted with two merchants who undertook to train 200–300 girls in lace work. The girls were 'apprenticed' for seven years, had a nine-hour working day, and received no pay for the first five years, and thereafter one-sixth of the usual wage. Manufacturers were doubtless delighted to be able to cloak this as 'patriotism'. Throughout central Europe orphanage labour was used in industrial production.[72] There were also attempts to harness the labour of poor children for purposes both of social control and of industrial output. Maria Theresa decreed in 1761 that the children of the poor 'should grow accustomed to hard work . . . Our manufacturers are in great need of spinners, and they would gladly employ children for this purpose', and Frederick II in 1775 wrote to the head of the provincial administration of Brandenburg that 'I would view it most favorably if you would see to it that children in the countryside who are presently idle devoted their free time to spinning.' Spinnschulen – spinning schools – became established in the 1760s, replacing the much more informal spinning bees which had functioned more as places for socialising.[73] Books for children drove home the message: in the fifth edition of his *Life of Jesus for Children* (1787), J.F. Feddersen advised children that 'It is God's will that people avoid all idleness and should work from their earliest years.'[74]

The hope in the second half of the eighteenth century that poor children could be turned into productive and well-disciplined subjects of the state was never fully realised. In England there were scandals associated with the employment of such children in factories. As to the foundling hospitals, opponents were able to deploy effectively the argument that an open-door foundling hospital was an inducement to immorality.[75] The catastrophic failure of the welfare policies of the French Revolution acted as an incentive to rein back on extensive state programmes. By this stage, however, at the end of the eighteenth century, many governments were deeply implicated in the running of foundling hospitals, and they could not easily disentangle themselves. Foundling hospitals had come to play a crucial role in the economy of states, the children functioning 'as a perishable commodity in a system of exchange between the city and the village'. In Russia in the 1880s 70,000 wet-nurses were employed annually to look after foundlings. Whole ways of life for thousands of people were linked to the existence of a system of abandonment of children. It is one of the recurring themes of the history of social policy that the populations which are targeted for help or control are often capable of undermining the intentions of policy makers, and of serving their own needs out of policies designed for other ends. In Russia the complex business of wet-nursing met the needs of entrepreneurs within it quite as much as it met those of the state.[76] Similarly in Canada in the mid-nineteenth century parents made use of so-called orphanages to leave their children, normally temporarily; 'other than in exceptional situations, most homes admitted many more non-orphans than orphans.'[77]

Faced with these ever-increasing demands on the services they had set up, governments and philanthropic agencies tried to stem the flow of clients. The turning cradle, set in an external wall of a foundling hospital, allowing a baby to be left anonymously, had been encouraged by Napoleon; existing in some 1,200 cities, towns and villages in Italy, as well as elsewhere, they began to be phased out: between the 1840s and the 1860s in France, in the 1850s in Spain, from the late 1860s in Portugal and Italy. The impact of closure on abandonment levels could be dramatic, admissions in Florence, for example, dropping by more than half between 1873 and 1877. By the end of the nineteenth century Italy, Spain and Greece were the only European countries with the turning cradle still in operation.[78] Support began to be offered to unwed mothers to try to persuade them to rear their own children. It was, suggests Jacques Donzelot, only a relatively small step to take from here to argue that there should be aid, with strings attached, for all mothers of the poor.[79]

That was to look some way into the future. By about the middle of the nineteenth century a phase of state policy towards children was drawing to a close, though obviously at different rates in different parts of the continent. That phase was marked by enlightened absolutism, a belief that central governments could intervene effectively to rear children who would be of service to the state. It reached its apogee in the French Revolution in Danton's claim that 'Children belong to society before they belong to their family', and in Robespierre's belief that 'The country has the right to raise its children; it should not entrust this to the pride of families or to the prejudices of particular individuals.'[80] Such claims were most unlikely to be uttered by the later stages of the French Revolution, but it took another half-century for rulers to disentangle themselves from the policies they had embraced so enthusiastically. So far as schooling was concerned there was no major retreat from state involvement – but nor was there any great advance. It is true that there were landmark acts to further education, in France in 1833, in Sweden in 1842, but the crucial next stage was postponed until the 1880s when states began to insist on compulsory schooling and to provide funds to make it free. In the meantime within a number of states initiatives were being taken which cumulatively were to construct a new image of a childhood which should be open to all.

Notes

1 P. Slack, *Poverty and Policy in Tudor and Stuart England* (London, 1988), pp. 73–80.

2 H. Cunningham, 'The employment and unemployment of children in England c.1680–1851', *Past and Present*, 126 (1990), p. 133.

3 H. Kamen, *European Society 1500–1700* (London, 1984), p. 168; C. Jones, *Charity and* Bienfaisance: *The Treatment of the Poor in the Montpellier Region 1740–1815* (Cambridge, 1982), p. 62.

4 N.Z. Davis, *Society and Culture in Early Modern France* (Cambridge, 1987), p. 22; Slack, *Poverty and Policy*, pp. 27, 65–6, 71.

5 T. Wales, 'Poverty, poor relief and the life-cycle: some evidence from seventeenth-century Norfolk', in R.M. Smith (ed.), *Land, Kinship and the Life-Cycle* (Cambridge, 1984), p. 375; Cunningham, 'Employment and unemployment', p. 128.

6 C.C. Fairchilds, *Poverty and Charity in Aix-en-Provence, 1640–1789* (Baltimore and London, 1976), pp. 85–6; O.H. Hufton, *The Poor of Eighteenth-Century France 1750–1789* (Oxford, 1974), p. 329.

7 V. Hunecke, 'The abandonment of legitimate children in nineteenth-century Milan and the European context', in J. Henderson and R. Wall (eds), *Poor Women and Children in the European Past* (London, 1994), pp. 119–21; Cf. J. Boswell, *The Kindness of Strangers: The Abandonment of Children in Western Europe from Late Antiquity to the Renaissance* (London, 1989), pp. 415–16 who argues for a more rapid spread in the fourteenth century.

8 L. Martz, *Poverty and Welfare in Habsburg Spain: The Example of Toledo* (Cambridge, 1983), pp. 224–5.

9 D.I. Kertzer, *Sacrificed for Honor: Italian Infant Abandonment and the Politics of Reproductive Control* (Boston, 1993), pp. 9–10.

10 P. Gavitt, *Charity and Children in Renaissance Florence: The Ospedale degli Innocenti, 1410–1536* (Ann Arbor, 1990), pp. 33–59.

11 Ibid., pp. 107–40; B. Pullan, *Rich and Poor in Renaissance Venice: The Social Institutions of a Catholic State, to 1620* (Oxford, 1971), pp. 163–9, 183–5; W.K. Jordan, *Philanthropy in England 1480–1660: A Study of the Changing Pattern of English Social Aspirations* (London, 1959), pp. 155–215, 268–70; J. Morgan, *Godly Learning: Puritan Attitudes Towards Reason, Learning, and Education, 1560–1640* (Cambridge, 1986), p. 185.

12 Fairchilds, *Poverty and Charity*, p. 21; Davis, *Society and Culture*, pp. 17–64, quoting pp. 51–2.

13 C. Lis and H. Soly, *Poverty and Capitalism in Pre-Industrial Europe* (Hassocks, 1979), pp. 87–9.

14 F.R. Salter (ed.), *Some Early Tracts on Poor Relief* (London, 1926), pp. 8–9; see also p. 47 on Ypres.

15 Davis, *Society and Culture*, p. 24; Pullan, *Rich and Poor*, p. 307.

16 B. Sandin, 'Education, popular culture and the surveillance of the population in Stockholm between 1600 and the 1840s', *Continuity and Change*, 3 (1988), pp. 370–1.

17 Fairchilds, *Poverty and Charity*, pp. 110–13; J.V. Melton, *Absolutism and the Eighteenth-Century Origins of Compulsory Schooling in Prussia and Austria* (Cambridge, 1988), p. 141.

18 Salter, *Some Early Tracts on Poor Relief*, pp. 18–19.

19 Fairchilds, *Poverty and Charity*, pp. 89–92; Davis, *Society and Culture*, pp. 42–4; R.A. Mentzer, 'Organizational endeavour and charitable impulse in sixteenth-century France: the case of Protestant Nîmes', *French History*, 5 (1991), pp. 11–16.

20 Pullan, *Rich and Poor*, pp. 307–8.

21 Fairchilds, *Poverty and Charity*, pp. 83, 24; Salter, *Some Early Tracts on Poor Relief*, pp. 18–19, and p. 93 for Luther's advice given to the town of Leisnig.

22 See, e.g., Gavitt, *Charity and Children in Renaissance Florence*, pp. 187–271, esp. p. 243; Mentzer, 'Organizational endeavour and charitable impulse', pp. 1–29.

23 I. d G. Sá, 'Child abandonment in Portugal: legislation and institutional care', *Continuity and Change*, 9 (1994), pp. 80–3.

24 D.L. Ransel, *Mothers of Misery: Child Abandonment in Russia* (Princeton, 1988), pp. 14–15; Hufton, *The Poor of Eighteenth-Century France*, pp. 320–4; P.C. Hoffer and N.E.H. Hull, *Murdering Mothers: Infanticide in England and New England* (New York and London, 1981).

25 M. Jackson (ed.), *Infanticide: Historical Perspectives on Child Murder and Concealment, 1550–2000* (Aldershot, 2002), p. 98.

26 Gavitt, *Charity and Children in Renaissance Florence*, pp. 295–6; Pullan, *Rich and Poor*, p. 261.

27 P. Ariès, *The Hour of Our Death* (London, 1981), pp. 165–8.

28 Davis, *Society and Culture*, p. 56; Fairchilds, *Poverty and Charity*, p. 15.

29 Martz, *Poverty and Welfare in Habsburg Spain*, p. 223.

30 Sandin, 'Education, popular culture and the surveillance of the population in Stockholm', pp. 370–6.

31 L. Stone, 'The educational revolution in England 1560–1640', *Past and Present*, 28 (1964), pp. 45–6; R.S. Tompson, 'English and English education in the eighteenth century', in J.A. Leith (ed.), *Facets of Education in the Eighteenth Century, Studies on Voltaire and the Eighteenth Century*, CLXVII (1977), pp. 68, 80–1.

32 G. Strauss, *Luther's House of Learning: Indoctrination of the Young in the German Reformation* (Baltimore and London, 1978), pp. 8, 13–28, 45, 130, 151–75.

33 Ibid., pp. 130, 197, 200–2, 279, 282.

34 R.A. Houston, *Literacy in Early Modern Europe: Culture and Education 1500–1800* (London, 1988), pp. 42–3; Sandin, 'Education, popular culture and surveillance of the population in Stockholm', pp. 359–62.

35 C. Rose, 'Evangelical philanthropy and Anglican revival: the Charity Schools of Augustan London, 1689–1740', *London Journal*, 16 (1991), pp. 35–65, quoting p. 36; M.G. Jones, *The Charity School Movement* (Cambridge, 1938), p. 72.

36 C. Rose, ' "Seminarys of Faction and Rebellion": Jacobites, Whigs and the London Charity Schools, 1716–1724', *Historical Journal*, 34 (1991), pp. 831–55.

37 Strauss, *Luther's House of Learning*, pp. 171–2.

38 P.F. Grendler, 'The Schools of Christian Doctrine in sixteenth-century Italy', *Church History*, 53 (1984), pp. 319–31; Pullan, *Rich and Poor*, pp. 401–4; L. Chatellier, *The Europe of the Devout: The Catholic Reformation and the Formation of a New Society* (Cambridge, 1989), p. 22.

39 Chatellier, *Europe of the Devout*, p. 22.

40 Houston, *Literacy in Early Modern Europe*, p. 19; R. Darnton, *The Great Cat Massacre, and Other Episodes in French Cultural History* (Harmondsworth, 1985), p. 132.

41 Houston, *Literacy in Early Modern Europe*, pp. 19–22; Morgan, *Godly Learning*, pp. 176–7; A. Fletcher, *Gender, Sex and Subordination in England 1500–1800* (New Haven and London, 1995), pp. 364–75.

42 H. Chisick, *The Limits of Reform in the Enlightenment: Attitudes toward the Education of the Lower Classes in Eighteenth-Century France* (Princeton, 1981), pp. 90–2, 239; R.R. Palmer, *The Improvement of Humanity: Education and the French Revolution* (Princeton, 1985), pp. 53–9.

43 G.L. Seidler, 'The reform of the Polish school system in the age of Enlightenment', in Leith, *Facets of Education*, p. 344.

44 B. Becker-Cantarino, 'Joseph von Sonnenfels and the development of secular education in eighteenth-century Austria', in Leith, *Facets of Education*, pp. 41, 29; see also, Houston, *Literacy in Early Modern Europe*, p. 46.

45 D. Beales, 'Social forces and enlightened policies', and H.M. Scott, 'Reform in the Habsburg Monarchy', in H.M. Scott (ed.), *Enlightened Absolutism: Reform and Reformers in Later Eighteenth-Century Europe* (London, 1990), pp. 50–1, 174–5.

46 Melton, *Absolutism and the Eighteenth-Century Origins of Compulsory Schooling*.

47 H. van der Laan, 'Influences on education and instruction in the Netherlands, especially 1750–1815', pp. 285–311; Seidler, 'Reform of the Polish school system', quoting p. 350; C. Gold, 'Educational reform in Denmark, 1784–1814', quoting p. 54, all in Leith, *Facets of Education*.

48 Scott, 'Reform in the Habsburg Monarchy', p. 175.

49 S. Schama, *Patriots and Liberators: Revolution in the Netherlands 1780–1813* (London, 1977), pp. 532–41, quoting p. 540; van der Laan, 'Influences on education and instruction in the Netherlands', pp. 271–311.

50 Beales, 'Social forces and enlightened policies', p. 51; Chisick, *Limits of Reform*, passim.

51 Melton, *Absolutism and the Eighteenth-Century Origins of Compulsory Schooling*, pp. 46, 174–5; Scott, 'Reform in the Habsburg Monarchy', p. 176; L. Hunt, *The Family Romance of the French Revolution* (Berkeley and Los Angeles, 1992), pp. 67, 161; Schama, *Patriots and Liberators*, p. 536; Gold, 'Educational reform in Denmark', pp. 54–5.

52 Houston, *Literacy in Early Modern Europe*, p. 47.

53 T.C.W. Blanning, 'Frederick the Great and Enlightened Absolutism', in Scott, *Enlightened Absolutism*, p. 267; see also R.S. Turner, 'Of social control and cultural experience: education in the eighteenth century', *Central European History*, 21 (1988), p. 303; Houston, *Literacy in Early Modern Europe*, p. 48.

54 Melton, *Absolutism and the Eighteenth-Century Origins of Compulsory Schooling*, pp. 46, 171–239; Beales, 'Social forces and enlightened policies', p. 53.

55 R.G. Fuchs, *Abandoned Children: Foundlings and Child Welfare in Nineteenth-Century France* (Albany, 1984), pp. 8–9; O. Ulbricht,

'The debate about Foundling Hospitals in Enlightenment Germany: infanticide, illegitimacy, and infant mortality rates', *Central European History*, XVIII (1985), p. 212.

56 Fairchilds, *Poverty and Charity*, pp. 131–46, quoting p. 144; Jones, *Charity and* Bienfaisance, pp. 87, 75, 253.

57 R.K. McClure, *Coram's Children: The London Foundling Hospital in the Eighteenth Century* (New Haven and London, 1981), pp. 76–123, 251, 261.

58 V. Fildes, 'Maternal feelings re-assessed: child abandonment and neglect in London and Westminster, 1550–1800', in V. Fildes (ed.), *Women as Mothers in Pre-Industrial England* (London, 1990), pp. 139–78.

59 K. Wrightson, 'Infanticide in earlier seventeenth-century England', *Local Population Studies*, 15 (1975), pp. 10–22; R.W. Malcolmson, 'Infanticide in the eighteenth century', in J.S. Cockburn (ed.), *Crime in England 1550–1800* (London, 1977), pp. 187–209; Hoffer and Hull, *Murdering Mothers*; M. Jackson, *New-Born Child Murder: Women, Illegitimacy and the Courts in Eighteenth-Century England* (Manchester, 1996).

60 McClure, *Coram's Children*, p. 173.

61 Ransel, *Mothers of Misery*, pp. 31–61, quoting p. 56.

62 B. Pullan, *Orphans and Foundlings in Early Modern Europe* (Reading, 1989), p. 8; Ulbricht, 'The debate about Foundling Hospitals in Enlightenment Germany', pp. 211–56.

63 J. Robins, *The Lost Children: A Study of Charity Children in Ireland, 1700–1900* (Dublin, 1980), pp. 15–100.

64 Ulbricht, 'The debate about Foundling Hospitals in Enlightenment Germany', passim, quoting 223; McClure, *Coram's Children*, pp. 14–15; see also, J. Sherwood, *Poverty in Eighteenth-Century Spain: The Women and Children of the Inclusa* (Toronto, 1988), pp. 100–2, 180–7; Sá, 'Child abandonment in Portugal', p. 77.

65 Quoted in J. Donzelot, *The Policing of Families* (London, 1980), p. 10.

66 Ransel, *Mothers of Misery*, pp. 31–61.

67 Fuchs, *Abandoned Children*, p. 24; A. Forrest, *The French Revolution and the Poor* (Oxford, 1981), pp. 122–3.

68 Ulbricht, 'The debate about Foundling Hospitals in Enlightenment Germany', 228; Donzelot, *Policing of Families*, p. 26.

69 Lis and Soly, *Poverty and Capitalism in Pre-Industrial Europe*, pp. 112–13.

70 Morgan, *Godly Learning*, p. 176; H. Cunningham, *The Children of the Poor: Representations of Childhood since the Seventeenth Century* (Oxford, 1991), pp. 24–6, 33–5, quoting p. 34.

71 Robins, *Lost Children*, pp. 103–7; Cunningham, *Children of the Poor*, pp. 26–32, quoting p. 32; H. Chisick, 'Institutional innovation in popular education in eighteenth century France: two examples', *French Historical Studies*, 10 (1977), pp. 44–5; M.J. Maynes, *Schooling in Western Europe: A Social History* (Albany, 1985), p. 44. In North America a society had been established in 1751 to promote the manufacture of cloth, employing 'women and children who are now in a great measure idle'; and in 1791 Alexander Hamilton reported that 'children are rendered more useful by manufacturing establishments than they otherwise would be'. W.I. Trattner, *Crusade for the Children: A History of the National Child Labor Committee and Child Labor Reform in America* (Chicago, 1970), pp. 25–7.

72 Lis and Soly, *Poverty and Capitalism in Pre-Industrial Europe*, pp. 162, 170; Melton, *Absolutism and the Eighteenth-Century Origins of Compulsory Schooling*, pp. 131–3.

73 Melton, *Absolutism and the Eighteenth-Century Origins of Compulsory Schooling*, pp. 132–41; see also, H. Medick, 'Village spinning bees: sexual culture and free time among rural youth in early modern Germany', in H. Medick and D.W. Sabean (eds), *Interest and Emotion: Essays on the Study of Family and Kinship* (Cambridge, 1984), pp. 317–39.

74 R.B. Bottigheimer, *The Bible for Children: from the Age of Gutenberg to the Present* (New Haven and London, 1996), p. 97.

75 Ulbricht, 'The debate about Foundling Hospitals in Enlightenment Germany', p. 254.

76 Ransel, *Mothers of Misery*, pp. 176–255, quoting p. 198.

77 P.T. Rooke and R.L. Schnell, 'Childhood and charity in nineteenth-century British North America', *Histoire Sociale–Social History*, XV (1982), pp. 167–8, 177, quoting p. 177; B. Bradbury, 'The fragmented family; family strategies in the face of death, illness, and poverty, Montreal 1860–1885', in J. Parr (ed.), *Childhood and Family in Canadian History* (Toronto, 1982), pp. 110–28. For further evidence of the advantages of the 'orphan' label, see C. Stansell, 'Women, children, and the uses of the streets: class and gender conflict in New York City, 1850–1860', in H.J. Graff (ed.), *Growing Up in America: Historical Experiences* (Detroit, 1987), pp. 307–8, 313.

78 Kertzer, *Sacrificed for Honor*, pp. 84, 103–6, 155–62; Ransel, *Mothers of Misery*, p. 68; L.A. Tilly, R.G. Fuchs, D.I. Kertzer and D.L. Ransel, 'Child abandonment in European history: a symposium', *Journal of Family History*, 17 (1992), p. 6.

79 Fuchs, *Abandoned Children*, pp. 28–61; Donzelot, *Policing of Families*, pp. 26–30.

80 Quoted in Hunt, *Family Romance of the French Revolution*, p. 67.

CHAPTER 6

Saving the children, *c*.1830–*c*.1920

Governments and philanthropists, as we have seen, had for centuries formulated and operated policies towards children. Why should the period between 1830 and 1920 be marked out for separate treatment? The answer is that for a significant number of reformers the purpose of a policy towards children was lifted clear of its old moorings: until the nineteenth century policies had been drawn up with a concern either for the child's soul or for the future manpower needs of the state. Both of these concerns remained in place in the nineteenth and early twentieth centuries, but they were joined by a new one, a concern to save children for the enjoyment of childhood. The ideology of childhood, the emergence of which was traced in Chapter 3, now began to influence public action.

Philanthropy was central to this child-saving activity. Philanthropists opened and ran homes for orphans and other neglected children, they organised schemes of emigration, they set up kindergartens and schools, they founded societies for the prevention of cruelty to children, and they had numerous programmes for visiting the poor. Although these things are not susceptible to measurement, there can be little doubt that this was on a scale greater than in the eighteenth century, and, outside some urban communities, than in the sixteenth or seventeenth centuries. It stands indeed in marked contrast to that decline of charity observable at least in France in the eighteenth century.

Who were these philanthropists and what impelled them to action? They certainly differed from those moved to charitable activity in earlier centuries who believed that the giving of gifts to the poor was a vital contribution to their own salvation. And yet the vast majority of them were

Christian, normally quite explicitly so, both in their own lives and in the organisations which they established. Denominational rivalry had a part to play in impelling them to action, but no more than a part. Much more important was a missionary zeal to reach out to people who, in the slums of the new big cities of an industrialising world, seemed as heathen as the 'savages' of Africa or Polynesia. Of course this missionary zeal had its limits: a rank fear of 'the dangerous classes' sometimes surfaced alarmingly; Shaftesbury in 1840 saw 'the two great demons in morals and politics, Socialism and Chartism . . . stalking through the land', and urged as a preventative that the neglect of children be ended. Leading Christian philanthropists in Europe, W.H. Suringar in the Netherlands and J.H. Wichern in Germany, both at the forefront of efforts to reclaim neglected children, invoked similar fears.[1] The voicing of these anxieties about revolution was perhaps as much a rhetorical device to stir up the apathetic as a motivating force for the active philanthropist, but the latter certainly had no desire to upset the existing social order, rather to re-enforce it. Philanthropists were not utopians or revolutionaries, and they worked with the grain of the economic, social and political structures of their times. It was this which gave them power and leverage. From time to time, of course, they exposed themselves to criticism: Henry Mayhew could argue that the Ragged Schools of nineteenth-century London contributed to rather than diminished the crime rate; more powerful critics could raise questions over the policies and practices of philanthropists in transporting children to Canada; both Barnardo's and the British National Society for the Prevention of Cruelty to Children were subject to serious criticisms of the scope and direction of their activities.[2] But by and large philanthropic organisations concerned with children received a favourable press, and were accepted both in the communities in which they worked and in society at large.

Children were not the only people to be on the receiving end of nineteenth-century philanthropy, but they featured largely in philanthropic plans. Children were thought to be unformed enough to be savable. They represented the future. Their 'plastic natures', thought the Boston Children's Friend Society, 'may be molded into images of perfect beauty, or as perfect repulsiveness'.[3] And it was relatively easy to tap the pockets of the public by a sentimental appeal on their behalf. Moreover, women played an increasingly important role in philanthropy in the nineteenth century, and it seemed both natural and politically safe that they should focus their work on charity towards children. In England in 1893 it was estimated that there were 500,000 women working 'continuously and semi-professionally' in philanthropy, and many of them were involved in charities for children.[4]

In the philanthropic/missionary discourse we can often sense shock at the distance between the actuality and ideals of childhood as experienced within the middle and upper classes, and what they observed within the mission field. They saw 'children without childhood'. The essentially romantic rather than Christian view of childhood as properly protected and dependent, and separate from adulthood, which had become dom-inant in the first half of the nineteenth century, provided a motivating reference point for any philanthropist. 'The ideal we place before us', wrote an American Progressive, Edward T. Devine, in 1910, 'is a protected childhood.' We can see this ideal in action in Florence Davenport-Hill's response to children in workhouses: 'It is painful to set aside our ideal of a childhood of innocence and bright playfulness, and to realise that there are among us thousands of children familiar with shocking vice . . .'; her remedy, of course, was to try to place these children in an environment where 'innocence and bright playfulness' could flourish.[5]

This view of childhood can be seen as a motivating influence in many countries from about the 1830s. In their study of charity for children in nineteenth-century British North America Patricia Rooke and R.L. Schnell argue that most of the ingredients of what we think of as a modern concept of childhood were present before the 1880s. There were in place policies which emphasised the need for protection and segregation of children and for making them dependent. All that was lacking was delaying the respons-ibilities of these children, for they were indeed expected to contribute to the economy at an early age. If this was true of Canada, it was even more the case for Britain which provided a number of models for policies towards children taken over by the Canadians.[6]

In trying to promote this view of childhood philanthropists aimed to immerse children in 'networks of good influence'.[7] Put another way, many working-class children came under some sort of surveillance or control by philanthropic organisations. Philanthropy had opened up huge areas for public intervention into working-class life – for, though its work rarely involved the state, it was emphatically public rather than private.

Philanthropists, however, were not the only people acting in the public sphere with a concern for children. Sometimes a distinction is drawn between a period of child rescue lasting from about the middle of the nineteenth century for some thirty years, and a more ambitious and far-reaching child-saving period from the 1880s onwards. Linked to this is the view that child rescue was primarily a task for philanthropists and voluntary agencies, and that in child-saving there was a more pronounced role for government and for a growing body of professionals concerned with childhood. Certainly in the period beginning in the 1880s there was a tipping of the balance in action on behalf of children from philanthropy to the state, and a growing involvement of professionals and experts in the task of saving the children. By the end of the century it was coming to be felt that only state action could secure a childhood for all children, and states began to take over from philanthropy the key role in so doing. In giving their impetus to 'saving the child', states had a variety of motivations, besides those which could be called child-oriented: concern about population levels; worry about the level of 'civilisation' of the masses; desire to breed a race capable of competing in the twentieth century. 'Saving the children' involved moving them somewhere close to the centre of the political agenda of the modern state.

Child labour

Child labour in Britain in the new conditions of the industrial revolution first brought the new ideology of childhood into play as a factor in policy-making. The regulation and control of child labour dates back centuries with an assumption that most children's first experience as full-time workers would be as servants or apprentices – that is to say, they would be living outside the parental home. Regulations defining the responsibilities of both masters and servants or apprentices had the full force of law. In addition the state had a responsibility to find apprenticeships for the children brought up in its care. What is sometimes seen as the first Factory Act in Britain in 1802 is better described as one of a long series of apprenticeship acts, seeking in this instance to protect pauper apprentices in the cotton mills. It was not therefore the principle of state intervention in the child labour market which was the novelty of the period beginning in 1830; that principle was well established. The novelty was the first voicing of the assertion that children had a right not to work at all.

That assertion had a long gestation period of some fifty years. From about 1780 we can begin to hear people questioning the prevalent assumption that children in poverty should be inured to work from an early age. In 1766 Jonas Hanway, in (significant title) *An Earnest Appeal for Mercy to the Children of the Poor*, had urged that when poor children were apprenticed out, 'it should be considered how to make labor as pleasant, or to speak more to the heart, as little *irksome* as possible, and with a tender regard to the measure of a young person's strength of body or mind'.[8]

Hanway was a mercantilist, fully alive to the importance of training young people for the future service of the state, but he clearly doubted the sense of Locke's view, still being cited as authoritative, that poor children should be put to work at the age of three, with a 'bellyful of bread daily' supplemented by, in cold weather, 'if it be thought needful, a little warm water-gruel'.[9] Hanway also took up the cause of the boys and the occasional girl who were employed cleaning chimneys. Thanks very largely to Hanway, the cruelty inflicted on the children began to be recognised: they had to be induced up the chimneys by pin pricks on their feet or by a fire lit in the grate; and if they avoided death by suffocation they were peculiarly liable to cancer of the scrotum. Hanway's *A Sentimental History of Chimney Sweepers* of 1785 did more than simply set forth these cruelties; it embellished them in a rhetoric in which Hanway worked on people's sentiments, appealing to humanity, to Christianity, to pity, to compassion, to reason, to passion, and to national honour and traditions. Climbing boys were 'as children', he wrote, 'objects of our mercy and tenderest kindness'. Hanway was the initiator of a genre of literature which marked out the climbing boys as the epitome of exploitation, stolen and sold like slaves, all the more scandalous because, as a Sheffield campaigner wrote in the 1830s, '*They are, of all human beings, the most lovely, the most engaging, the most of all others claiming protection, comfort, and love. They are CHILDREN.*'[10]

Initially it was the damage to children's physique which attracted attention to the work of children in cotton factories. Alerted by an outbreak of fever in a cotton works, doctors in Lancashire in the 1780s laid down as an axiom that for children under fourteen 'the active recreations of childhood and youth are necessary to the growth, the vigour and the right conformation of the human body'. Childhood was being seen as at least in part a time for play. Without it children would not develop the bodily strength necessary for a successful adulthood, and in the cotton factories they were not receiving it. But over and above this utilitarian attitude there was an admixture of the sentimentalism which Hanway and the Romantic poets had legitimated. People began to be moved in curious ways by the sight of children at work; for most of the eighteenth century the response had been one of admiration for those who had organised such work, but by the end of the century people like Mrs Trimmer, an Evangelical who was not notably soft-hearted, found themselves unable to 'think of little children, who work in Manufactories, without the utmost commiseration'. Like the climbing boys, they began to be thought of as slaves, 'our poor little White-Slaves, the children in our cotton Factories', as S.T. Coleridge expressed it.[11]

Coleridge himself campaigned for an Act of Parliament to control the work of children. The 1802 Act had been largely concerned with pauper apprentices, but it soon became necessary to widen the focus to consider the so-called 'free labour' of children, that is the labour of children who were living in their families rather than being in the care of the state. The factories had begun to recruit such children. Critics poured scorn on the idea that this labour was in any sense 'free': 'If the labor were indeed free', wrote Coleridge, 'the contract would approach, on the one side, too near to suicide, on the other to manslaughter.' The Act of 1819, the first to address this 'free' labour, was something of a disappointment to reformers, but the campaign to improve conditions had a momentum which was not easily halted. It came to a head in the early 1830s, coinciding precisely with the campaigns for the emancipation of slaves in British colonies, part of its emotive force stemming from the claim that the British government seemed more concerned for the black than for the white slave. 'It is notorious', wrote Richard Oastler in 1833, 'that the health of the negro slave, of the adult felon, of the horse, of the ass, of the hare, of the rabbit, of the part-ridge, of the pheasant, of the cabbage, and of the strawberry, is protected by law; but at the same time, the Children of the Poor are unprotected by the law . . .'[12]

The government conceded that something had to be done, but was determined not to give in to the demands of the campaigners for a ten-hour day, for this would have had the effect of limiting the hours worked not only by children but also by adults; instead it focused on the children, banning work in factories by children under nine, and restricting the hours to eight a day for children up to the age of fourteen. Backing up the Act with an inspectorate, the government was effectively defining childhood as a period in which people needed protection by the law; and the period of childhood was carefully marked out by the utilitarian Royal Commission which had advised the government. The Commission argued that at the beginning of the fourteenth year 'the period of childhood, properly so called, ceases, and that of puberty is established, when the body becomes more capable of enduring protracted labour . . .' This physiological change coincided with a change in social status for

in general at or about the fourteenth year young persons are no longer treated as children; they are not usually chastised by corporal punishment, and at the same time an important change takes place in what may be termed their domestic condition. For the most part they cease to be under the complete control of their parents and guardians.

They begin to retain a part of their wages. They frequently pay for their
own lodging, board, and clothing. They usually make their own
contracts, and are, in the proper sense of the words, free agents.

A child was becoming defined as someone who was not a 'free agent', who
was dependent, and therefore in need of protection by law.[13] No children
seemed more in need of protection than those who worked underground,
hauling and pushing the coal wagons to the mine shaft. Another Royal
Commission in 1842 not only described what happened, but included
drawings of the children at work (Plate 4), shocking contemporaries and
standing ever since as an encapsulation of the conditions of child labour in
the industrial revolution.

Government action was aimed in part against unscrupulous parents
who would put their children to early and harmful work. Leonard Horner,
the factory inspector, set the blame for what was going wrong in the factories at the feet of parents, and had little truck with paternal rights; 'If the
father has his natural rights', he wrote, 'so has the child; and if the father
robs him of these, the State must become his guardian, and restore them to
him.' But alongside this willingness to contemplate an invasion of long-
established parental rights went a recognition that economic forces were
operating to the disadvantage of children; there was a strong demand for
child labour. The Royal Commission saw that demand increasing 'in consequence of the tendency of improvements in machinery to throw more
and more of the work upon children, to the displacement of adult labour'.
That tendency, some thought, had causes 'as steady in their operation as
a physical law'. Manufacturers, in competition with one another, would
seek to reduce labour costs, and one way of doing that was to introduce
machinery which could be operated by the cheapest labour, that of children. Defenders of the factory system pointed out how this was solving the
problem which had been endemic for centuries, that of finding sufficient
employment for children. But others, including the utilitarians, who had
considerable influence on official thinking in Britain in the 1830s and
1840s, were forced to recognise that the hidden hand of capitalism might
not always work to the benefit of all, and that there was a need for a corpus
of law, reinforced by inspection, to prevent market forces from progressively employing more children and fewer adults.[14]

The extent to which market forces were already doing this needs
emphasis. The young were crucial to the profitability of late eighteenth-
and early nineteenth-century industry. In the British cotton industry in
1835 43 per cent of the workers were under eighteen. In the north-eastern

United States the percentage of women and children in the manufacturing labour force rose from 10 per cent to 40 per cent from the early nineteenth century up to 1832. In 1852 in Manchester and Salford, 76 per cent of all fourteen-year-old girls and 61 per cent of all fourteen-year-old boys were employed in mills. In the words of a foreman in a wool mill in 1833, 'factories cannot be carried on without children . . . One effect of the present system is that children come to do the same work instead of the fathers; boys are worked in place of men.'[15] Nor was this process confined to the textile industry. When Henry Mayhew investigated the London artisan trades at mid-century, he found that the point put to him by the tailors and the boot and shoe makers and the woodworkers was not that machinery or technological innovation was leading to the substitution of child for adult labour: the cause lay rather in competition and the division of labour. Masters were driven to reduce their costs in order to survive. 'Twenty years ago', a small master in the woodworking trades told Mayhew, 'I don't think there was a young child at work in our business.' Now, 'our trade's come to such a pass that unless a man has children to help him he can't live at all'.[16] There seemed to be a process whereby competition drove down the cost of labour by the increasing use of child labour.

The utilitarians did not object to child labour in principle, only to its excess. Time in childhood, they argued, must be set aside for schooling and physical growth. But beyond that, and beyond a certain minimum age, there was no reason why children should not go to work and contribute to the family economy. Children therefore should be half-timers, half at work and half at school, a solution to the problem of factory work which won wide support in the middle decades of the nineteenth century. It was acceptable to Evangelicals like Lord Shaftesbury, one of the most passionate advocates of a Ten Hour Act, for his chief concern, as he never ceased to reiterate, was to ensure that children went to school.[17]

But for those touched by Romanticism a childhood in which children did any work at all was beginning to be seen as unnatural. The romantic view of childhood was widely disseminated and elaborated upon, and became embedded in the rhetoric of the factory movement of the 1830s and 1840s. Thus Philip Gaskell in his survey of factory conditions in his book *Artisans and Machinery* (1836) referred directly to Wordsworth's 'Intimations of Immortality from Recollections of Early Childhood' in writing that:

It has been truly observed, and not less beautifully than truly, that 'heaven is around us in our infancy'. This might have been extended, and

said, that 'heaven is around and within us in our infancy', for the
happiness of childhood springs full as much from an internal
consciousness of delight, as from the novelty of its impressions from
without. Its mind, providing the passions are properly guided, is indeed
a fountain of all that is beautiful – all that is amiable – overflowing with
joy and tenderness; and its young heart is a living laboratory of love,
formed to be profusely scattered on all around.

Childhood here was a fountain irrigating the arid soils of adulthood. It
came indeed to be seen as some recompense to mankind for the loss of
Eden. It was, or should be, 'the weary life's long happy holyday', the
archaic spelling of holiday emphasising the place which childhood had in
God's plan for mankind.[18]

Armed with this kind of vision, the assertion of the rights of childhood
became imbued with an emotional quality lacking in the utilitarian and
evangelical perspectives. Reason gave precedence to feelings, and those
feelings were brought to bear on children in the factories and mines and up
the chimneys. Parental rights became as nothing in conflict with the rights
of children. Indeed, the issue became not children versus parents, but children versus 'the factory system', a new and unnatural mode of production.
Whereas in nature the young devoted their time to growing and playing, in
human society, or at least in the factory system, the young were put to
work. As Elizabeth Barrett Browning put it in 'The Cry of the Children',

> *The young lambs are bleating in the meadows,*
> *The young birds are chirping in the nest,*
> *The young fawns are playing with the shadows,*
> *The young flowers are blowing toward the west –*
> *But the young, young children, O my brothers,*
> *They are weeping bitterly!*
> *They are weeping in the playtime of the others,*
> *In the country of the free.*

To the English the offence against childhood was compounded by the fact
that it was occurring in 'the country of the free' – in England. But in
essence what Browning and others influenced by Romanticism were
demanding was a childhood for all children everywhere which was in harmony with nature, and in which manual labour had no part. 'Ever a toiling
Child doth make us sad', wrote Samuel Roberts of Sheffield in 1837. Three
years later Douglas Jerrold, one of the founders of *Punch*, was to write of
factory children that they were 'children without childhood'.[19] He did not

need to elaborate: the romantics had helped to fix in the British mind an idea of what childhood should be.

Until the mid-nineteenth century the debates on child labour under industrialisation were concentrated in Britain. But as they industrialised, other countries also began to legislate to protect children. In France the 1841 Child Labour Law 'marked the emergence of a serious state concern with the supervision and protection of childhood'. Although this law was not very effectively implemented, it was followed up in the mid–late 1860s by 'a dramatic intensification of concern over child labor', which is partly explained by the historian of these events as stemming from the fact that a 'new understanding of childhood as a period to be prolonged and devoted to nurturing and education was a normative feature of the mentality of the comfortable classes in France by the late 1860s'.[20] The momentum of reform was only briefly interrupted by the events of 1870–1, and in 1874 France passed a Child Labour Law which set twelve as a minimum age for work. In Prussia the law of 1853 established twelve as the minimum age for employment in industry, with consistent enforcement only after a further act of 1878. In industrialised New England it was in the period from the 1840s that child labour laws were passed.[21] In industrialising countries, it may be asserted with some confidence, the crucial steps to control child labour were taken prior to the 1880s, and although utilitarian and evangelical arguments often helped shape the legislation, competing with them and influencing them was a growing belief that children should not work. When Progressives in the United States rather belatedly in the early twentieth century sought to move beyond a state to a federal response to child labour, they did so because, in the words of one spokesman, 'The term child labor is a paradox for when labor begins . . . the child ceases to be'; and in the words of another, 'a child is industrially taboo' and 'to violate its rights is to touch profanely a holy thing'.[22] The magnitude of the shift that had been made needs emphasis; for most of the eighteenth century philanthropists and governments tried to create work opportunities for children from about the age when in the later nineteenth century they would be sent to school; for by that date few people could be found who would publicly deny that children should be saved from work.

Street children

The work conditions for children in the industrial revolution were something new, and it was not surprising that they provoked a sharp response. Street children, by contrast, were a centuries-old problem. Yet the response to that problem in the middle and later decades of the nineteenth century contained within it elements of the romantic wish to save the child for childhood, rather than inure it to regular labour. Perhaps it was the sheer number of the children which had something to do with this. In New York in 1849 the chief of police reported on 'the constantly increasing numbers of vagrant, idle and vicious children', whose numbers were, he claimed, 'almost incredible'. In London Shaftesbury reckoned that there were probably more than 30,000 'naked, filthy, roaming, lawless, and deserted children'. In Paris in the first half of the nineteenth century the numbers of vagrant and abandoned children were greater than before the Revolution.[23] For needy children the cities were magnets. In France for centuries they had travelled from Savoy and the Auvergne to Paris to eke out a living as chimney sweeps and street traders. In the nineteenth century in poor villages in the Apennines in Italy, families apprenticed their children to *padrones* who put the children to work on the streets of Paris, London, New York, Moscow and many other cities, to perform with animals or musical instruments.[24]

There was sympathy for these children, particularly if they exhibited signs of proper childish demeanour. Sometimes philanthropic individuals, hearing of particularly pitiful cases, agreed in effect to adopt a child who would otherwise go to prison.[25] But there was also fear. To Shaftesbury children who behaved like 'tribes of lawless freebooters', rendered 'the state of society more perilous than in any former day'. In Paris Delacroix's painting of *The Barricade* had set up in the public mind the role of urchins in the revolution of 1830, a point reiterated by de Tocqueville with respect to 1848 when he wrote that 'It is the Paris urchins who usually start insurrections.' The two cities vied with one another in writing up the threats posed by such children. In London, claimed one writer in 1849, 'we have a class as wild, and perhaps even more incorrigible than those spawned forth by the dangerous classes in Paris'.[26]

Did this alarm about what was increasingly called 'juvenile delinquency' have any basis in reality? Probably not much. Boys (they were nearly all boys) arrested and awaiting trial in London were interviewed, and the picture which emerged was of working-class children from poor families who engaged in subsistence crime. Henry Underwood, for example, 'stole provisions – such as bread and bacon'. It was often chance that led to one boy rather than another getting caught up in the criminal justice system, and once within it further criminal activity was highly likely: once you had been inside an institution it was difficult to find employment and to return to a crime-free life. Perhaps for this reason some of the boys welcomed the prospect of transportation, imagining a fresh start in a new country.[27]

Middle-class commentators who had contact with juvenile delinquents or other street children found them to lack all of what had become the accepted characteristics of children. A mark of this was their independence from adults. They enjoyed, said Shaftesbury, a 'barbarian freedom from all superintendence and restraint'. They became known as 'savages' or 'street arabs', a designation which stamped them as 'indolent, averse from any settled or steady employment, averse from restraint of any kind'. The freedom of this life had rapidly removed from them any of the marks of childhood, a fact all too visible in their body language. Henry Mayhew, interviewing a girl, aged eight, who sold watercress, found that she 'had entirely lost all childish ways', and that her face was wrinkled 'where the dimples ought to have been'. The delinquent boy, it was said, presented 'the face of a child with no trace of childish goodness'.[28]

From this diagnosis stemmed the solution: the delinquent 'has to be turned again into a child'. In England Mary Carpenter in the 1850s set out an agenda of the utmost simplicity. Children, she said, needed love; without it, 'they are no longer children'. Young offenders, therefore, must be treated with consideration for 'the nature of the child, *as a child*. We must not treat him as a man.' And finally, the offender must 'gradually be restored to the true position of childhood . . . he must . . . be placed in a *family*'. This was not simply sentimentalism, a regret for childhoods which had not been allowed to happen, though doubtless this was part of it; it was also the outcome of an internalisation of the romantic belief that the enjoyment of a proper childhood was the only foundation for a tolerable adult life. And that childhood must be one of dependence and protection within the bounds of a family, or a substitute family.[29]

The method dating back to the fifteenth century for dealing with abandoned or delinquent children was to place them in an institution. From the 1830s there was an intensified phase of institution building, catering for children of all kinds thought to be in need. In Europe two institutions, the Rauhe Haus near Hamburg, opened in 1833, and Mettray, near Tours, opened in 1840, became much-visited and inspirational models for what Jeroen Dekker has described as 'an archipelago of homes' for the re-education of children, housing 'hundreds of thousands of children . . . in thousands of homes'.[30] In the United States asylum building swept across the country in the period after 1830. By 1850 in New York State alone there were twenty-seven public and private institutions caring for children. In the country as a whole, the seventy-seven private orphanages of

1851 had increased to 613 by 1880, and there were a further 474 established over the following twenty years. By 1910 there were over 150,000 dependent, neglected and delinquent children cared for in 1,151 institutions. In English-speaking Canada in 1891 there were no less than forty-one orphanages, housing 3,827 children.[31] In Ireland there was a huge influx of children into institutional care in the aftermath of the Famine of the late 1840s, the numbers totalling 120,000 in 1850. By the mid-1860s this number had been sharply reduced to 18,000, but there were in addition a large number of children looked after by religious bodies; in Dublin twenty-four Catholic organisations caring for orphans had increased the number of children in their care from 800 to 3,500 between 1834 and 1864, and they were matched by an equal number of Protestant organisations.[32]

These institutions, whether established for orphan children, for the neglected, or for juvenile delinquents, had many characteristics in common. Orphanages had a wider catchment clientele than one might imagine, some two-thirds of the inmates of four orphanages in one Midwestern state in the 1920s having both parents alive.[33] It was difficult to keep a clear distinction between institutions designed for those who had been convicted of an offence and those aiming to prevent children from offending. Of all the institutions it may be said that their mission, as they saw it, was to place children where they were 'sheltered from the perils of want and the contamination of evil example'. They were asylums, houses of refuge, places where children were protected.[34] It is easy to think of them simply as agencies for social control, but parents and other responsible adults frequently sought admission to them for children in their charge. Thus in the Dutch town of Delft neither hardship nor lack of kin can explain the placing of children in the orphanage; it received children because it provided good care and good prospects for the children in its care.[35]

Despite this kind of evidence, most contemporaries and modern scholars have been highly critical of the lives led by children in institutions. Although ostensibly they modelled themselves on Christian families, institutions subjected children to a highly-disciplined regime where the prime objective seemed to be to instil obedience, and where, in the words of one visitor, 'Everything moves by machinery, as it always must with masses of children never subdivided into families.'[36] The criticisms of these institutions mounted in the second half of the nineteenth century. There were acute health problems, in particular the prevalence of an eye infection, ophthalmia. But more than this, it was recognised that in the massing of children together 'no account is made of the child's natural desire for home life, for affection, and above all for parental love. Deprived of these, it feels an outcast and is only too likely some day or other to retaliate on that society which has wronged it. If we take home and love from the poor, we reduce their fate to that of the beasts of burden.' It was apparently Americans who coined the word 'institutionalised' to refer to a child who was 'mechanical and helpless from the effect of asylum life'.[37]

There were numerous attempts in the later nineteenth century to provide some kind of home life for children who were in care. Sometimes they might be restored to their natural families; in Paris about half of the children who came into conflict with the law were returned to their own families.[38] But for many children the natural family was seen as the cause of the child becoming dependent or delinquent; substitute families had to be found. There were two main ways of so doing. The first was to separate out young offenders from old, and to try to secure for the former an institutional life which bore some resemblance to that within a family. The origins of this movement lie back in the eighteenth century with, for example, the foundation in England in 1788 of the Philanthropic Society to rescue abandoned and criminal children. But the model for residential institutions was the Rauhe Haus established near Hamburg in 1833, on which were based Mettray in France, Mettray in the Netherlands, Ruysselede in Belgium and Red Hill in England. These were agricultural colonies for young offenders or deprived children which had the dual advantage of removing children from the contaminating influence of the city and of placing them in houses where there could be a semblance of family life.[39] For all kinds of children in care institutions began to be designed on the block or cottage rather than the barrack system; that is there were relatively small units within the boundaries of a large institution. But these were expensive, and many doubted whether they did in fact effectively reproduce the feel of a home.[40]

It was only in the twentieth century that there was established a separate system of criminal justice rather than different treatment after conviction. The initiative for separate children's courts stemmed from the United States where in 1899 the State of Illinois passed a Juvenile Court Act. Over the next four years the Illinois initiative was replicated in Wisconsin, New York, Ohio, Maryland and Colorado, and in 1908 it crossed the Atlantic to Britain and Germany. Four key ideas underlay the establishment of juvenile courts. The first was that the prime purpose of the court should be reform rather than punishment. Secondly, it followed from this that the courts should take preventive action, and should have powers to deal with those who in Illinois were called 'pre-delinquents', that is those who had not actually committed a criminal offence, but were thought likely to do so. Thirdly, since reform was the aim, sentences should be indeterminate, the length depending on the response of the juvenile to the treatment regime. Finally, there should be a probation system to provide guidance to and oversight of those who were outside institutions.[41]

The second initiative on behalf of deprived or delinquent children was even more radical than the attempt to establish institutions with a family feel: it was to place children in foster families. To do this within a state's boundaries was in some ways no more than an extension of the wet-nursing schemes used for foundlings for centuries. The children would be taken out of the unhealthy environment of the city, and placed in the countryside; the downside of such schemes was the question of inspection, recognised to be essential, but hard to implement, and there was always the danger that a fostered child might be exploited.[42]

The 'social engineering' involved in breaking a child's ties with its family was even more apparent if the child was sent overseas, or at a great distance from its place of origin.[43] In the 1820s both in London and in Paris schemes of this kind were floated, and in 1831 fifty-nine girls from Cork Foundling Hospital went to New South Wales at the expense of the government, but the movement did not achieve any momentum until mid-century.[44] In London Shaftesbury wanted to send the graduates of his Ragged Schools to South Australia. In New York Charles Loring Brace's Children's Aid Society began in 1854 to send economically productive children to farms in New York State and Midwestern states, eventually placing out more than 60,000 children.[45] Another 80,000 were 'emigrated' by the British to Canada between 1870 and 1914. This took place in part because of the demand for child labour in agriculture or domestic service on the frontier, and it might on that account be seen as at odds with the campaigns to save children from labour. But agricultural work for children, provided that it was consonant with their strength, could be presented as natural and in all key respects different from work in factories. Moreover it had the crucial added advantage that children were placed in an environment of nature, away from city streets. It might be necessary that they should work, but at least they would be doing so under the skies and not the factory roof; something of a childhood could be restored to them, and no effort should be spared in trying to achieve this. Barnardo, the most important figure in the British child emigration movement of the later nineteenth and early twentieth centuries, resorted to 'philanthropic abduction' in order to rescue children from the cities and from their inadequate families.[46]

Cruelty to children

It is often said of the British that they were more concerned about cruelty to animals than cruelty to children. Whereas there was a Royal Society for the Prevention of Cruelty to Animals from the 1820s, the National Society for the Prevention of Cruelty to Children was founded only in the 1880s. But in fact adult abuse of children had met with strong community sanctions and sometimes legal action in the eighteenth and early nineteenth centuries. *The Times* between 1785 and 1860 reported 385 cases of child neglect and sexual abuse, with only 7 per cent resulting in a 'not guilty' outcome. In sentencing, magistrates expressed their horror and revulsion at the cruelties inflicted, for the most part by parents, on children.[47] Child victims featured increasingly prominently in cases coming before the northeast circuit in England between 1770 and 1845, and there was a similar upward trend in London and the West Riding of Yorkshire after 1830. These legal actions had community support. Most cases which came to court originated in neighbours or family approaching the police. A London magistrate in 1830 acquitted, because of insufficient evidence, a shoemaker accused of intending to abuse girl children, but told the court that 'If I were the father . . . and had a good horsewhip in my hand, I know where I should apply it.' Outside the court, the shoemaker 'was met by a posse of women, who began to hoot and pelt him, and a sturdy coal-heaver tripping up his heels rolled him for several yards in the kennel, to the no small delight of the bystanders'.[48]

Set against this background, there was rather less novelty than is often suggested when reformers in the United States in the 1870s, and then in Britain in the 1880s, set up Societies for the Prevention of Cruelty to Children. By the end of the 1870s there were thirty-four SPCCs in the United States and fifteen elsewhere.[49] In continental Europe, France and Belgium were at the forefront of international discussions of measures to protect children: of fifteen international conferences on the theme held between 1872 and 1914, seven were in Belgium and two in Paris; and, particularly in the 1890s, these two countries pioneered campaigns to reform laws and institutions and to extend protection to children at risk.[50]

The novelty involved in these initiatives was twofold. First, there were now organisations deliberately designed to protect children. It is true that there were forerunners, but the aims of the new organisations were wider:

they sought to enforce existing laws, to make it a criminal offence to mis-treat or abuse a child, and to set up a system of inspection to investigate cases of suspected neglect or abuse. In Britain the NSPCC by 1910 had 250 inspectors who dealt with over 50,000 complaints. It was in the period 1880–1914, argues Harry Ferguson, that 'the modern concept of "child abuse" was socially constructed'.[51] Secondly, the societies and associated movements represented a deliberate attempt to restrict the power of par-ents and in particular fathers. The issue was not a new one. Thus in Britain there were long-recognised limits to the punishment parents could inflict on children. In 1850 a barrister was sentenced to prison for overstepping these limits, parents being reminded that they 'must take care not to exceed the bounds of moderation in chastising them'.[52] It was in France that parental, or to be more precise paternal, rights raised the deepest conflict. Under the Napoleonic Civil Code a father whose child afforded 'com-pelling grounds for dissatisfaction . . . can cause him to be imprisoned for a period of one month if he is less than sixteen years of age, and for a period of six months if he is older'.[53] In the later nineteenth century, how-ever, the paternal authority embedded in the Napoleonic Code began to be challenged. Philanthropic organisations had been established for the protection of children in the 1860s, and there emerged in the 1880s the concept of the child who was '*moralement abandonné*', a threat as well as a victim, but in need of rescue. When fathers applied to have a child imprisoned, social workers began as a matter of routine to see if it was the parent rather than the child who needed punishment. And after experience of parents reclaiming children who had been taken into the care of the state, a law in 1889 threatened a permanent loss of parental authority when 'fathers and mothers . . . through their habitual drunkenness, their notorious and scandalous misconduct, or through ill treatment, com-promise the safety, health or morality of their children'. Over the next quarter of a century, all western European countries passed laws, modelled on the French one, restricting parental rights. In France itself, by 1899 there were over 20,000 children '*moralement abandonné*' in the care of the state.[54] The British Prevention of Cruelty to Children Act, also of 1889, the 'Children's Charter' as it was called, similarly provided for the removal of children from parental care. It marked, in the view of its most ardent advocate, Benjamin Waugh, the beginning of 'Parliamentary con-test on behalf of children, as children, in their merely human interests . . . Then the absolutism of the State prevailed over the absolutism of the parent . . .'[55] Institutions designed to save children from adult cruelty were now in place.

Philanthropy, the state and children

The Societies for the Prevention of Cruelty to Children were in some sense privately-organised and funded agents of the state. The New York SPCC, for example, was a private corporation, but its agents were 'duly constituted officers of the law'. It was as though the state itself hesitated to be seen to be interfering too heavily in the daily lives of the people, and preferred to allow a private agency to act on its behalf. In contrast to many other SPCCs in the United States, the New York SPCC held to a policy of institutional care for children, and brought on its head considerable criticism both for this policy in itself, and for its general lack of accountability.[56] The relationship between philanthropy and the state in the care for children was fraught with difficulties.

In one perspective philanthropy had prepared the ground for later state intervention, with an easy transition from one to the other as the scale of the task outstripped philanthropic resources. But in another and more realistic one, philanthropists can be seen resisting state intervention in the fields which they had mapped out as their own. In the early twentieth century there was a growing critique of philanthropy as an agency for dealing with issues to do with childhood. Despite its own insistence on careful casework and on a separation out of the deserving and undeserving, or the helpable and unhelpable, philanthropy was condemned for indiscriminacy of another kind: it simply did not cover the whole population; there might be pockets of good coverage by philanthropic agencies next to areas without any.[57] There was still a good deal of support, perhaps majority support, within governments for what may be called the philanthropic solution to social problems, but in the first decade of the twentieth century there began to be voiced open criticism of philanthropy normally combined with condescending recognition of the philanthropists' good intentions.[58] It began to be argued that the state must act as the central and co-ordinating agency on behalf of children. In the United States and in Britain the phrase 'the children of the state', once used to refer exclusively to children in the direct care of the state, began to be used to refer to all children by advocates of a wider state role. 'All children are children of the state, or none are', declared Rev. Lloyd Jenkins Jones of Illinois in 1898.[59]

The identification of childhood as an area for state policy was accompanied and to some extent caused by a declining confidence in the family. Some argued that if families were doing their jobs properly, there would be no call for a state policy for children; the solution was not to resort to state policies, but to force families to face up to their responsibilities. Others argued that many families were unable to look after their children properly, and that the state ought positively to intervene on behalf of children while at the same time enabling families to function more effectively. The provision of school meals by local authorities could thus be seen either as the removal from the family of a proper and valued role, or as a welcome relief to families who could concentrate their inadequate resources on other matters. But in both cases the family was in some kind of interrogation from philanthropists or the state; it was certainly no longer assumed that the rearing of children could simply be left to families with the state or voluntary organisations picking up the casualties.

The rate of infant mortality, which in many countries remained as high in the late nineteenth century as at its outset, provided the most obvious arena for intervention. By the early twentieth century there was in existence 'an international infant welfare movement of truly immense dimensions', with national organisations in Denmark, Germany, Italy, Luxemburg, the Netherlands, Norway, Rumania, Russia, Spain, Switzerland, the United Kingdom and the United States.[60] Although there were some differences in emphasis from country to country in the policies recommended for bringing about a reduction in infant mortality, what was more remarkable was the speed with which solutions initiated in one country were adopted in others. Thus the French *Gouttes de Lait* – milk depots – were tried out in Canada, the Netherlands, Sweden, the United Kingdom, the United States, and doubtless elsewhere, the message being spread by international conferences in Paris in 1905 and in Brussels in 1907.

The essence of the international infant welfare movement was the constitution of babyhood as a medical problem in which mothers were the front-line defence against germs.[61] Doctors asserted for themselves a new role in promoting the gospel of hygiene. 'The future of the race', claimed the *British Medical Journal* in 1904, '. . . rests largely with the medical profession.'[62] Mothers, it was said, too often careless and indifferent, were responsible for the high rate of infant mortality, and it was the task of doctors, with their ancillary staff of nurses and health visitors, to bring home to them their duties, not only to their own offspring but also to the future of the race.

This task was embarked on with enthusiasm, and accompanied by pronounced social action. There were determined efforts both to encourage breastfeeding, backed up by such statistics as those produced by the Children's Bureau in the United States showing infant mortality rates three to four times higher for those not breastfed;[63] and to improve the quality of milk supply for those mothers who were not breastfeeding. This was accompanied by campaigns to teach mothers or potential mothers lessons in hygiene and in childminding. Instinct was not enough. The National Congress of Mothers in the United States in 1912 was determined to 'battle down the old wall of belief that mother instinct teaches a woman all she needs to know about child nurture'.[64] Motherhood, it was insisted, carried with it heavy responsibilities, amongst them the duty to exit from the labour market unless there were very strong countervailing reasons why this should not happen. Schools for Mothers began to proliferate. Nurses gained access to working-class homes where they could try to enforce the gospel of hygiene.[65] Girls at elementary school were taught how to look after babies. In France, under the flag of *puériculture*, they were prepared for their biological destiny. In the United States, Little Mothers' Leagues for girls aged twelve and upwards, were designed so that the girls could pass on the message of hygiene to their immigrant parents; there were 239 of them in New York City alone in 1911, and by 1915 there were branches in forty-four American cities.[66]

Publicity was a key part of these campaigns. Better Baby contests in the United States in 1912 and 1913 were replaced by non-commercial but extremely successful Baby Weeks from 1916; Britain had its first National Baby Week in July 1917.[67] Few mothers can have escaped entirely the barrage of advice directed at them. In 1929 the United States Children's Bureau estimated that half of American babies had benefited from the government's child-rearing information. In Britain in 1918 there were 700 municipal and 578 voluntary maternity and child welfare centres, the number having nearly doubled since the beginning of the war in 1914.[68]

Concern about infant mortality was international and the solutions proposed differed only at the margin; and yet the motivations for action, and the structures of campaigns differed quite substantially from one country to another. Thus in France the campaigns had a strong pro-natalist flavour, being designed to increase French population, while in the United States the concern was much more to Americanise recent immigrants and to promote economic efficiency. Doctors played a key role in all countries, but whereas in France their authority was recognised from the outset, elsewhere, in the United States and in the Netherlands for example, they were in some sense using the concern about infant mortality to promote their own status, and were anxious, as one American doctor expressed it in 1913, not to open the 'portals of this important field of preventive medicine to social workers and philanthropists'.[69] The latter were in fact already within the portals, some of them accepting medical leadership, but others campaigning for policies which not only taught hygiene, but provided material support for mothers. Little, however, was likely to be achieved unless the state, often for reasons of its own, thought it fit to provide support for mothers.

The state's role was certainly more conspicuous in the spread of compulsory schooling. Many states had introduced schooling laws before the 1880s which were designed to provide a network of schools for all children. Some of these, as we have seen, date from the eighteenth century. Yet what marked nearly every school law prior to the 1880s was the gap between the intention and the reality. Take, for example, the Guizot law passed in France in 1833. Every commune or group of communes was to have at least one elementary school which had to be officially certified, and there were provisions made for training school teachers. On one level the law was an enormous success; there was a substantial increase in both the number of schools and the number of enrolments in the 1830s and 1840s, though it needs to be noted that the upturn began before 1833. By 1850, it is claimed, 'the principle of universal schooling, if not its practice can be said to have been established', and over the next quarter of a century 'the practice of full enrolment became the accepted norm'.[70] Nevertheless, in 1876 nearly 800,000 out of 4.5 million children of school age (18 per cent) were not registered in any school. Moreover, the schools and their teachers left much to be desired. 'Dark, humid, crowded, unventilated, unfurnished, unlit, unheated or smelly and smoky when a fire or stove was lit, drafty, unwelcoming, and ugly, such was the great majority of schools right through the end of the 1870s', writes Eugen Weber. Teachers were part-time, supplementing their inadequate salaries with other jobs.[71] Many rural schools opened in winter only, knowing that children would be required for agricultural work in the summer; summer attendance remained at less than three-quarters of winter attendance into the twentieth century. Furthermore, distance from school, bad roads, and lack of footwear meant that many children did not attend, or at least not with any regularity even when the school was open.[72] It is certainly possible to be too negative; the vast majority of children did attend a school before the 1880s, and there is evidence that they did so because their parents and their communities wanted and expected them to, rather than because central government tried to enforce attendance. Moreover, the system had an inbuilt mechanism for growth. Nevertheless, even if it was mainly at the level of the quality of provision rather than the quantity, the reforms of the 1880s had a marked impact.[73] In 1881 fees were abolished in public elementary schools; in 1882 enrolment in a school was made compulsory; in 1883 every village or hamlet with more than twenty children of school age was required to maintain a public elementary school; in 1885 the budget for the building and maintenance of schools and for the pay of teachers was substantially increased; and in 1886 there was put into place an elaborate system of inspection and control.[74] In the aftermath of defeat by Germany in 1870–1, the French schools may be seen as a national investment in a system which would make the French language universal (something by no means the case prior to the 1880s), and instil in the population a sense of pride in being French. But at the same time, and for different reasons, they began to be accepted by the people. The elementary skills of reading and writing and arithmetic were becoming more obviously a necessity for daily life, and the possession of the prized certificate could open up possibilities of economic and social advancement.[75]

In England and Wales the chronology was very similar. It was in 1833 that there was the first public grant of money for elementary schooling – though it was on a much smaller scale than in France. But a combination of church schools, Sunday schools and cheap private schools meant that a considerable majority of all children were receiving some schooling before the larger state interventions from the 1870s. The Act of 1870 was designed to ensure that there was a school in every neighbourhood, but it was only in 1880 that attendance was made compulsory for those aged five to ten, followed up in 1891 by the abolition of fees. The state's purpose in making schooling compulsory went beyond a desire to ensure that every child was taught the three Rs; it wanted to instil morality, and patriotism, and to train children in regular habits. Schools were designed to become a reference point for order; in the 1870s in London, it was 'like planting a fort in an enemy's country . . . the symbol of tyranny and oppression'. The more neighbourly private schools were harried out of existence.[76]

In many countries it was in the last quarter of the nineteenth century that the way was opened to a major transformation in both the experience and the conceptualisation of childhood, the shift from a situation where children were thought of as members of the labour force to one where they were schoolchildren. Figures for numbers in school are notoriously difficult to interpret, for they sometimes refer to registrations and sometimes to attendances, but some leave no doubt of the extent of the change which was occurring. Thus in England and Wales the proportion of children aged five to fourteen who were in school rose from 24 per cent in 1870 to 48 per cent in 1880 to 70 per cent in 1900. In Austria the rise was less dramatic but significant nevertheless, from 43 per cent in 1870 to 53 per cent in 1880 to 66 per cent in 1900. Elsewhere, it is true, the figures lend no support to the proposition that it was in this period that a transformation occurred. In the Netherlands and in Norway the proportion of children in the age range at school was at or only slightly below two-thirds throughout the period 1870–1900; and on the other side in Italy the percentage of children at school was still only 39 in 1900. But this low figure for Italy must not be interpreted as implying that only 39 per cent of children in Italy received any schooling; if, say, the school leaving age was ten or eleven, then one would not expect very high percentages of those aged five to fourteen to be at school.[77] Moreover, even if, as in France, the figures for the proportion of children at school do not show any significant increase in this period, other measures suggest the importance of what was happening: illiteracy amongst bridegrooms and military recruits, which had been about 25 per cent in the late 1860s had dropped to 5 or 6 per cent by 1900.[78]

What was probably more important than the proportion at school was the fact that nearly all countries were making schooling compulsory. In the United States, for example, although in some areas child labour continued to vie with schooling, twenty-eight states passed compulsory schooling laws in the post Civil War period, and school attendance figures rose steadily.[79] Furthermore, states were putting in place measures to enforce that compulsion, and this undoubtedly changed the experience of schooling for children and for working-class parents who now came under a form of control which led to numerous conflicts with the state. In England and Wales there were nearly 100,000 prosecutions a year for truancy in the 1880s, and, although the number had dropped to 37,000 by 1910, the offence was second only to drunkenness out of all those brought before the courts.[80]

Attendance at school was not the only way in which working-class children and their parents found their lives to a novel extent shaped by the state. The schools themselves often placed a priority on the inculcation of 'the habits of order and obedience'. This frequently involved corporal punishment, and attitudes towards it could sharply divide families and schools. It also involved what Stephen Heathorn, with respect to England, has called 'a near-systematic process of national-identity construction . . . initiated . . . between 1880 and 1914'. In the stories of the nation which children learned there were different roles for boys and girls, and this was reinforced by the emphasis in the syllabus on needlework, cookery and laundry for girls, preparing them for lives as servants or housewives. In some ways this fitted working-class expectations, for girls were more likely than boys to be kept back at home to help their mothers, and the schools quietly sanctioned this.[81]

Compulsory attendance was not achieved without a struggle, but the bitter phase of that struggle was over by the 1920s, if not before. Parents and children had come to accept regular schooling as a norm. Despite the emphasis on national uniformity and regulation from above, there were many differences at local level in the experience of schooling, and while some children looked back on their schooling with what seems justified outrage, and took the very earliest opportunity to leave, for others it was a largely positive experience, and one which they would have wished to have prolonged.[82]

From the state's point of view, compulsory schooling provided opportunities for surveillance beyond anything that could be hoped for in the home. As the French psychiatrist Georges Heuyer put it in 1914, school was 'a laboratory for the observation of antisocial tendencies'.[83] From a rather different perspective, the evidence from schooling over a period of time provided ammunition for those concerned about the possible deterioration of the race in the urban civilisation of the nineteenth and early twentieth centuries. Dr Alfred Eicholz, an inspector of schools in Britain, presented photographs of children at a school in south London to an Interdepartmental Committee on Physical Deterioration, seeing improvement (Plate 5). In the 1902 photograph there was, he said, 'a more civilised intelligent look about the children. They are better filled out and straighter.'[84] School was both the site of improvement and the provider of evidence for it.

The forty years between 1880 and 1920 were not in any simple sense a period when governments suddenly moved into surveillance and policing of areas of social life previously unknown territory to them. There is a long history of state concern with childhood, in some countries highly visible at national level, in others more obscure but nonetheless a presence at local level. Industrialisation, in Britain first and then in other countries, led governments into closer control than previously of child labour. A mixture of motives, including child unemployment, led them to impose compulsory schooling, which vastly increased the range and scope of the state's activities. Meanwhile philanthropic projects of the nineteenth century, on a scale and with a scope beyond the imagination of previous centuries, had attempted to deal with the social problems associated above all with urbanisation. By the early twentieth century there was increasing feeling that the task was beyond the scope of philanthropy on its own, and that the state must take a more active role. There ensued battles between philanthropy and the state, not all of which ended up with a victory for more state involvement – for the philanthropists had powerful bodies of support. But there can be no doubt that the state's role was increasing, and that it was taking over from philanthropy the key role in 'saving the children'.

State concerns and children's rights

Compulsory schooling was not introduced simply or mainly to try to provide all children with an experience of childhood. It has to be understood in a context of state rivalry, and a worry about the effectiveness of the socialisation of children in the reproduction of the social order. The same context underlay schemes for the emigration of children or for their care within institutions in their own countries. How far, then, were policies which affected children in fact child-centred, how far was 'child-saving' actually about providing a childhood for children? The answer may lie in a consideration of the movement to enshrine 'the rights of the child'.

Reformers and philanthropists were deeply imbued with the romantic belief that childhood should be happy, the best time of life. 'God made childhood to be happy' wrote a Scottish Evangelical in the 1840s. It was something to which one would look back later both with nostalgia and for inspiration. 'A happy childhood', wrote Kate Wiggin in 1892, 'is an unspeakably precious memory. We look back upon it and refresh our tired hearts with the vision when experience has cast a shadow over the full joy of living.'[85] If these happy childhoods were to be achieved, childhood had to be sharply separated from adulthood, and its characteristics and needs had to be recognised. Childhood and adulthood, in this thinking, became almost opposites of one another. If adults were burdened with responsibilities, children should be carefree. If adults worked, children should play: 'play is the highest phase of child development', wrote Froebel.[86] If sex was part of the life of adults, it should play no part in that of children: in England and Wales the age of consent for girls was raised from twelve to sixteen. And if adults had to live in towns, children were entitled to contact with nature.

Philanthropists who had so wholeheartedly embraced the ideology of childhood and who were confronted with the realities of actual childhoods on city streets, began to formulate theories of the rights which properly belonged to children. We have seen how the idea of the rights of the child as against its parents or employers began to be set out in the 1830s in England. Towards the end of the century these rights came to be seen as more than rights to maintenance, education and protection, but as very specifically the rights to childhood. 'The rights of a child', wrote Benjamin

Waugh, 'are its birthrights. The Magna Carta of them, is a child's nature. The Author, is its Creator.' God and nature between them laid out a plan for childhood which adults interfered with at their peril. A child, wrote Kate Wiggin, has an 'inalienable . . . right to his childhood'.[87] These rights were precisely the opposite of the rights which adults might claim to independence or freedom. As the Board of Public Charities in Illinois put it, 'Dependence is a child's natural condition.'[88] In 1913 Alexander McKelway, a leader in the campaign to restrict child labour in the United States, drew up a 'Declaration of Dependence by the Children of America in Mines and Factories and Workshops Assembled' in which the children 'declare ourselves to be helpless and dependent; that we are and of right ought to be dependent, and that we hereby present the appeal of our helplessness that we may be protected in the enjoyment of the rights of childhood'.[89] Children's rights therefore were the right to be protected, a theory which fitted well with the thrust of child-saving efforts.

Children themselves, the evidence suggests, on balance did not feel themselves to be beneficiaries of this discourse of rights. In its name, some of them were removed from their families, incarcerated in institutions, and transported across oceans. Some undoubtedly felt that it had been the saving of them. But most who were rescued found it difficult to come to terms with the institutional norms and practices which now shaped their lives. The girls who had been sexually abused found that they were regarded as polluted and potentially polluting, and were hidden away. Children sent to institutions to be saved, many without having committed any offence, saw it 'as a punishment'. Fostered and emigrated children were often mistreated, and adjusted with difficulty to the communities and rural environments which it was hoped would be the saving of them. Their sense of personal identity, derived from their families, was systematically undermined by discouraging the maintenance of any links with their past lives.[90]

There was nevertheless, in the early twentieth century, a growing international body of adult opinion campaigning for the right of children to protection. Swiss officials wrote in 1912 that 'In many . . . states the powerful idea of protecting children and youth is becoming more and more the dominant preoccupation, not only of official spheres, but also of all the classes of the population', and they hoped for the creation of an *Office international de protection de l'enfance*. It required the jolt of the First World War and its aftermath to bring to a head the disparate efforts of those thinking about drawing up a declaration of children's rights. Competing organisations lobbied the newly-formed League of Nations for the central role in co-ordinating children's rights. The successful initiative lay with an Englishwoman, Eglantyne Jebb, who had taken up the cause of children in the defeated countries; as children, she argued, they could hardly be blamed for and therefore should not suffer as a consequence of defeat. The Save the Children Fund was the outcome. Rather than winding down the organisation as the immediate crisis passed, Jebb found herself confronted with a succession of new situations where the children needed to be saved, and she was moved to draw up a simple declaration of children's rights which was adopted by the League of Nations in 1924. These rights were in fact duties of adults, it being formally recognised that 'mankind owes to the Child the best that it has to give'.[91]

Important as international organisations were in setting the tone of discussions, it was at the level of the state that laws were passed and action taken. In the thinking of the late nineteenth and early twentieth centuries the rights of children were entirely consonant with an increased role for the state in the lives of children. For it was the state alone which could enforce those rights. If, as was claimed, a first consequence of employing children was 'that they cease almost at once to be children', then it was the state's responsibility to prevent that too-early employment.[92] If home and school were the only two proper environments for children, then the state must ensure that children were indeed in homes which deserved the name or in school. And all this protection of the newly-defined children's rights was in harmony with the larger purposes of the state in securing the reproduction of a society capable of competing in the harsh conditions of the twentieth century. In the phrasing of the time, the interests of the child and the interests of the state were one and the same. A child-centred policy was one from which the state could only gain. Families might be the losers. They sometimes took the initiative in handing over their children to the care of the state, but, as Donzelot noted, the more that children's rights are proclaimed, 'the more the strangle hold of a tutelary authority tightens around the poor family'.[93] Child-saving aimed both to provide the child with what was thought of as a childhood, and to ensure the future of society. The two aims were thought to be entirely consonant with one another.

Notes

1 H. Cunningham, *The Children of the Poor: Representations of Childhood since the Seventeenth Century* (Oxford, 1991), p. 86; J. Dekker, *The Will to Change the Child: Re-education Homes for Children at Risk in Nineteenth Century Western Europe* (Frankfurt am Main, 2001), p. 69.

2 *The Morning Chronicle Survey of Labour and the Poor: The Metropolitan District*, Vol. 4 (Horsham, 1981), pp. 34–78, 131–53; G. Wagner, *Barnardo* (London, 1979), pp. 86–172; G.K. Behlmer, *Child Abuse and Moral Reform in England, 1870–1908* (Stanford, 1982), pp. 119–60.

3 Quoted in D.J. Rothman, *The Discovery of the Asylum: Social Order and Disorder in the New Republic* (Boston and Toronto, 1971), p. 213.

4 F.K. Prochaska, *Women and Philanthropy in Nineteenth-Century England* (Oxford, 1980), pp. 30–2, 224–5.

5 Devine quoted in R.A. Meckel, *Save the Babies: American Public Health Reform and the Prevention of Infant Mortality 1850–1929* (Baltimore and London, 1990), p. 103; F. Davenport-Hill, *Children of the State* (2nd edn, London, 1889), p. 22.

6 P.T. Rooke and R.L. Schnell, 'Childhood and charity in nineteenth-century British North America', *Histoire Sociale–Social History*, XV (1982), pp. 157–79.

7 B. Finkelstein, 'Casting networks of good influence: the reconstruction of childhood in the United States, 1790–1870', in J.M. Hawes and N.R. Hiner (eds), *American Childhood: A Research Guide and Historical Handbook* (Westport, Conn. and London, 1985), pp. 111–52.

8 Quoted in Cunningham, *Children of the Poor*, p. 31.

9 H. Cunningham, 'The employment and unemployment of children in England c.1680–1851', *Past and Present*, 126 (1990), pp. 129–30.

10 Cunningham, *Children of the Poor*, pp. 53–64.

11 Ibid., pp. 64–76.

12 Ibid., pp. 70–83.

13 Ibid., pp. 94–5.

14 Ibid., pp. 83–95; on the demand for child labour, see C. Tuttle, *Hard at Work in Factories and Mines: The Economics of Child Labor During the British Industrial Revolution* (Boulder, 1999).

15 C. Nardinelli, *Child Labor and the Industrial Revolution* (Bloomington and Indianapolis, 1989), p. 109; C. Goldin and K. Sokoloff, 'Women, children, and industrialization in the early Republic: evidence from the manufacturing censuses', *Journal of Economic History*, XLII (1982), p. 743; British Parliamentary Papers, *Industrial Revolution: Children's Employment* (Shannon, 1968), Vol. 3, C1, p. 96.

16 E.P. Thompson and E. Yeo (eds), *The Unknown Mayhew* (Harmondsworth, 1973), pp. 477–8.

17 H. Silver, 'Ideology and the factory child: attitudes to half-time education', in P. McCann (ed.), *Popular Education and Socialization in the Nineteenth*

Century (London, 1977), pp. 141–66. For similar concerns in Sweden, see B. Sandin, ' "In the large factory town": child labour legislation, child labour and school compulsion', in N. de Coninck-Smith, B. Sandin and E. Schrumpf (eds), *Industrious Children: Work and Childhood in the Nordic Countries 1850–1990* (Odense, 1997), pp. 17–46.

18 Cunningham, *Children of the Poor*, pp. 88–94.

19 Ibid., pp. 51, 83–96.

20 L.S. Weissbach, *Child Labor Reform in Nineteenth-Century France* (Baton Rouge and London, 1989), pp. 84, 140, xiii.

21 Nardinelli, *Child Labor and the Industrial Revolution*, pp. 127–9.

22 V.A. Zelizer, *Pricing the Priceless Child: The Changing Social Value of Children* (New York, 1985), p. 55; R.H. Bremner (ed.), *Children and Youth in America: A Documentary History*, 2 vols (Cambridge, Mass., 1971), Vol. 2, p. 653.

23 J.M. Hawes, *Children in Urban Society: Juvenile Delinquency in Nineteenth-Century America* (New York, 1971), p. 91; Cunningham, *Children of the Poor*, p. 106; L. Chevalier, *Labouring Classes and Dangerous Classes in Paris During the First Half of the Nineteenth Century* (London, 1973), pp. 117–20.

24 J.E. Zucchi, *The Little Slaves of the Harp: Italian Child Street Musicians in Nineteenth-Century Paris, London, and New York* (Montreal, 1992).

25 C. Nilan, 'Hapless innocence and precocious perversity in the courtroom melodrama: representations of the child criminal in a Paris legal journal, 1830–1848', *Journal of Family History*, 22 (1997), pp. 256–60.

26 Cunningham, *Children of the Poor*, pp. 106–8; Chevalier, *Labouring Classes and Dangerous Classes in Paris*, pp. 115–16.

27 H. Shore, *Artful Dodgers: Youth and Crime in Early Nineteenth-Century London* (Woodbridge, 1999); L.R. Berlanstein, 'Vagrants, beggars, and thieves: delinquent boys in mid-nineteenth century Paris', *Journal of Social History*, 12 (1978–9), pp. 531–52; I. Pinchbeck and M. Hewitt, *Children in English Society*, 2 vols (London, 1969–73), Vol. 2, pp. 431–78.

28 Cunningham, *Children of the Poor*, pp. 106–12. For further discussion of this famous interview, see C. Steedman, *Strange Dislocations: Childhood and the Idea of Human Interiority, 1780–1939* (London, 1995), pp. 117–29.

29 Cunningham, *Children of the Poor*, p. 112.

30 Dekker, *The Will to Change the Child*, passim, quoting p. 237.

31 P.F. Clement, 'The city and the child, 1860–1885', in Hawes and Hiner, *American Childhood*, p. 252; Bremner, *Children and Youth in America*, Vol. 2, pp. 283–4; Rothman, *Discovery of the Asylum*, pp. 206–36;

N. Sutherland, *Children in English-Canadian Society: Framing the Twentieth-Century Consensus* (Toronto, 1976), p. 12.

32 J. Robins, *The Lost Children: A Study of Charity Children in Ireland, 1700–1900* (Dublin, 1980), pp. 119, 192–3, 275–6, 294.

33 Bremner, *Children and Youth in America*, Vol. 2, pp. 272, 426; B. Bradbury, 'The fragmented family: family strategies in the face of death, illness, and poverty, Montreal 1860–1885', in J. Parr (ed.), *Childhood and Family in Canadian History* (Toronto, 1982), p. 128; L. Abrams, *The Orphan Country: Children of Scotland's Broken Homes From 1845 to the Present Day* (Edinburgh, 1998), p. 86.

34 Rothman, *Discovery of the Asylum*, p. 210, quoting the Orphan Society of Philadelphia, 1831.

35 H. van Solingo, E. Walhout and F. van Poppel, 'Determinants of institutionalization of orphans in a nineteenth-century Dutch town', *Continuity and Change*, 15 (2000), pp. 139–66; for a similarly positive assessment of the lives of children in a foundling hospital, see D.I. Kertzer, 'The lives of foundlings in nineteenth-century Italy', in C. Panter-Brick and M.T. Smith (eds), *Abandoned Children* (Cambridge, 2000), pp. 41–55.

36 Rothman, *Discovery of the Asylum*, pp. 210–36, quoting p. 229.

37 Davenport-Hill, *Children of the State*, pp. 72–86, 222; cf. Bremner, *Children and Youth in America*, Vol. 2, p. 296 for W.P. Letchworth in 1886 referring to children becoming 'institutionized'.

38 Berlanstein, 'Vagrants, beggars, and thieves', pp. 532–3.

39 Pinchbeck and Hewitt, *Children in English Society*, Vol. 2, pp. 468, 474, 518, 525; Dekker, *The Will to Change the Child*.

40 L.D. Murdoch, 'From barrack schools to family cottages: creating domestic space for late Victorian poor children', in J. Lawrence and P. Starkey (eds), *Child Welfare and Social Action in the Nineteenth and Twentieth Centuries: International Perspectives* (Liverpool, 2001), pp. 147–73.

41 A.M. Platt, *The Child Savers: The Invention of Delinquency* (2nd edn, Chicago and London, 1977), pp. 133–9; S. Schlossman and S. Wallach, 'The crime of precocious sexuality: female juvenile delinquency in the Progressive era', *Harvard Educational Review*, 48 (1978), pp. 65–92; E.R. Dickinson, *The Politics of German Child Welfare from the Empire to the Federal Republic* (Cambridge, Mass., and London, 1996), pp. 20–2, 50.

42 Abrams, *Orphan Country*, pp. 35–77.

43 Ibid., p. 247.

44 J. Parr, *Labouring Children: British Immigrant Apprentices to Canada, 1869–1924* (London, 1980), pp. 28–9; Chevalier, *Labouring Classes and Dangerous Classes in Paris*, p. 456; Robins, *Lost Children*, p. 198.

45 Cunningham, *Children of the Poor*, p. 106; Hawes, *Children in Urban Society*, pp. 87–111.

46 Parr, *Labouring Children*, pp. 62–81.

47 L.A. Pollock, *Forgotten Children: Parent–Child Relations from 1500 to 1900* (Cambridge, 1983), pp. 92–5; see also J. Warner and R. Griller, ' "My pappa is out, and my mamma is asleep": minors, their routine activities, and interpersonal violence in an early modern town, 1653–1781', *Journal of Social History*, 36 (2003), pp. 561–84. For evidence of state concern about bad parents in sixteenth-century Germany, see J.F. Harrington, 'Bad parents, the state, and the early modern civilizing process', *German History*, 16 (1998), pp. 16–28.

48 L.A. Jackson, *Child Sexual Abuse in Victorian England* (London, 2000), pp. 20–1, 38.

49 L. Gordon, *Heroes of Their Own Lives: The Politics and History of Family Violence* (London, 1989), p. 27.

50 M-S. Dupont-Bouchat, 'Du tourisme pénitentiaire à "l'internationale des philanthropes". La création d'un réseau pour la protection de l'enfance à travers les congrès internationaux (1840–1914)', *Paedagogica Historica*, XXXVIII (2002), pp. 533–63.

51 Behlmer, *Child Abuse and Moral Reform*, pp. 162, 239; H. Ferguson, 'Cleveland in history: the abused child and child protection, 1880–1914', in R. Cooter (ed.), *In the Name of the Child: Health and Welfare, 1880–1940* (London, 1992), pp. 148–9.

52 *Report of the Prosecution of Dr Kenealy for Cruelty to a Child with the Sentence* (London, n.d.[1874]). See also C.A. Conley, *The Unwritten Law: Criminal Justice in Victorian Kent* (Oxford, 1991), p. 107.

53 J. Donzelot, *The Policing of Families* (London, 1980), p. 85.

54 Ibid., pp. 30, 83–8; S. Schafer, *Children in Moral Danger and the Problem of Government in Third Republic France* (Princeton, 1997), pp. 67–86, 100–2, 130; Dekker, *The Will to Change the Child*, p. 104.

55 R. Waugh, *The Life of Benjamin Waugh* (London, 1913), p. 306.

56 Bremner, *Children and Youth in America*, Vol. 2, pp. 117–18, 185–222.

57 S. Tiffin, *In Whose Best Interest? Child Welfare Reform in the Progressive Era* (Westport, Conn. and London, 1982), pp. 187–214; B. Harrison, *Peaceable Kingdom* (Oxford, 1982), pp. 240–59.

58 J.E. Gorst, *The Children of the Nation: How their Health and Vigour should be promoted by the State* (London, 1906), pp. 12–14.

59 Cunningham, *Children of the Poor*, p. 211; Tiffin, *In Whose Best Interest?*, p. 218.

60 Meckel, *Save the Babies*, pp. 101–9.

61 P. Wright, 'The social construction of babyhood: the definition of infant care as a medical problem', in A. Bryman, B. Bytheway, P. Allatt and T. Keil (eds), *Rethinking the Life Cycle* (London, 1987), pp. 103–21.

62 Quoted in D. Dwork, *War is Good for Babies and Other Young Children: A History of the Infant and Child Welfare Movement in England 1898–1918* (London, 1987), p. 21.

63 S.H. Preston and M.R. Haines, *Fatal Years: Child Mortality in Late Nineteenth-Century America* (Princeton, 1991), p. 27.

64 Quoted in A. Klaus, *Every Child a Lion: The Origins of Maternal and Infant Health Policy in the United States and France, 1890–1920* (Ithaca and London, 1993), pp. 142–3.

65 J. Lewis, *The Politics of Motherhood: Child and Maternal Welfare in England, 1900–1939* (London, 1980), pp. 27–113; C. Dyhouse, 'Working-class mothers and infant mortality in England 1895–1914', *Journal of Social History*, 12 (1978), pp. 248–67; Dwork, *War is Good for Babies and Other Young Children*.

66 Meckel, *Save the Babies*, pp. 144–5; Klaus, *Every Child a Lion*, p. 77–80.

67 Klaus, *Every Child a Lion*, pp. 144–54; Dwork, *War is Good for Babies and Other Young Children*, p. 211.

68 T. Skocpol, *Protecting Soldiers and Mothers: The Political Origins of Social Policy in the United States* (Cambridge, Mass. and London, 1992), p. 481; Dwork, *War is Good for Babies and Other Young Children*, p. 211.

69 Klaus, *Every Child a Lion*, passim, quoting p. 88; H. Marland, 'The medicalization of motherhood: doctors and infant welfare in the Netherlands, 1901–1930', in V. Fildes, L. Marks and H. Marland (eds), *Women and Children First: International Maternal and Infant Welfare, 1870–1945* (London, 1992), pp. 74–96.

70 R. Grew and P.J. Harrigan, *School, State, and Society: The Growth of Elementary Schooling in Nineteenth-Century France: A Quantitative Analysis* (Ann Arbor, 1991), pp. 31–89, quoting pp. 78–9.

71 E. Weber, *Peasants into Frenchmen: The Modernization of Rural France 1870–1914* (London, 1977), pp. 304–8.

72 Ibid., pp. 318–23; Grew and Harrigan, *School, State, and Society*, pp. 67, 270.

73 Grew and Harrigan, *School, State, and Society*.

74 Weber, *Peasants into Frenchmen*, pp. 308–9.

75 Ibid., pp. 328–38.

76 D. Rubinstein, 'Socialization and the London School Board 1870–1904: aims, methods and public opinion', in McCann (ed.), *Popular Education and Socialization in the Nineteenth Century*, pp. 231–64; J.S. Hurt, *Elementary Schooling and the Working Classes 1860–1918* (London, 1979); P. Gardner, *The Lost Elementary Schools of Victorian England: The People's Education* (London, 1984).

77 Calculated from B.R. Mitchell, *European Historical Statistics* (2nd edn, London, 1981), pp. 38–66, 785–806.

78 C.M. Cipolla, *Literacy and Development in the West* (Harmondsworth, 1969), p. 119.

79 J.P. Felt, *Hostages of Fortune: Child Labor Reform in New York State* (Syracuse, 1965), p. 7; W.I. Trattner, *Crusade for the Children: A History of the National Child Labor Committee and Child Labor Reform in America* (Chicago, 1970); D.I. Macleod, *The Age of the Child: Children in America, 1890–1920* (New York, 1998), p. 76.

80 Hurt, *Elementary Schooling and the Working Classes*, p. 203.

81 A. Davin, *Growing Up Poor: Home, School and Street in London 1870–1914* (London, 1996), pp. 85–153, quoting p. 134; S. Heathorn, *For Home, Country, and Race: Constructing Gender, Class, and Englishness in the Elementary School, 1880–1914* (Toronto, 2000), quoting p. ix; N. de Coninck-Smith, 'Copenhagen children's lives and the impact of institutions, c.1840–1920', *History Workshop*, 33 (1992), pp. 57–72.

82 Rubinstein, 'Socialization and the London School Board', pp. 250–8; J. Rose, 'Willingly to school: the working-class response to elementary education in Britain, 1875–1918', *Journal of British Studies*, 32 (1993), pp. 114–38.

83 Donzelot, *Policing of Families*, p. 132.

84 Interdepartmental Committee on Physical Deterioration, British Parliamentary Papers, 1904, vol. xxxii, p. 179.

85 T. Guthrie, *Seed-Time and Harvest of Ragged Schools* (Edinburgh, 1860), pp. 7–8; K.D. Wiggin, *Children's Rights: A Book of Nursery Logic* (London, n.d., c.1892), p. 31; cf. R. Bray, 'The children of the town', in C.F.G. Masterman (ed.), *The Heart of the Empire* (1901; Brighton, 1973), p. 127.

86 F. Froebel, *The Education of Man* (New York and London, 1887), p. 54.

87 Waugh, *Life of Benjamin Waugh*, p. 296; Wiggin, *Children's Rights*, p. 10.

88 Platt, *Child Savers*, p. 135.

89 Trattner, *Crusade for the Children*, frontispiece.

90 Jackson, *Child Sexual Abuse in Victorian England*, pp. 86–9, 135; L. Mahood, *Policing Gender, Class and Family: Britain, 1850–1940* (London, 1995), p. 148; Abrams, *Orphan Country*, pp. 35–77, 122–61, 251–4.

91 D. Marshall, 'The construction of children as an object of international relations: the Declaration of Children's Rights and the Child Welfare Committee of League of Nations, 1900–1924', *The International Journal of Children's Rights*, 7 (1999), pp. 103–47, quoting p. 115; F.M. Wilson, *Rebel Daughter of a Country House: The Life of Eglantyne Jebb, Founder of the Save the Children Fund* (London, 1967), passim, quoting p. 224.

92 Bremner, *Children and Youth in America*, Vol. 2, p. 658.

93 Mahood, *Policing Gender*, pp. 141, 143; Donzelot, *Policing of Families*, p. 103.

CHAPTER 7

'The century of the child'?

In 1900 the Swedish feminist Ellen Key published a book with the title *The Century of the Child*. The idea for it had come from a drama, *The Lion's Whelp*, in which one character states that 'The next century will be the century of the child, just as much as this century has been the woman's century. When the child gets his rights, morality will be perfected.' Key's vision of the future was one in which children would be conceived by parents who were physically fit and in a loving relationship, and who would then grow up in homes where mothers were ever-present. Women's role was emphatically to bring up children; they should prepare themselves for motherhood by a period of service 'devoting themselves to the care of children, hygiene, and sick nursing'. Such systems of care for children as crèches or kindergartens were very much second best, and school itself should strive 'to make itself unnecessary'. Success in child-rearing lay in becoming 'as a child oneself', and then if this happened, 'the simplicity of the child's character will be kept by adults. So the old social order will be able to renew itself.' Key was in no doubt that the future would be determined by the way children were reared, and she blamed failures in child-rearing for what she saw as three of the scars of the modern world, capitalism, war and Christianity. Thus if the twentieth century was going to be 'the century of the child' it was going to be so not simply for the sake of the child but, in addition, for that of humanity as a whole.[1]

Key's book was both a reflection of some of the common ideas of her time, as in her emphasis on eugenics, and also an elaboration of the belief of the late nineteenth century that 'saving the child' was of the most fundamental political and social significance. The book became a world bestseller, and the phrase of the title caught on, becoming a commonplace in the United States in the Progressive era.[2] It probably quickly came to shed some of what would have been seen as Key's quirkier ideas, such as her opposition to school or to Christianity, and settled down to an abiding belief in the first half of the twentieth century that 'Of all the assets of which the State stands possessed, none are more valuable than the children', or that children were 'the greatest asset of any civilization'.[3] They should be valued accordingly, and it became more emphatically than before the responsibility of the state to ensure a proper childhood for all children. As Lillian Knowles wrote in a history textbook of the 1920s, indicative of this enhanced role for the state, 'The factory restrictions led eventually to the State education of the child, the scope of which is ever widening as is also the scope of the protective measures designed to help children. Indeed, the twentieth century promises to be the century of the child.'[4] As we have seen in Chapter 6, this involved some recasting of the relationship between philanthropy and the state. Equally the search was on for the discovery of the true nature of childhood, for successful policies towards children were increasingly seen as dependent on 'scientific' knowledge.

This vision of a 'century of the child' attracted reformers for most of the first half of the twentieth century. Their overriding aim was to map out a territory called 'childhood', and put in place frontier posts which would prevent too early an escape from what was seen as desirably a garden of delight. Within this garden children would be cared for and would acquire 'the habit of happiness'.[5] Ahead of them, depicted in *The Twentieth Century Child* (Plate 6), lay the thorns of adolescence and adulthood. The barefoot girl, her sunlit childhood coming to an end, holds some lilies as a symbol of purity, but they hardly seem adequate protection for the path ahead. In the second half of the twentieth century it was the sense of an erosion or even disappearance of childhood which dominated discussion: children began to claim and be given rights which enabled them to break out of the garden; some of them, like the killers of James Bulger in Britain, failed spectacularly to live up to the innocence supposedly innate in all children; many more, perhaps all, seemed to be losing their childhood early under the pressures of the twin forces of the media and of mass consumption.

Science, experts and childhood

In 1909 a United States Congress report on a proposal to set up a Federal Children's Bureau stressed the need 'to get scientific data, and at actual facts, as well as the results of the best scientific treatments with regard to children'.[6] The belief that science held the key to a better childhood for children was at its height in the late nineteenth and first half of the twentieth centuries. Mothers were the target readership for magazines which thrived on science-endorsed advertisements of products for babies; 'scientific child care was part of the everyday life of the middle classes'.[7] Science, it was believed, could improve life chances for children; more than this, science could help to unlock the mysteries of how children's minds worked, could measure the intelligence of children, could tell mothers how to rear children, and could provide guidance for children whose development or behaviour did not conform to standard norms.

The most urgent task at the beginning of the century was to ensure that children stayed alive. As we have seen, the infant mortality rate in many countries remained obstinately high right through the nineteenth century. Northern Europe led the way in reducing the rate in the second half of the nineteenth century, and from the very beginning of the twentieth century the rate in nearly all countries began to decline and has continued to do so. At the beginning of the twentieth century the rate for most countries was within the range of 100 to 250 deaths per 1,000 live births; by 1950, in twenty-six European countries, only three had rates above 100, and fourteen were below 60. By 1975 half of the European countries had rates below 20, and in only four were they above 30. At the end of the century, the rate for Europe as a whole was down to 11, and for Northern America to 7.[8] This decline in itself marks out the twentieth century from the whole of the rest of the history of childhood, and it is difficult to exaggerate its importance. By the middle of the twentieth century the death of a baby was something which few parents would experience, whereas in all previous centuries it had been something which parents would have been lucky to avoid. This did not mean that they had treated those deaths with indifference; as we have seen, there is much evidence of parental grief. The change of substance was that parents could now reasonably assume that all children born to them would survive to adulthood, and consequently that the notion of family planning could take on new meaning; not surprisingly the decline in infant mortality was accompanied by a sharp decline in fertility. Children in the twentieth century had fewer siblings than their predecessors, and those siblings were likely to be close to them in age, whereas previously they might be separated from them by up to twenty years, with gaps where death had taken its toll.

The downward trend in infant mortality has been so pronounced that it might be thought easy to determine its causes; but in fact this has been far from the case. We have seen in Chapter 6 that there was considerable social action designed to reduce infant mortality, but it is not clear what part this played in that reduction. In the first half of the century the reduction occurred mainly amongst babies aged one month and older. They were particularly likely to die from diarrhoea in the hot summer months when flies carried contamination from faeces to food; adherence to the gospel of hygiene could help to reduce this danger. It is, however, likely that the decline in deaths from diarrhoea owed more to improved sanitation than to the activities of teachers, doctors, nurses and social workers. Thus in Britain water closets were installed in many towns in the early twentieth century; in 1899 26.4 per cent of houses in Manchester had water closets, in 1913 97.8 per cent.[9] Changes of this kind made it feasible to attain a reasonable standard of hygiene. It has also been argued that the decline in infant mortality owed much to improved standards of living, quite irrespective of medical intervention and social action.[10]

The conclusion must be that it would be mistaken to assume that any one factor can explain the sharp decline in infant mortality, though equally some factors, such as improved sanitation, may be more important than others. Recent studies of both England and Austria, for example, 'show very effectively that the secular decline of infant mortality [in the first half of the twentieth century] was chiefly achieved through environmental improvements in the more disadvantaged areas (towns and cities in England, the lowlands in Austria)'. In the more recent past medical science has been the key driver in sustaining a decline in mortality, particularly among very young babies.[11]

Concern with mortality and morbidity naturally stretched beyond babyhood. In a range of European countries (England and Wales, Finland, Italy, Spain and Sweden), there seems to have been a decline in the mortality of one- to five-year-olds up to about 1840, a worsening of the situation through to the mid-1860s, and then almost steady decline. In Britain the death rate for those aged one to five had fallen by 33 per cent between 1861 and 1900, and in the United States for white children it had been declining for two decades prior to 1900.[12] The mother's role was again thought to be crucial, and she was encouraged to keep young children at home; in England the percentage of children aged three to five who were at school fell from 43.5 per cent in 1899 to 33.8 per cent in 1906.[13] This was accompanied by a growing professionalisation of medicine for children. The novelty of this must not be exaggerated, for as we have seen in previous chapters medicine had always recognised a set of diseases peculiar to children. Moreover, as early as 1802 there was a special children's hospital in Paris, followed up by a wave of foundations in Germany in the 1840s, by the Hospital for Sick Children in Great Ormond Street in London in

1852, and by children's hospitals in New York and Philadelphia in the mid-1850s. These early hospitals, however, were essentially isolation hospitals, and it was only towards the end of the century that there began to be a shift towards therapy, particularly with the development in the 1890s of a serum for diphtheria. Chairs in paediatrics were established in Paris in 1879 and in Berlin in 1894. In 1888 the American Pediatric Society was formed, and paediatricians were able, through the work they carried out in hospitals, to gain acceptance against those who doubted whether paediatrics should be a distinct branch of medicine. The next stage in the United States was the development of practices limited to paediatrics, their numbers growing from 138 in 1914 to 6,567 in 1955, and then nearly doubling again by 1966. A new profession had become established.[14]

Once children had reached the age for the commencement of compulsory schooling, it became possible and perhaps necessary to make some kind of assessment of their mental and physical capacities. There developed ways of categorising children by intelligence, and of measuring their physical development against newly-conceived norms. Both arose from the sense that a significant proportion of children, through mental or physical defect, were unable to benefit from compulsory schooling. So far as mental capacity was concerned, the first concern was to identify and separate out the mentally handicapped and 'feeble-minded' for whom the favoured solution in the late nineteenth and early twentieth centuries was the 'special school', followed ideally by lifetime segregation in an institution.[15] The IQ test was developed in France by Victor Simon and Alfred Binet, and after 1905 quickly gained international acceptance as one of the tools by which one could predict the capacity for development of any child.

The norms established for physical development were often those of the middle and upper classes living in rural areas, and not surprisingly urban working-class children failed to meet the required standards, but the extent to which they failed was still an eye-opener; in Glasgow in 1905, for example, even within the lower classes, boys living in two-roomed households were on average 11.7 lb. lighter and 4.7″ smaller than boys from four-roomed houses, and girls from one-roomed houses were 14 lb. lighter and 5.3″ smaller than girls from four-roomed houses.[16] To remedy these physical deficiencies there were developed programmes for drill and other physical exercises in the school curriculum, school meals and medical inspection. Organised school medical services date from the 1870s in Brussels, Sweden and Paris; after a precarious start in New York in the 1870s, American school medical inspection began to take shape in the

1890s. In England and Wales anything beyond local initiatives waited until the first decade of the twentieth century, but thereafter there was a substantial development of programmes of medical inspection and treatment based on the school; between 1910 and 1935 the number of school dentists rose from twenty-seven to 852, of school nurses from 436 to 3,429, and of school clinics from thirty to 2,037. Publicly-funded school meals also became widely available, particularly in the inter-war depression years. In the United States in the 1930s some 130,000,000 meals were served over a five-year period; in England and Wales in 1938 nearly 9 per cent of elementary schoolchildren ate school lunches, and the number was to increase sharply in the Second World War.[17] All of this entailed an unprecedented degree of surveillance of the working-class population – for it extended beyond the classroom to the home – and a corresponding emergence of experts in such surveillance. Increasingly these experts were medically trained. 'In 1880', writes Roger Cooter, 'child health and welfare was not yet medicalized . . . But by the 1920s child health and welfare was not only medicalized, it was serving as a powerful argument for extending the role of the state in health and welfare generally.'[18]

The contribution of science towards the understanding of childhood was by no means confined to orthodox medicine. In at least three other respects science had a crucial role to play. First, it made a claim to understand children's minds: were they, for example, biologically programmed to speak their native language, or did they need to be taught? How did they learn? These were questions of enormous importance for understanding human beings as a whole, but they began to be studied as above all contributions to the study of children. In 1877 the English journal *Mind* published Hippolyte Taine's 'On the Acquisition of Language by Children' and Charles Darwin's 'A Biographical Sketch of an Infant'. This gave rise to a spate of amateur scientific enquiries by enthusiastic fathers; as James Sully reported to the readers of the *Cornhill Magazine* in 1881 'The tiny occupant of the cradle has had to bear the piercing glance of the scientific eye.' In Germany Wilhelm Preyer's *Die Seele des Kindes* (1881), translated as *The Mind of a Child*, encouraged further enquiries of this sort.[19] In America G. Stanley Hall's study of 1883, 'The contents of children's minds', acquired classic status, and inspired the formation of Child Study Associations on both sides of the Atlantic. Hall's fairly indiscriminate use of material from questionnaires distributed to parents eventually began to be criticised, and the way was open for psychologists to lay claim to the field. Psychology was struggling to establish itself as a profession in the early twentieth century; its advance was helped immeasurably by the search on the part of educationalists for a means of assessing children in schools – the tests devised by psychologists provided the solution. Guided by psychology, education could become a science. In 1916 in Britain Cyril Burt, in post as a psychologist for the London County Council, could set out to create 'a *Scientific Profession of Teaching*', and in the same year in Illinois an official could claim that 'the study of the child from the standpoint of the scientific interpretation of mind and its making is a new science – but it is here to stay'.[20] He was correct in his forecast. Collectively and individually children were subjected to the scientific gaze of the psychologist.

Secondly, science was thought capable of contributing to the under-standing of children's instincts as well as their minds. This was a more contentious field of study for in the nineteenth century the idea of the innocence of children had nearly laid to rest theories of their innate wickedness; yet the findings of science were only with difficulty consonant with theories of innocence. Nineteenth-century psychiatrists had encoun-tered and described children whose behaviour hardly suggested innocence, but they were uncertain whether such disorders stemmed from heredity or from some initiating factor in the child's upbringing, nor did they have a conception of a normal maturational development. Notoriously they were instrumental in spreading the view of the unnaturalness and inherent dangers of masturbation in children. Thus although psychiatrists were well aware that the child could be a sexual being, they tended to regard this as an abnormality.[22] It was Freud's ambiguous contribution to the century of the child to claim at its outset that every child had an innate sexuality which manifested itself in predictable ways from infancy onwards.

In one sense Freud destroyed ideas of the innocence of the child, for in the nineteenth century innocence and asexuality were closely connected. But it was equally possible to argue that the sexual instincts of a baby were part of nature; innocence was destroyed only if adults interfered in a clumsy way with the sexual play and enjoyment of children. Freud, with the exception of the five-year-old Little Hans, saw only adult patients, and his apparent ability to trace difficulties in adulthood to traumas in child-hood, and in particular to the mishandling of the sexuality of the child by adults, served to make parenting seem a task beset with difficulties in which neither common sense nor tradition could provide reliable guidance. Parents needed advice from experts, and they received it in overflowing abundance. Most of these experts were medically qualified.

Thirdly, practitioners began to look for the origins of delinquency in childhood, and in what was often seen as psychological maladjustment.

Delinquency, which had previously been traced at least in part to environment and poverty, began to be seen as psychological in origin. One source of this, and a sharp reminder that notions of the innocence of the child were by no means universal, was the development in Germany and the Netherlands of 'pedagogical pathology'; this focused on children's deficiencies: 300 of them, such as obstinacy, short-sightedness and lying, were identified and listed.[23] Another source was William Healy's Chicago Juvenile Psychopathic Institute, founded in 1909, and of enormous influence in encouraging endeavours to pick up the seeds of delinquency in childhood. It was therefore not surprising that when the Commonwealth Fund was established in the United States in 1918 'to do something for the welfare of mankind', it should put its resources to setting up Child Guidance Clinics as a contribution to the prevention of delinquency. The 'problem child' was the focus of attention, but it soon became clear that there were 'problem children' who were not heading for a career of crime, but exhibiting mild emotional or behavioural symptoms with which neither parents nor teachers could easily cope. Child Guidance Clinics – there were sixty of them in the United States by 1942 – offered these problem children and their carers professional help from teams of psychiatrists, psychologists and social workers.[24]

An initiative in child care in one country rarely remained confined within its borders. There were international conferences on School Hygiene, in London in 1907 and in Paris in 1910. Germany led the way in pioneering open-air schools for unhealthy city children, and its 'oral hygiene crusade' was the model in dentistry. Much of Ontario's 'Children's Charter' of 1893 was lifted directly from Britain's of 1889.[25] Child labour was one of the concerns of the International Association for Labour Legislation, founded in 1900, and holding biennial conferences before the First World War.[26] Child Guidance Clinics on the American model reached Britain in the mid-1920s.[27] Although national differences obviously remained, there were in existence international networks which provided a common standardised framework within which assessments could be made of the extent to which the twentieth century was indeed 'the century of the child'.

Children and social policy

In democracies governments and publicists routinely throughout the twentieth century described children as 'the future'. Get things right now for children and the future would be bright; get them wrong, and disaster loomed. On the one hand this justified expenditure on children, on the other it presented children as actually or potentially dangerous. Either way, the importance of childhood could not be denied. It raised questions, and often led to fierce debates on the respective roles of the state, voluntary organisations, and the family or individual. Some political parties, for example both the Independent Labour Party and the Social Democratic Federation in Britain, placed issues to do with childhood at the head of their political agendas in the early twentieth century. This was more than a matter of domestic politics, for childhood became caught up in the international rivalry of states; children were seen as the most valuable asset a nation had, one which, if not properly nurtured, would lead to a process of degeneration and to a loss of power and status relative to other countries. It was therefore almost inevitable that states would be drawn further and further into issues of child policy.

Harry Hendrick sees three dichotomies or oppositions informing much policy-making in the twentieth century: an emphasis on either the bodies or the minds of children; the child as victim or threat; and the child as normal or abnormal. In the early part of the century it was the bodies of (working-class) children which attracted attention: ill-fed, too small and liable to disease, the children were both victims of their environment or parentage, and a threat if left untreated. Hence the thrust towards medical inspection and provision of school meals. Some bodies (and minds) were so damaged as to be abnormal, in need of special treatment, perhaps incarceration or even sterilisation. Towards the middle of the century the focus shifted from the bodies to the minds and emotions of children, this coming to a head in the Second World War when, in Britain, evacuated children showed signs of mental distress. Since the 1960s there has been renewed emphasis on the bodies of children. The 'battered baby syndrome' and a succession of scandalous abuses of children's bodies have fuelled public concern, and governments have been drawn into making a response.[28]

Children continued to loom large in the statistics of poverty. Their removal from the labour market made them to a much higher age than previously a continuing expense to their families rather than a potential source of income. B. Seebohm Rowntree's famous study of York, *Poverty: A Study of Town Life* (1901), showed how young children could impoverish a family and how many children were living in poverty, and a multiplicity of further studies confirmed these facts. Thus in the southern England town of Reading at the outbreak of the First World War nearly half the schoolchildren were living in primary poverty, and children there and elsewhere constituted over half of all those living in primary poverty.

In Rowntree's follow-up study of York in 1936 he found nearly half of those in primary poverty to be children under fourteen.[29] Politicians, bureaucrats, social workers and publicists wrestled with the problem of how to prevent the poverty of working-class families from depriving their children of the kind of childhood increasingly thought appropriate. Should there be direct benefits in kind to children in poverty, through the provision of meals or clothes? Or was it necessary to begin to think of 'family endowment', payments by the state or by employers to parents? It was in the first half of the twentieth century that some form of payment to families with children became almost universal everywhere outside the United States. Governments' willingness to pay these family allowances was not entirely or even mainly due to their acceptance of the arguments of pressure groups who had campaigned for them from a child-centred perspective; rather governments saw in family allowances a means of stabilising employer–labour relationships, or of controlling wage inflation, or of encouraging a higher birth rate.[30] Children, however, did undoubtedly benefit from these moves which made it less likely that they would pass their childhoods in poverty.

The achievements of one generation, however, could receive setbacks in another: there was no sustained reduction in child poverty. Britain, admittedly, had a record worse than anywhere outside the United States, but its figures for child poverty in the late twentieth century indicate the way in which a reinforcing mix of economic trends, especially high unemployment, demographic changes, and government policies could impinge on the lives of hundreds of thousands of children: in the 1980s and 1990s the proportion of children in poverty rose from one in ten to about one in three.[31] There has been a reduction since then, but in the twenty-first century the disproportionate number of children living in poverty blights the lives of children and remains a standing embarrassment and challenge to the rhetoric of children as the future.

It went almost without saying for reformers that if children were to enjoy a proper childhood they must be prevented from too early an entry into the labour market. As we have seen, by the end of the nineteenth century nearly all countries had passed laws which prohibited or restricted child labour. An exception, at national level, was the United States, and it was there in the early twentieth century that a National Child Labor Committee was established both to encourage action and legislation at state level, and eventually to push, with only limited success, for federal legislation. For the campaigners of the Committee there was little doubt that, in the words of one of them, 'when labor begins . . . the child ceases to be', but up to the 1920s they met with considerable opposition especially in the south where there was demand for child labour in the textile industry. But the opposition was more widespread than that; it encompassed Catholic priests who defended child labour on the grounds of the income it brought to poor immigrant families, farmers who wanted the seasonal labour of children, and declared it to be positively healthful, and working people who resented intrusion by government into their family work traditions.[32] These factors, combined with a staunch defence of states' rights, meant that the National Child Labor Committee had to be content with piecemeal measures in the slow erosion of child labour in the United States, an erosion which doubtless owed much to changes in technology as well as to public opinion and law.[33]

Outside the United States national legislation with regard both to work and to compulsory schooling had limited the scope for child labour by the beginning of the twentieth century, but there were parts of the economy, such as home industries, where it was difficult for the arm of the law to reach, and there was a continuing concern about work done by schoolchildren out of school hours. In Austria in 1908 a survey of 400,000 school children reported that one-third of them had jobs, especially in domestic industries, and in the 1920s children in working-class homes were said to work between four and six hours each day.[34] On the eve of the First World War it was estimated that in the United Kingdom there were over half a million children under fourteen in employment, most of them schoolchildren who had part-time jobs, typically as messengers or deliverers of newspapers. The same niche in the labour market was filled by schoolchildren in Scandinavia, though there, particularly in rural and fishing communities, it met with less disapproval than in Britain: in Denmark compulsory full-time rather than part-time schooling was introduced only in the 1950s.[35]

The First World War stimulated the demand for and the amount of child labour, but thereafter it seems to have been in decline, and increasingly at the margins of the economy. Nevertheless, most schoolchildren continued to do some work, both to help the family economy and, particularly from the middle of the century onwards, to fund their own consumption. Officialdom denied its extent, overconfident that child labour was a problem which had been solved, but the evidence is strong that children continued to work.[36]

School, not the workplace, was the proper place for children to be when they were not at home. Many saw the end of schooling as the end of childhood. As governments have raised the school-leaving age, childhood has been progressively prolonged. Thus in England and Wales it was set at ten when compulsory schooling was introduced in 1880, rose by stages but with local exemptions up to the First World War, and was consolidated at fourteen in 1918, at fifteen in 1944 and at sixteen in 1972. Less than half of those aged twelve to fourteen were at school in 1900, virtually all of them by mid-century. Roughly 5 per cent of those aged fifteen to eighteen were at school in the first quarter of the century, 37 per cent of them after the rise in the school-leaving age in 1972. By the mid-twentieth century in most of Europe all children from the school starting age (which varied between five and seven) up to at least fourteen could be expected to be at school; the exceptions were in southern Europe, where Spain and Portugal were laggards, with less than half of those aged between five and fourteen at school. But they would soon catch up, Spanish statistics showing, a touch implausibly, that in 1970 there were more children in school than there were in the age range five to fourteen.[37] The precise figures may be open to doubt, but the trend cannot be: governments were ensuring that schooling was taking up more and more of a person's life, and the more they did so the longer people thought of themselves and were treated as children.

Poverty, child labour and schooling were central elements of policy-making with regard to children, but they did not define it. There was another large and amorphous field of government activity concerned with the tripartite relationship between government, parents and children. For governments the focus was on children 'in trouble': the field covered children removed from their families to state care, children coming into contact with the criminal justice system, and children subjected to cruelty within the home. A marker of the importance of these issues is indicated by the increasing volume of legislation devoted to them. In England and Wales, for example, to highlight only the most important pieces of legislation, 'the century of the child' witnessed the Children Act 1908, the Children and Young Persons Act 1933, the Children Act 1948, the Children and Young Persons Acts of 1963 and 1969, and the Children Acts of 1975 and 1989. All of these Acts sought to steer a path between two concerns: that for the 'best interests of the child' and that for the protection of society at large from the threat posed by troublesome children both in the present and the future. In the Second World War and its welfare state aftermath, much influenced by studies of the impact on children of evacuation and of John Bowlby's theories on the harmful effects on children of 'maternal deprivation', the aim was to keep children with their families, even 'problem families'. What these deprived families needed, it was felt, was help, and social workers were the government agents who would provide it. In the late 1960s and 1970s, the reaction against the welfare state, together with the emergence of concern about cruelties to children inflicted within the home, led to reconsideration of these policies. Over the last quarter of the century the state tried to find structures to help mediate between the welfare of the child, held to be of 'paramount' importance, the responsibility of parents for the rearing of children, and the media and public concern that, as the *Daily Star* put it, 'much of Britain is facing a truly frightening explosion of kiddie crime'. Although legislation made more than a nod in the direction of children's rights, it was the rights and responsibilities of parents which were most emphasised. At the end of 'the century of the child', society was still grappling to find some resolution of the issue that first came to prominence in the 1880s, that of the proper relationship between government, parents and children.[38]

Parents and children

Since the invention of print there has been advice to which parents could turn, but the volume of it began to escalate in the twentieth century and has gone on escalating. For much of the first half of the twentieth century the tone of advice literature presents a considerable challenge to anyone claiming that this was 'the century of the child'. The impact of science was to encourage in parents a distancing of parent and child; as Reinhard Spree writes with reference to German advice literature, 'towards the end of the nineteenth century the idea of subjugating the everyday treatment of the child to exact, scientifically founded rules became more and more common. Making the life of the child a technically controlled science was completed by attempting to make the parent–child interaction into a science. What should be displaced is spontaneity, emotions, and individuality.'[39] Spree wonders whether this was specific to Germany, and the answer is that it was not. In 1914 the United States Children's Bureau was advising that 'The rule that parents should not play with the baby may seem hard, but it is without doubt a safe one.'[40] The major input of science in the 1920s was behaviourism, the belief that children can be trained to behave in desired ways by suitable rewards and punishments. For Cyril Burt, 'superintending the growth of human beings is as scientific a business as cultivating plants or training a race horse'.[41] Parents were not always best suited to do this. In the United States John Watson was in no doubt that there were 'much more scientific ways of bringing up children [than by parents in individual homes] which will probably mean finer and happier children'. But, on the assumption that parents were in charge, his advice was uncompromising: 'There is a sensible way of treating children. Treat them as though they were young adults . . . Never hug and kiss them, never let them sit in your lap.' In Britain the *Mothercraft Manual*, running into twelve editions between 1923 and 1954, advised mothers that 'Self-control, obedience, the recognition of authority, and, later, respect for elders are all the outcome of the first year's training.' Truby King, an authoritative voice, particularly in Britain, told readers in 1937 that 'The leading authorities of the day – English, foreign and American – all agree that the first thing to establish in life is *regularity of habits* . . . The establishment of perfect regularity of habits, initiated by "feeding and sleeping by the clock", is the ultimate foundation of all-round obedience.' Here was a combination of Locke, with his insistence on learning by habit formation, and Puritan belief in the importance of obedience. As the Newsons have noted, 'we have seen a deity-centred morality giving way to a science-centred morality, both with curiously similar results in the tone of parental behaviour'.[42]

A challenge to this dominant behaviourism began to emerge in the 1930s, with the stress by psychoanalysts on the will, emotions and passions of children, and the advice that if these were suppressed they would simply come to the surface later in adolescence or adulthood; a repressive mode of child-rearing – 'training' – began to be associated with fascism, attempts to understand the child and work with it with democracy. In the United States Anderson and Mary Aldrich's *Babies are Human Beings* (1938) marked the end of the dominance of behaviourism, and in the period after the Second World War parents were being advised to enjoy parenting rather than to look on it as an intimidating scientific task.[43] The appetite for literature of advice was enormous. *Parents' Magazine* reached sales of 100,000 a month within a year of its launch in the late 1920s, and within thirty years of its first publication in 1946, Dr Spock's *The Common Sense Book of Baby and Child Care* had sold 28 million copies, making it, next to the Bible, the best-selling book of the twentieth century.[44]

Parents were not, however, released from the knowledge that child-rearing was supremely important for the future of the child and of humanity, and it was this insistence on the significance of parenting which justifies the use of the 'century of the child' label. As Max Lerner commented of America in the 1950s, 'It is evident that in no other culture has there been so pervasive a cultural anxiety about the rearing of children.'[45] Behaviourists and psychoanalysts might differ in their understanding of children and in the nature of the advice they gave, but they were in agreement on the importance of childhood. And it would have required a supremely self-confident parent to ignore in its totality the advice which percolated through in magazines and broadcasts, and in clinics.[46]

How did all these developments affect the lives of children? For the great majority of them the major change of the first half of the twentieth century was that they lost any productive role within the economy, and increasingly gained a new role as consumers. This undoubtedly altered the way in which children were viewed by parents. It was not that children had previously been valued above all for the contribution they could make to the family economy; rather that contribution had been understood as a norm. Once it was removed, parents had to adjust to a new valuation of children. Their response was to have fewer of them, but to value them individually more, and to value them for emotional reasons only rather than for a rarely-analysed combination of emotional and economic reasons.

This transition, probably the most important to have occurred in the history of childhood, was worked through in the late nineteenth and first half of the twentieth centuries. Children did not necessarily experience it as liberation. There is much evidence of children's self-esteem rising at the point where they began to contribute to the family economy. Clifford Hills, born to an agricultural labourer's family in East Anglia, remembered with pride how his part-time earnings at the age of nine were sufficient to buy the family's Sunday roast meat. Robert Roberts, in a slum school in Salford, recalled how his proposal in a school debate that the school-leaving age should be raised to fifteen so that children would have a greater chance to enter the professions was met with derision by his victorious opponent who stated simply, to thunderous applause, that 'we should gerrout to work at fourteen and fetch some money in for us parents'. Recalling the depression years in the United States, Margot Hentoff commented that there was 'a sense of great satisfaction in being a child with valuable work to do'.[47]

Those children who enjoyed or did well at school might well resent the pressure they felt to leave at the earliest possible moment so that they could contribute to the family economy. Most, however, accepted the necessity for this, sometimes even deliberately failing an exam so that their school career was curtailed. The pressures exerted by community and family outweighed any desire for more education. In the New England textile industry 'Most families expected children to begin working just as soon as they were able or permitted to enter the labor force', and some forged birth certificates or lied in order to hasten that day. And when they started work children were not earning primarily for themselves but for their families. In the United States in the 1920s sons contributed 83 per cent and daughters 95 per cent of their earnings to the family.[48]

At a speed which varied by country this assumption of an early end to schooling and the making of an immediate contribution to the family economy faded away in the first half of the century. The process was not uninterrupted. In the United States, in the depression years, families, particularly those with large numbers of children, came again to rely on the contributions which children could make to the family economy, typically with boys bringing in some income and girls becoming responsible for an increased number of domestic tasks.[49] But the trend, made possible by rising standards of living and by state support for families, was unmistakable. Children were ceasing to have any economic value, and if they did earn any money in a part-time job they kept it for themselves. More important than this, they became the focus for expenditure, parents determining to give their children a better childhood than they themselves had had, and seeing the means to this in expenditure.[50]

For working-class children another major change of the twentieth century was the shift from a life focused on the street to one focused on the home. Cramped conditions made the home an undesirable location for anything other than sleep and perhaps food. At the turn of the century in Vienna 'we were all street kids. In those days everyone was just a street kid. We grew up in the alley, the street . . .' For most of the London working class, too, 'the centre of the boy's life lies in the street, and his leisure time is spent there'. Girls, too, would be in the street, though they would not venture so far from the home as boys, often having childminding responsibilities.[51] As housing condition improved, homes could offer greater comfort, and the street may have lost some of its attraction. This was accompanied by a change in the social organisation of the home. Parents, and in particular fathers, became less remote and authoritarian, less the centre of attention when they were present.

Childhood under threat

War most dramatically highlighted the difficulty of preserving the territory of childhood. On the one hand, and positively, it impelled nation states to focus on children as the future, and to put more emphasis on reforms that reduced infant mortality and provided some protection against childhood poverty.[52] But, on the other, it exposed children to life-threatening dangers, and, in the Second World War, to the extermination of one and a half million of them as a matter of state policy. Children's vulnerability in warfare first became apparent in the chaos in eastern Europe at the end of the First World War. One positive outcome was the founding of the Save the Children Fund, dedicated to the idea that the protection of children in warfare should be a priority. But this and other internationalist and humanitarian initiatives on behalf of children had no purchase in Germany and countries dominated by it in the Second World War.

Jewish children suffered severe segregation and discrimination even before the war. Once war had begun they were increasingly isolated, first at home or in hiding, then in transit camps or ghettos, and ultimately in the slave labour and death camps. For some children in the illegal ghetto schools there was a welcome discovery of common Jewish roots and culture, but a much more common experience was gross impoverishment and starvation. Mary Berg, aged sixteen, wrote of the Warsaw ghetto, that 'There are a great number of almost naked children, whose parents have died, and who sit in rags on the streets. Their bodies are horribly emaciated; one can see their bones through their parchment-like yellow skins ... Some of these children have lost their toes; they toss around and groan ... They no longer beg for bread, but for death.' If they did not die of starvation or from diseases associated with lack of nutrition, the younger of them, lacking any usefulness as workers, were the first to be shepherded into the gas chambers. Only 11 per cent of Jewish children survived the war. There is remarkable evidence of children's ability to sustain some kind of child life, to play and to exercise the imagination, in the ghettos or even at the very doors of the gas chambers, but the play, or the pictures they drew, were often not so much attempts to escape into some happier world as reflections of the ghastly lives they led and the deaths that awaited them.[53] It was a mockery to invoke 'the century of the child' when so many of them were killed as a matter of state policy.

In the second half of the twentieth century the vision of the century of the child faded for more mundane reasons. It was not that people ceased to accord significance to childhood – far from it; rather, they began to doubt that it was possible to preserve in any integrity the territory mapped out as childhood. Invasions threatened from every quarter, and childhood, so it was argued, could no longer survive. In consequence children themselves became alien creatures, a threat to civilisation rather than its hope and potential salvation.

A symptomatic text was Neil Postman's *The Disappearance of Childhood* (1982). Writing from California, Postman reported that there were no longer games, or food, or clothes specifically for children.

Children showed little respect for their elders, they figured prominently in the crime statistics, and above all they lacked the sense of shame, especially in regard to sex, which was fundamental to Postman's conception of childhood. In a way we are transported back into that world which Ariès had imagined for the middle ages in which the boundaries between adulthood and childhood were fluid or non-existent. Ariès, interestingly, in the 1950s in France could see the fencing-off of childhood as the peculiarity of the modern world. A quarter of a century later in California the ending of it was being lamented.

Postman's dirge would hardly deserve special attention but for the explanation which he gave for the disappearance of childhood. He argued that a sense of childhood had emerged with the invention of print; reading became a valued skill, and increasingly one which it was thought that everyone should acquire. Childhood was set aside as the time in which to do this, and school was the place where it would happen. To learn to read required certain characteristics: delayed gratification, persistence, sitting still and sequentiality. By contrast a visual culture, represented by television, requires no such qualities; we do not have to be taught to watch. Childhood therefore rose with one form of communication and fell when print culture was replaced by visual culture. Technological determinism could hardly be taken further.

Two points of interest may be extracted from Postman. The first is that his vision of a good childhood is not one in which the essence is freedom and happiness; rather it is good behaviour, a deference to adults, and a commitment to learning skills essential for the adult world. Secondly, television is not simply a medium of communication; embedded in it is a commercialism which turns the child into a consumer. There is a long history of fears that children will be corrupted by forms of communication; the reading of 'penny dreadfuls' in the Victorian era was thought to be damaging. Visual culture was probably always considered worse, and there had been much fear throughout the twentieth century that films would corrupt the young. But at least films could be and were censored, and some controls could be placed on the age at which people could see particular categories of film. Television, and even more video, and then, in the late twentieth century, the internet were not susceptible to anything like the same degree of control. In part the fear has been that children will be presented with images of sexuality and violence which may disturb them. But more insidiously a visual culture may present values in advertisements, and in the games show with cash prizes, which place before children images of the good life hardly consonant with the delayed gratification endorsed by Postman and before him by a long tradition within Christianity. Children become consumers, and they want to buy not for the family economy, but for themselves.

Pessimists, both on the right and the left of the political spectrum,[54] argued that childhood had been corrupted by commercialism. In the late twentieth and early twenty-first centuries rapid changes in media technology reinforced these Postman-like fears, but also gave rise to the optimistic interpretation that the internet provided the means to liberate children from paternalistic adult control. 'Media-savvy' children, it was argued, exploiting the 'interactive' nature of the internet, could begin to create a culture of their own. These hopes invested in the media curiously shared much with the fears. In different ways, they exaggerated and simplified the impact of the media. Both generalised about 'children' of all ages and all social classes, and both misunderstood the complex ways in which children respond to the media. But they were a testimony to the ways in which hopes and anxieties about the modern world became focused on children.[55]

The critique associated with Postman highlighted the ideal of childhood which had become entrenched in the first half of the century – one in which children were insulated from the adult world. It suggested that adults themselves viewed adulthood as the fall from Eden, childhood being the time for happiness and safety. Childhood should therefore be prolonged as long as possible. Postman's lament takes on a further meaning when he explains that for him children are aged between seven and seventeen; childhood starts and ends late.

It was not surprising that it was in America that the breakdown of the separate world of childhood seemed to have gone furthest, for to Europeans the American child had always shown alarming tendencies towards a precocity much deplored in the later nineteenth and twentieth centuries. In 1875 Therese Yelverton had lamented that in travelling through the United States, 'I never discovered that there were any American *children*. Diminutive men and women in process of growing into big ones, I have met with; but the child in the full sense attached to that word in England – a child with rosy cheeks and bright joyous laugh, its docile obedience and simplicity, its healthful play and disciplined work, is a being almost unknown in America.'[56] American children were contrasted with French children who were kept within the bounds of the family, and yet lived in a world separated from that of adults, including their own parents.[57] J.B. Priestley, in Arizona in the late 1930s, found 'something very disconcerting' about American children:

They seemed to be living at too fast a pace; they were not solid enough; they appeared to be over-excited . . . All of them were more adult in their tastes and style of life, though not in temperament, than our own children and others I know in England. Most of them had a tremendous precocity, sometimes amusing, sometimes alarming. To outsiders they were civil enough, but often they were very rude to their parents, who had travelled so far from the old-fashioned notion of parental authority that now they were oddly apologetic and conciliatory in their attitude towards these children, who were most exacting and shrill in their demands.[58]

Priestley was mixing in professional and middle-class circles, and it was at this social level that the lack of deference of American children was most shocking to a European. For in Europe the children of the bourgeoisie were closeted in a world of servants and of school where adult authority was not questioned, and where parents kept a distance which preserved for them an air of unchallengeable invincibility. It was doubtless in Britain, with its tradition of boarding schools, that this was carried furthest, but it could be found throughout Europe. It began to break down when, primarily for financial reasons, it became difficult to hire the nannies and other servants necessary to maintain this way of life. Parents, and in particular mothers, were forced into closer contact with their children, and modified their behaviour.

This collapse of adult authority took effect at varying rates. In France in the 1950s a majority of parents still wanted to see more rather than less discipline of children.[59] But when working-class mothers in Nottingham in the early 1960s were asked the question, 'Would you say you are bringing up your children the same way as you yourself were brought up, or differently?' they were in no doubt about the differences. In large part they stemmed from an improved standard of living, and a consequent ability to provide children with more material goods. As one mother expressed it, 'I think myself you give in to your own where you couldn't have it – you think to yourself, well I didn't get this, and I'll see that he gets it. I think that's the whole attitude of a lot of people.' But there was more to this 'giving in' to children than simply the provision of material goods. Respondents were in no doubt that their parents had been much stricter disciplinarians than they themselves were. Many had found their own mothers remote and rigid, and not easy to talk to, and were seeking in their own parenting to encourage a closer companionship with their children. But they were also conscious of social pressures which led them to 'give in' against their better judgement: 'Television advertising jingles replace nursery rhymes; supermarkets, by siting enticing packets at the child's eye-level, make use of him as an efficient agent in the wheedling of shillings from his mother's purse; and every council estate seems to have at least three ice-cream firms continually patrolling its roads.'[60]

What this amounted to was a shift in the balance of power between adults and children. It was most evident at the economic level. In Bethnal Green in East London in the early 1950s a working-class mother explained how 'When I was a kid Dad always had the best of everything. Now it's the children who get the best of it. If there's one pork chop left, the kiddy gets it.'[61] As non-workers children became recipients of weekly pocket money, and of increasingly expensive presents at Christmas and on birthdays. The issue of pocket money greatly exercised middle-class commentators in the later nineteenth and early twentieth centuries, for pocket money gave children a degree of independence, and one which they showed themselves unfit to bear. In 1899 the American Society for the Study of Child Nature expressed many reservations about it.[62] In a survey of towns in Britain in the 1940s it was reported that 'school children in the poorer districts had far more pocket-money than those of the better class', and that they spent it 'largely on sweets, ice-cream and comics', the sweets being 'often of the most wretched quality' and the comics 'poor to a degree'.[63] Obviously they thought the money was ill spent and without any compensating advantages in teaching children some elementary economics.

It is clear that even before the Second World War children constituted a market with some significant purchasing power. The biggest profits lay in the spin-offs from films and cartoons; by 1933 Disney was selling over $10 million of merchandise, mainly models of famous cartoon characters.[64] The coming of television was to increase enormously the opportunities for marketing products to the extent that they came to shape the form and content of children's television. As Stephen Kline has put it, 'Television constituted children as an audience so they could be integrated into the market.'[65] By the late 1980s Disney enterprises were making $3.44 billion worldwide from the licensing of cartoon and fantasy characters; in the United States the total market for licensed character toys was $8.2 billion, these toys themselves constituting nearly 70 per cent of the total toy market. In the United Kingdom at the end of the twentieth century the market in children's consumer goods was estimated at more than £10 billion per year.[66]

In the early twentieth century the choice and purchase of toys lay mainly with adults. They had become aware that children learned through play, and saw in appropriate toys (mechanical objects for boys, dolls for girls) ways of preparing their children for adulthood. Advice books encouraged consumption: until the early twentieth century, children, the advice went, should seek to control an emotion such as envy; between 1915 and 1930 parents were told to respond to a child's envy by buying it what it wanted.[67] This was a sign of, and a step towards, greater involvement of children in the purchase of toys. In the United States, first in the 1930s, and with a new spurt in the 1960s, the balance in the purchasing of toys switched more decisively towards children, parents being cut out of a direct relationship between manufacturers and children. Barbie dolls (1959 onwards) and action men became the prototype toys of a new era in which children made the key decisions about purchase.[68]

For parents children were an expense only partially met by welfare policies. They had always, to a much greater extent than often is realised, been an expense, but it had been accompanied by a sense of economic obligation of child to parent which the child began to meet when it turned over its wages to its mother. In the second half of the century children rarely contributed anything to the family economy. When they started work, they assumed that their earnings were for themselves alone. Parents might hope for some care from their children in old age, but until then they had a responsibility to provide for their children to the point where in Britain in the 1990s a child cost over £100,000 (and by 2004, £164,000).[69] Children of course had no absolute right to such sums, and might feel themselves to be in a situation of relative powerlessness. But although parents might lament the extent to which children were 'spoiled', they lived within a culture in which the forces of competitive emulation were so strong that any failure to provide children with what their peers had was likely to induce guilt.

But the shift in the balance of power between adult and child was more than simply economic – it was also emotional. Parents now looked to children for emotional gratification. Nowhere is this clearer than in the development of adoption in the twentieth century. Every society has had some system for transferring children from parents to non-parents, but the grounds for doing so have been primarily economic – the receiving family had some use for the child; affectionate relationships might develop, but they were not the grounds on which adoption occurred. In the twentieth century married couples, normally childless themselves, adopted children who would be nothing but an expense. Sometimes their motivation was to save the child, but, as their frequently stated preference for fair-haired girls indicated, they also sought to gratify themselves. Adults needed children to satisfy their own emotional needs, and were prepared to pay large sums in order to acquire them. Parents in America insured themselves against the deaths of their children, not, as in the past, on the grounds of the loss of the child's earning power, but because of the emotional loss they would suffer – and the sums they received vastly exceeded the sums granted for loss of earning power.[70] Children might be only dimly aware of the value which was being placed upon them, but in effect an economic and emotional transformation meant that parents could easily become, as was noted in America in the early twentieth century, 'slaves of their children'. Put another way, there had been, in Zelizer's phrase, a sacralisation of childhood, that is, children had been 'invested with sentimental or religious meaning'.[71] One indication of this lies in the power accorded to images of children; on the one hand Americans take approximately 10 billion snapshots of children every year; on the other, images of children sell goods: approximately half of advertisements with photos show children.[72]

Children also began in the late twentieth century to acquire rights which placed them more nearly on a par with adults. As we have seen in Chapter 6, when people first began urging that children had rights, the rights they had in mind were rights to a protected childhood. The 1989 United Nations Convention on the Rights of the Child not only provides for the protection of the child but also for his or her right to be heard in any decision that may affect his or her life. Under national laws, in the United States and in Britain for example, children acquired the right to bring proceedings against their own parents, an indication that the shift in the balance of power between parents and children extended beyond the economic and emotional spheres.

This shift of power towards children was counterbalanced by two interlocking and reinforcing factors. Parents became increasingly anxious to do what they perceived to be the best for their children, and local and global events seemed to make that more and more difficult. The outcome was a shift towards greater protection for children, admixed with nostalgia for a world which existed only in the imagination, one which was safe for children. The threats to childhood seemed multiple. If the home and the school had become by the early twentieth century spaces which should be inhabited by children, neither was in any way safe by the century's end. As the abuse of children mounted the political agenda, 'home' was identified as the place where it was most likely to occur, unless it was in 'homes', for children notionally 'in care'. Horrific events in schools rendered them also dangerous. Adults entered them to shoot randomly at children and teachers; in the United States, even worse, at Columbine Heights it was children who did the killing. Cyberspace was no safer than terrestrial: children could both witness violence unsuitable for their or perhaps any age, and, in the shape of child pornography, were the victims of adult perversion. Danger to childhood came not only from the adult world, but also from children themselves: reports of bullying mounted, but it could go beyond that. In 1993 in England James Bulger, aged three, was led away from a shopping mall (another dangerous space) to be eventually killed by two ten-year-old boys. In the British press, the killers were 'evil', an indication that the innocence of the child could not be taken for granted.[73]

This trend towards protection of children was accompanied by a plethora of studies of children and childhood which cumulatively suggested that the late twentieth century was 'marked by both a sustained assault on childhood and a concern for children'. The message of these studies was that adults should try to visualise the world through the eyes of children, rather than seeing in the child only the adult to be; but the actuality they described was one in which childhood and children had become controlled by anxious adults. The shift in the power balance in this perspective was away from rather than towards children.[74]

The century of the child ended in ways unforeseen at its commencement. The essence of the vision of childhood at the beginning of the century was the powerlessness of children, their dependence; good parenting consisted of preserving and prolonging this in part at least by the exercise of parental authority. What happened in the second half of the century was that parental authority declined, and children demanded and received an earlier access to the adult world; they were not willing to accept the attempt to prolong childhood to the late teenage years. In some ways this represented a return to a historical norm in which childhood did not extend beyond fourteen at the maximum. But there were two key differences. First, childhood had become a major issue in politics and in everyday discourse, and the greater freedoms of children were balanced by greater adult concern for and attempts to control their time, their space, their bodies and their minds. Second, in earlier centuries at the age of fourteen a person was economically productive whereas in the late twentieth century he or she would have a minimum of two years and quite probably a further seven or more years of non-productivity. Not surprisingly 'adolescence' came to be seen as a time of stressful conflict between parents and children.

Notes

1 E. Key, *The Century of the Child* (1900; New York and London, 1909), passim, quoting pp. 45, 109, 183, 257, 317.

2 S. Tiffin, *In Whose Best Interest? Child Welfare Reform in the Progressive Era* (Westport, Conn. and London, 1982), p. 14.

3 W. Clarke Hall, *The State and the Child* (London, 1917), p. xi; C.W. Waddle, *An Introduction to Child Psychology* (London, n.d. [1918?]), p. 3.

4 L.C.A. Knowles, *The Industrial and Commercial Revolutions in Great Britain during the Nineteenth Century* (1921; revised edn, London, 1926), p. 96.

5 E. Sharp, *The London Child* (London, 1927), p. 37.

6 R.H. Bremner (ed.), *Children and Youth in America: A Documentary History*, 2 vols (Cambridge, Mass., 1971), Vol. 2, p. 763.

7 L.G. Gurjeva, 'Child health, commerce and family values: the domestic production of the middle class in late-nineteenth and early-twentieth century Britain', in M. Gijswijt-Hofstra and H. Marland (eds), *Cultures of Child Health in Britain and the Netherlands in the Twentieth Century* (Amsterdam and New York, 2003), pp. 103–25, quoting p. 105.

8 B.R. Mitchell, *International Historical Statistics: Europe 1750–1988* (3rd edn, Basingstoke, 1992), pp. 116–23; R. Meckel, 'Infant mortality', in P.S. Fass (ed.), *Encyclopedia of Children and Childhood in History and Society*, 3 vols (New York, 2004), Vol. 2, p. 477. See also G. Masuy-Stroobant, 'Infant health and infant mortality in Europe: lessons from the past and challenges for the future', in C.A. Corsini and P.P. Viazzo (eds), *The Decline of Infant and Child Mortality: the European Experience, 1750–1990* (The Hague, 1997), pp. 1–34.

9 M.J. Daunton, *House and Home in the Victorian City: Working-Class Housing 1850–1914* (London, 1983), pp. 246–59; F. Bell and R. Millward, 'Public health expenditures and mortality in England and Wales, 1870–1914', *Continuity and Change*, 13 (1998), pp. 221–49; but for evidence that improved sanitation seems to have played little part in the reduction of urban infant mortality in Germany, see J. Vögele, 'Urbanization, infant mortality and public health in Imperial Germany', in Corsini and Viazzo (eds), *The Decline of Infant and Child Mortality*, pp. 109–27.

10 J.M. Winter, 'Aspects of the impact of the First World War on infant mortality in Britain', *Journal of European Economic History*, 11 (1982), pp. 713–38.

11 C.A. Corsini and P.P. Viazzo (eds), *The Decline of Infant Mortality in Europe 1800–1950: Four National Case Studies* (Florence, 1993), p. 13. This volume, together with its successor, Corsini and Viazzo (eds), *The Decline of Infant and Child Mortality*, provide an excellent introduction to recent research. See also Meckel, 'Infant mortality', pp. 476–7.

12 D.M. Fariñas and A.S. Gimeno, 'Childhood mortality in Central Spain, 1790–1960: changes in the course of demographic modernization', *Continuity and Change*, 15 (2000), pp. 235–67; A. Hardy, 'Rickets and the

rest: child-care, diet and the infectious children's diseases, 1850–1914', *Social History of Medicine*, 5 (1992), p. 391; S.H. Preston and M.R. Haines, *Fatal Years: Child Mortality in Late Nineteenth-Century America* (Princeton, 1991), p. xviii.

13 P. Wright, 'The social construction of babyhood: the definition of infant care as a medical problem', in A. Bryman, B. Bytheway, P. Allatt and T. Keil (eds), *Rethinking the Life Cycle* (London, 1987), p. 116.

14 P. Weindling, 'From isolation to therapy: children's hospitals and diphtheria in *fin de siècle* Paris, London and Berlin', in R. Cooter (ed.), *In the Name of the Child: Health and Welfare, 1880–1940* (London, 1992), pp. 124–45; S.A. Halpern, *American Pediatrics: The Social Dynamics of Professionalism, 1880–1980* (Berkeley, Los Angeles and London, 1988), pp. 35, 40, 53–4, 57–79, 82.

15 M. Jackson, ' "Grown-up children": Understandings of health and mental deficiency in Edwardian England', in Gijswijt-Hofstra and Marland (eds), *Cultures of Child Health*, pp. 149–68.

16 S.R.S. Szreter, 'The first scientific social structure of modern Britain 1875–1883', in L. Bonfield, R.M. Smith and K. Wrightson (eds), *The World We Have Gained: Histories of Population and Social Structure* (Oxford, 1986), pp. 337–54; 'Report by Dr W. Leslie Mackenzie and Captain A. Foster, on a collection of statistics as to the physical condition of children attending the public schools of the School Board for Glasgow . . .', *Parliamentary Papers 1907* (Cd 3637), p. v.

17 G. Rosen, *A History of Public Health* (New York, 1958), pp. 365–74.

18 Cooter, *In the Name of the Child*, p. 12.

19 D. Riley, *War in the Nursery: Theories of the Child and Mother* (London, 1983), pp. 43, 51–2.

20 H. Cunningham, *The Children of the Poor: Representations of Childhood since the Seventeenth Century* (Oxford, 1991), pp. 196–200; Tiffin, *In Whose Best Interest?*, p. 267.

21 N. Rose, *Governing the Soul: The Shaping of the Private Self* (London and New York, 1990), pp. 132–50.

22 S. Kern, 'Freud and the discovery of child sexuality', *History of Childhood Quarterly*, I (1973), pp. 117–41.

23 J. Dekker, *The Will to Change the Child: Re-education Homes for Children at Risk in Nineteenth Century Western Europe* (Frankfurt am Main, 2001), pp. 120–8.

24 M. Horn, *Before It's Too Late: The Child Guidance Movement in the United States, 1922–1945* (Philadelphia, 1989).

25 N. Sutherland, *Children in English-Canadian Society: Framing the Twentieth-Century Consensus* (Toronto, 1976), pp. 52–3, 59, 111, 233–6, 258.

26 A.M. Allen, *Sophy Sanger: A Pioneer in Internationalism* (Glasgow, 1958), p. 54; E. T[ownshend] (ed.), *Keeling Letters and Recollections* (London, 1918), p. 320.

27 D. Thom, 'Wishes, anxieties, play and gestures: child guidance in inter-war England', in Cooter, *In the Name of the Child*, pp. 200–19.

28 H. Hendrick, *Child Welfare: Historical Dimensions, Contemporary Debate* (Bristol, 2003), esp. pp. 1–18.

29 A.L. Bowley and A.R. Burnett-Hurst, *Livelihood and Poverty* (1915; New York and London, 1980), pp. 43–5; J. Macnicol, *The Movement for Family Allowances, 1918–45: A Study in Social Policy Development* (London, 1980), pp. 48–50; J. Lewis, 'Models of equality for women: the case of state support for children in twentieth-century Britain', in G. Bock and P. Thane (eds), *Maternity and Gender Policies: Women and the Rise of the European Welfare States, 1880s to 1950s* (London, 1991), p. 85.

30 J. Macnicol, 'Welfare, wages and the family: child endowment in comparative perspective, 1900–50', in Cooter, *In the Name of the Child*, pp. 244–75.

31 Hendrick, *Child Welfare*, pp. 181–6, 209–16.

32 V.A. Zelizer, *Pricing the Priceless Child: The Changing Social Value of Children* (New York, 1985), pp. 55–72.

33 W.I. Trattner, *Crusade for the Children: A History of the National Child Labor Committee and Child Labor Reform in America* (Chicago, 1970); J.P. Felt, *Hostages of Fortune: Child Labor Reform in New York State* (Syracuse, 1965).

34 R. Sieder, ' "Vata, derf i aufstehn?": childhood experiences in Viennese working-class families around 1900', *Continuity and Change*, I (1986), p. 53.

35 F. Keeling, *Child Labour in the United Kingdom* (London, 1914); N. de Coninck-Smith, B. Sandin and E. Schrumpf (eds), *Industrious Children: Work and Childhood in the Nordic Countries 1850–1990* (Odense, 1997), esp. pp. 149–50.

36 P. Horn, 'The employment of elementary school children in agriculture 1914–1918', *History of Education* 12 (1983), pp. 203–16; S. Cunningham, 'The problem that doesn't exist? Child labour in Britain 1918–1970', in M. Lavalette (ed.), *A Thing of the Past? Child Labour in Britain in the Nineteenth and Twentieth Centuries* (Liverpool, 1999), pp. 139–72; H. Cunningham, 'The decline of child labour: labour markets and family economies in Europe and North America since 1830', *Economic History Review*, LIII (2000), pp. 409–28.

37 A.H. Halsey (ed.), *British Social Trends since 1900* (Basingstoke, 1988), p. 230; Mitchell, *International Historical Statistics*, pp. 12–45, 854–77.

38 Hendrick, *Child Welfare*, passim, quoting p. 189; for a wider geographical study, and the conclusion that 'Across Europe massive numbers of children are subject to a complex interplay of a range of social oppressions', see K. Pringle, *Children and Social Welfare in Europe* (Buckingham and Philadelphia, 1998), quoting p. 181.

39 R. Spree, 'Shaping the child's personality: medical advice on child-rearing from the late eighteenth to the early twentieth century in Germany', *Social History of Medicine*, 5 (1992), pp. 317–35.

40 Bremner, *Children and Youth in America*, Vol. 2, p. 37.

41 Quoted in Cunningham, *Children of the Poor*, p. 220.

42 J. and E. Newson, 'Cultural aspects of childrearing in the English-speaking world', in M. Richards (ed.), *The Integration of a Child into a Social World* (Cambridge, 1974), pp. 53–82.

43 C. Hardyment, *Dream Babies: Child Care from Locke to Spock* (London, 1983), pp. 157–229.

44 H. Cravens, 'Child-saving in the age of professionalism, 1915–1930' and C.E. Strickland and A.M. Ambrose, 'The baby boom, prosperity, and the changing worlds of children, 1945–1963', both in J.M. Hawes and N.R. Hiner (eds), *American Childhood: A Research Guide and Historical Handbook* (Westport, Conn., and London, 1985), pp. 441, 538.

45 Quoted in Strickland and Ambrose, 'The baby boom, prosperity, and the changing worlds of children', pp. 540–1.

46 Riley, *War in the Nursery*, pp. 80–108; Newson, 'Cultural aspects of childrearing', pp. 62–3.

47 T. Thompson, *Edwardian Childhoods* (London, 1981), pp. 44, 57–8; R. Roberts, *A Ragged Schooling* (1976; London, 1979), p. 152; Hentoff quoted in G.H. Elder, *Children of the Great Depression: Social Change in Life Experience* (Chicago and London, 1974), p. 64.

48 S. Humphries, *Hooligans or Rebels? An Oral History of Working-Class Childhood and Youth* (Oxford, 1981), pp. 59–61; T.K. Hareven, *Family Time and Industrial Time: The Relationship between the Family and Work in a New England Industrial Community* (Cambridge, 1982), pp. 189, 214–16, 226–7.

49 Elder, *Children of the Great Depression*, pp. 64–70; in Canada, 'until after the Second World War, most working-class children turned their earnings over to their parents'. N. Sutherland, *Growing Up: Childhood in English Canada from the Great War to the Age of Television* (Toronto, 1997), pp. 131–2.

50 Zelizer, *Pricing the Priceless Child*; J. Seabrook, *Working-Class Childhood: An Oral History* (London, 1982), pp. 117–18.

51 Sieder, ' "Vata, derf i aufstehn?" ', pp. 63, 68–9; R.A. Bray, 'The boy and the family', in E.J. Urwick (ed.), *Studies of Boy Life in our Cities* (1904; New York and London, 1980), pp. 71–3.

52 See, e.g., D. Dwork, *War is Good for Babies and Other Young Children: A History of the Infant and Child Welfare Movement in England 1898–1918* (London, 1987); Masuy-Stroobant, 'Infant health and infant mortality', p. 26; B. Harris, *The Health of the Schoolchild: A History of the School Medical Service in England and Wales* (Buckingham and Philadelphia, 1995), pp. 82–7, 165–71. For the impact of the Napoleonic wars on policies towards children, see Dekker, *The Will to Change the Child*, pp. 47–8.

53 D. Dwork, *Children with a Star: Jewish Youth in Nazi Europe* (New Haven and London, 1991); G. Eisen, *Children and Play in the Holocaust: Games among the Shadows* (Amherst, 1988), quoting p. 25; N. Stargardt, 'Children's Art of the Holocaust', *Past and Present*, 161 (1998), pp. 191–235.

54 Seabrook, *Working-Class Childhood*.

55 D. Buckingham, *After the Death of Childhood: Growing Up in the Age of Electronic Media* (Cambridge, 2000).

56 R.L. Rapson, 'The American child as seen by British travellers, 1845–1935', *American Quarterly*, 17 (1965), pp. 520–34, quoting p. 521.

57 T. Zeldin, *France 1848–1945*, 2 vols (Oxford, 1973), Vol. I, pp. 328–9, 338–42.

58 J.B. Priestley, *Midnight on the Desert* (London, 1940), pp. 150–2.

59 Zeldin, *France 1848–1945*, Vol. I, pp. 338–42.

60 J. and E. Newson, *Infant Care in an Urban Community* (London, 1963), pp. 219–40, quoting pp. 223, 231.

61 M. Young and P. Willmott, *Family and Kinship in East London* (1957; Harmondsworth, 1968), p. 28.

62 B. Wishy, *The Child and the Republic: The Dawn of Modern American Child Nurture* (Philadelphia, 1968), pp. 117–19; Zelizer, *Pricing the Priceless Child*, pp. 97–112.

63 Women's Group on Public Welfare, *Our Towns* (Oxford, 1943), p. 22.

64 S. Kline, *Out of the Garden: Toys and Children's Culture in the Age of TV Marketing* (London and New York, 1993), p. 136.

65 Ibid., p. 74.

66 Ibid., pp. 136, 138, 321; Buckingham, *After the Death of Childhood*, p. 65.

67 S.J. Matt, 'Children's envy and the emergence of the modern consumer ethic, 1890–1930', *Journal of Social History*, 36 (2002–3), pp. 283–302.

68 M. Formanek-Brunell, *Made to Play House: Dolls and the Commercialization of American Girlhood, 1830–1930* (New Haven, 1993); G. Cross, *Kids' Stuff: Toys and the Changing World of American Childhood* (Cambridge, Mass., 1997).

69 *Guardian*, 5 May 2004.

70 Zelizer, *Pricing the Priceless Child*, pp. 138–65.

71 Rapson, 'The American child', p. 523; Zelizer, *Pricing the Priceless Child*, p. 11.

72 A. Higonnet, *Pictures of Innocence: The History and Crisis of Real Childhood* (London, 1998), p. 9.

73 The Bulger case, and the response to it, had a precedent in Paris in 1834 when Honorine Pellois, aged eleven, received a twenty-year sentence for murdering two toddlers by pushing them into a well. Described as 'a little monster', Pellois's crime led to the reflection that 'the human species contains undefinable beings who seem to find instinctual pleasure in evil'. C. Nilan, 'Hapless innocence and precocious perversity in the courtroom melodrama: representations of the child criminal in a Paris legal journal, 1830–1848', *Journal of Family History*, 22 (1997), pp. 273–4.

74 A. James, C. Jenks and A. Prout, *Theorizing Childhood* (Cambridge, 1999), p. 3. For other important works in this tradition, see A. James and A. Prout (eds), *Constructing and Reconstructing Childhood* (1990; London, 1997); C. Jenks, *Childhood* (London, 1996); Hendrick, *Child Welfare*.

CHAPTER 8

Conclusion

In 1971 David Rothman described how 'many historians have experienced that middle-of-the-night panic when contemplating how thin a line sometimes separates their work from fiction. But on this score the study of childhood seems especially nerve-racking, threatening to turn us all into novelists.'[1] Over thirty years on, despite a huge amount of work on the history of children and of childhood, it is still possible to feel that panic. It is heightened rather than diminished by the knowledge that the conclusions acceptable to the 1970s were overturned by historians of the 1980s. Moreover, it is not simply that the conclusions of one year are challenged the next; we are not even certain what questions to ask. The questions which this book has most centrally asked have been about the relationship between public action and thought and private experience. It is these questions, I believe, which should provide the agenda for historians of children and of childhood. They are, as it happens, the questions addressed by Philippe Ariès.

Until recently, however, the emphasis has been different, and the question which has been asked is: did parents in the past love their children? Diaries, autobiographies, letters and wills, the archives of foundling hospitals and the deposits of Poor Law authorities, have all been exhaustively tapped to find the answer to this question. It is in many ways a vain quest, an attempt to answer a question wrongly posed for it assumes that 'love' is something we would recognise if we encountered it. And it further sets up a false dichotomy between parents who did love their children, and those who did not, quite failing to recognise that some parents might both love and not love their children, might have ambivalent and contradictory feelings.[2]

The obsession with this question placed the history of children and childhood within the history of private life, that attempt to uncover the emotional tempo of intimate human relationships in the past. In this book, I have argued that it also belongs to public life, both in the sense that public policies towards children were articulated and often implemented, and in the sense that children played a part in the economic, social and political life of communities. In the 1960s and early 1970s it might legitimately have been complained that the history of childhood consisted far too exclusively of a study of public policies towards children;[3] in the 1980s and 1990s it was a contrary danger which threatened, an ignoring of anything outside the private sphere. This book has sought to right the balance, aiming to show the interaction between, on the one hand, economic developments, public policies and ways of imagining the world, and, on the other, thinking about childhood and the experience of being a child.

Is it possible, in conclusion, to map out the continuities and changes in this history? Taking his stance in the middle of the twentieth century Ariès argued that if there was a moment of transformation in both conceptualisation of childhood and in treatment of children it lay in the seventeenth century – though he accepted that it was a long time before it worked its way through the social ranks. Pollock's counter-argument was that in the period 1500–1900 the continuities in the treatment of children by parents stood out more markedly than the changes. Ariès paid little attention to the nineteenth century; Pollock stopped short of the twentieth century. It is my argument that it is in the twentieth century that there has been most rapid change in conceptualisation and experience of childhood, but that there is a long lead-in to this. In the long view, and allowing for the changes to which we have drawn attention, continuity is the key to the medieval and sixteenth and seventeenth centuries, the crucial imprint being made by Christianity. The beginning of a secular view of children and childhood in the eighteenth century marks the onset of a period of significant change both in conceptualisation of childhood and in treatment of children. The popularity of the ideas of Locke and Rousseau, and later of the Romantic poets, indicates the beginning of a period when children began to cease to be seen as the embodiment of souls in need of salvation, and became instead either like the young of some domestic pet in need of habit training or like a seed which should be allowed to grow naturally.

There is considerable evidence that both Locke and Rousseau deeply influenced a significant number of well-to-do parents, some of whom went to extraordinary lengths to use their books as blueprints for parenting. But there was no automatic way in which these new ideas spread throughout the middle classes or descended the social scale. Rather what happened was that the industrial revolution placed the children of the poor in a visible and public situation where it was manifest that their upbringing was in stark contrast to the precepts of nature. Campaigners and reformers fought to bring an end to this, and some of them used as their weapons arguments from nature. Governments were generally unimpressed by these arguments but were nevertheless driven into legislating to control child labour and to make illegal its worst manifestations.

Putting an end to child labour was one way of 'saving the child'. This became the aim of innumerable voluntary organisations in the nineteenth and early twentieth centuries. It carried with it the idea of saving the soul of the child, for nearly all those involved in these organisations were Christians. And yet even for committed Christians 'saving the child' came to take on a dominant meaning of preserving for the child what was thought of as a proper childhood; and this implied a childhood separated from the adult world in innocence and dependence. Children, for most Christians, ceased to be tainted with original sin. Slowly this vision of a proper childhood for all children began to be put into place, with the child and adult worlds separated out as far as humanly possible.

Compulsory schooling was introduced for a variety of reasons, some of them far removed from concepts of child-saving. Nevertheless, it was the key change which made possible the spread of the idea that all children should have a proper childhood. Children ceased to have any economic value. The 'century of the child' set itself the task of providing a childhood for all children, and was in many ways triumphantly successful, most notably in increasing the survival chances of children.

The twist came in the second half of the twentieth century. Children began to break out of the ghetto of dependency in home and school to which they had been assigned. Acquiring a degree of emotional, economic and legal power in relation to their parents, they were able to become participants in a commercial culture dominated by the search for profits. Most adults found this an alien culture, but were able to exercise control over it, or over their child's participation in it, only at the margin. The childhood of many children in western society at the end of the twentieth century was hardly in accordance with the hopes held out for a 'century of the child'.

In some ways, however, the 'century of the child' lived up to its billing in ways not anticipated at its outset. Children began to acquire rights which brought them closer to adults rather than separated them from them. In legal processes and in family disputes, adults tried to elicit and respect the views of children in ways unimaginable at the century's beginning. Statements of the rights of children at the end of the century put the emphasis not only on protection of children, but also on children's rights to a degree of self-determination, an emphasis which thoroughly muddied the earlier attempt to separate out the worlds of adults and children.

When Norbert Elias and Philippe Ariès looked back over the history of childhood and saw an increasing differentiation between adults and children they were observing a set of changes which from their mid-twentieth-century perspective made considerable sense. If we, like them, start from the present, we will see something different, for the trend which they traced over centuries has gone into reverse. Similarly, in the wake of recent revelations of adult abuse of children, such as the Belgian Marc Dutroux's kidnapping, rape and murder of children, it is hard now not to shudder at the naivety of Lloyd de Mause's belief that things were continually getting better. Nevertheless the apparent polarity of views between Elias and Ariès on the one hand and de Mause on the other demands some consideration. Were adulthood and childhood up to the mid-twentieth century moving further apart or closer together? Elias and Ariès were right to note the trend towards separating out childhood as a special time of life, yet de Mause may not have been entirely wrong in thinking that parents were moving closer to the child's world. That is to say, what was happening to childhood was apparently at odds with what was happening to children; but only apparently. It was part of the ethos of Romanticism that childhood should be acknowledged as a special time of life, but also that adults should keep the child in themselves alive; they must in some sense continue to be children. And in so far as they did this, they were able to move closer to actual children in ways which de Mause described.

A romantic view of childhood as a special time of life has both sunk deep into and had a remarkable tenacity in western societies. Nor has it been confined to the west. In the twentieth century, international organisations, both voluntary and official, often themselves competing for public attention, have sought to export western ideas of childhood. The successive statements of children's rights, from the League of Nations Declaration of Children's Rights in 1924, through the United Nations Declaration of the Rights of the Child in 1959, to the Convention on the Rights of the Child of 1989, embody western ideas of childhood.[4] In 1973 the International Labour Organization, charged at its formation in 1919 with 'the abolition of child labour', was envisaging a world where no child under the age of sixteen engaged in any form of productive work, a notion distinctly at odds with ideas and practices outside the west.[5]

The romantic ideal has faced, and largely withstood, many challenges. Up to the middle of the twentieth century it could be said that the actuality of childhood in western society was coming closer to the ideal. Adherents of the romantic view of childhood could feel confident that things were indeed getting better. In 1942 Sylvia Lynd rejoiced, even in the middle of war, that 'the story of English children . . . is a story that moves towards a happy ending'.[6] What happened in the late twentieth century, however, was an increasing disjunction between romantic ideal and lived reality. It was a disjuncture to which Zlata gave expression in the extreme conditions of the siege of Sarajevo, but at different levels it affected all parents and most children.

In most societies children have had as little power as did Zlata to bring reality nearer to ideal. Parental power determined how children were reared. In the late twentieth and early twenty-first centuries, however, matters are different. Adults portray the world external to the home as full of danger, and seek correspondingly to protect their children by denying them autonomy. At the same time, their confidence in their own authority has been weakened by a variety of factors – commercial, legal, psychological – which make it difficult to carry out that protection as they would wish to. The result is that, to a much greater extent than in previous centuries, child-rearing has become a matter of negotiation between parent and child, with the state and other agencies monitoring and inspecting the process. In this process ideas about childhood which exist in the public domain act as a framework within which adults and children work out ways of living. The peculiarity of the late twentieth and early twenty-first centuries, and the root cause of much present confusion and angst about childhood, is that a public discourse which argues that children are persons with rights to a degree of autonomy is at odds with the remnants of the romantic view that the right of a child is to be a child. The implication of the first is a fusing of the worlds of adult and child, and of the second the maintenance of separation.

Notes

1   D.J. Rothman, 'Documents in search of a historian: toward a history of children and youth in America', *Journal of Interdisciplinary History*, 2 (1971–2), p. 369.

2   A. Farge, *Fragile Lives: Violence, Power and Solidarity in Eighteenth-Century Paris* (Cambridge, 1993), pp. 46–51.

3   Typical books were I. Pinchbeck and M. Hewitt, *Children in English Society*, 2 vols (London, 1969–73) and R.H. Bremner (ed.), *Children and Youth in America: A Documentary History*, 2 vols (Cambridge, Mass., 1971).

4   D. Marshall, 'The construction of children as an object of international relations: the declaration of children's rights and the Child Welfare Committee of League of Nations, 1900–1924', *International Journal of Children's Rights*, 7 (1999), pp. 103–47; id., 'The Cold War, Canada, and the United Nations Declaration of the Rights of the Child', in G. Donaghy (ed.), *Canada and the Early Cold War 1943–1957* (Ottawa, 1999), pp. 183–212; P.T. Rooke and R.L. Schnell, ' "Uncramping child life": international children's organisations, 1914–1939', in P. Weindling (ed.), *International Health Organisations and Movements, 1918–1939* (Cambridge, 1995), pp. 176–202; J. Boyden, 'Childhood and the policy makers: a comparative perspective on the globalization of childhood', in A. James and A. Prout (eds), *Constructing and Reconstructing Childhood: Contemporary Issues in the Sociological Study of Childhood* (London, 1997), pp. 190–229.

5   H. Cunningham, 'The rights of the child and the wrongs of child labour: an historical perspective', in K. Lieten and B. White (eds), *Child Labour: Policy Options* (Amsterdam, 2001), pp. 13–26.

6   S. Lynd, *English Children* (London, 1942), p. 8.

Guide to further reading

What follows is a guide to further reading, and not a bibliography of the history of childhood; it is selective. The principles of selection have been that a book or article should either be on the history of childhood, making a significant contribution to it, or, if it is wider in scope, in the pages in which it deals with childhood, should contain important information or argument.

1. Books

Abrams, L., *The Orphan Country: Children of Scotland's Broken Homes From 1845 to the Present Day* (Edinburgh, 1998).

Alexandre-Bidon, D. and Lett, D., *Children in the Middle Ages, Fifth–Fifteenth Centuries* (Notre Dame, Indiana, 1999).

Anderson, M., *Approaches to the History of the Western Family, 1500–1914* (London, 1980).

Ariès, P., *Centuries of Childhood* (Harmondsworth, 1960).

Ariès, P. and Duby, G. (eds), *A History of Private Life*, 5 vols (London, 1987–91).

Avery, G. and Reynolds, K. (eds), *Representations of Childhood Death* (Basingstoke, 2000).

Bedaux, J.B. and Ekkart, R. (eds), *Pride and Joy: Children's Portraits in the Netherlands, 1500–1700* (Ghent and Amsterdam, 2000).

Behlmer, G.K., *Child Abuse and Moral Reform in England, 1870–1908* (Stanford, 1982).

Behlmer, G.K., *Friends of the Family: The English Home and Its Guardians, 1850–1940* (Stanford, 1998).

Boas, G., *The Cult of Childhood* (London, 1966).

Bolin-Hort, P., *Work, Family and the State: Child Labour and the Organization of Production in the British Cotton Industry, 1780–1920* (Lund, 1989).

Bonfield, L., Smith, R.M. and Wrightson, K. (eds), *The World We Have Gained: Histories of Population and Social Structure* (Oxford, 1986).

Boswell, J., *The Kindness of Strangers: The Abandonment of Children in Western Europe from Late Antiquity to the Renaissance* (1988; London, 1989).

Bottigheimer, R.B., *The Bible for Children: From the Age of Gutenberg to the Present* (New Haven and London, 1996).

Bremner, R. (ed.), *Children and Youth in America: A Documentary History*, 2 vols (Cambridge, Mass., 1971).

Brown, M.R. (ed.), *Picturing Children: Constructions of Childhood Between Rousseau and Freud* (Aldershot, 2002).

Buckingham, D., *After the Death of Childhood: Growing Up in the Age of Electronic Media* (Cambridge, 2000).

Calvert, K., *Children in the House: The Material Culture of Early Childhood, 1600–1900* (Boston, 1992).

Casey, J., *The History of the Family* (Oxford, 1989).

Chatellier, L., *The Europe of the Devout: The Catholic Reformation and the Formation of a New Society* (1987; Cambridge, 1989).

Chisick, H., *The Limits of Reform in the Enlightenment: Attitudes toward the Education of the Lower Classes in Eighteenth-Century France* (Princeton, 1981).

Clement, P.C., *Growing Pains: Children in the Industrial Age 1850–90* (New York, 1997).

Collinson, P., *The Birthpangs of Protestant England: Religious and Cultural Change in the Sixteenth and Seventeenth Centuries* (London, 1988).

Cooter, R. (ed.), *In the Name of the Child: Health and Welfare, 1880–1940* (London, 1992).

Corsini, C.A. and Viazzo, P.P. (eds), *The Decline of Infant Mortality in Europe 1800–1950: Four National Case Studies* (Florence, 1993).

Corsini, C.A. and Viazzo, P.P. (eds), *The Decline of Infant and Child Mortality: The European Experience, 1750–1990* (The Hague, 1997).

Coveney, P., *The Image of Childhood* (1957; Harmondsworth, 1966).

Crawford, S., *Childhood in Anglo-Saxon England* (Stroud, 1999).

Cross, G., *Kids' Stuff: Toys and the Changing World of American Childhood* (Cambridge, Mass., 1997).

Cunningham, H., *The Children of the Poor: Representations of Childhood since the Seventeenth Century* (Oxford, 1991).

Cunningham, H. and Viazzo, P.P. (eds), *Child Labour in Historical Perspective 1800–1985: Case Studies from Europe, Japan and Colombia* (Florence, 1996).

Darnton, R., *The Great Cat Massacre, and Other Episodes in French Cultural History* (1984; Harmondsworth, 1985).

Davidoff, L. and Hall, C., *Family Fortunes: Men and Women of the English Middle Class, 1780–1850* (London, 1987).

Davin, A., *Growing Up Poor: Home, School and Street in London 1870–1914* (London, 1996).

Davis, N.Z., *Society and Culture in Early Modern France* (Cambridge, 1987).

De Coninck-Smith, N., Sandin, B. and Schrumpf, E. (eds), *Industrious Children: Work and Childhood in the Nordic Countries 1850–1990* (Odense, 1997).

Dekker, J., *The Will to Change the Child: Re-education Homes for Children at Risk in Nineteenth Century Western Europe* (Frankfurt am Main, 2001).

Dekker, R., *Childhood, Memory and Autobiography in Holland: From the Golden Age to Romanticism* (Basingstoke, 2000).

De Mause, L. (ed.), *The History of Childhood* (1974; London, 1976).

Demos, J., *A Little Commonwealth: Family Life in Plymouth Colony* (New York, 1970).

Dickinson, E.R., *The Politics of German Child Welfare from the Empire to the Federal Republic* (Cambridge, Mass. and London, 1996).

Dixon, S., *The Roman Family* (London, 1992).

Donzelot, J., *The Policing of Families* (1977; London, 1980).

Dwork, D., *War is Good for Babies and Other Young Children: A History of the Infant and Child Welfare Movement in England 1898–1918* (London, 1987).

Dwork, D., *Children with a Star: Jewish Youth in Nazi Europe* (New Haven and London, 1991).

Eisen, G., *Children and Play in the Holocaust: Games among the Shadows* (Amherst, 1988).

Elder, G.H., *Children of the Great Depression: Social Change in Life Experience* (London, 1974).

Elder, G.H., Modell, J. and Park, R.D., *Children in Time and Place: Developmental and Historical Insights* (Cambridge, 1993).

Elias, N., *The History of Manners: The Civilizing Process, Vol. 1* (1939; New York, 1978).

Fairchilds, C.C., *Poverty and Charity in Aix-en-Provence, 1640–1789* (London, 1976).

Farge, A., *Fragile Lives* (Cambridge, 1993).

Farge, A. and Revel, J., *The Rules of Rebellion: Child Abductions in Paris in 1750* (Cambridge, 1991).

Fass, P.S., *Kidnapped: Child Abduction in America* (New York, 1997).

Fass, P.S. (ed.), *Encyclopedia of Children and Childhood in History and Society*, 3 vols (New York, 2004).

Felt, J.P., *Hostages of Fortune: Child Labor Reform in New York State* (Syracuse, 1965).

Fildes, V., *Wet Nursing: A History from Antiquity to the Present* (Oxford, 1988).

Fildes, V. (ed.), *Women as Mothers in Pre-Industrial England* (London, 1990).

Fildes, V. et al. (eds), *Women and Children First: International Maternal and Infant Welfare, 1870–1945* (London, 1992).

Finucane, R.C., *The Rescue of the Innocents: Endangered Children in Medieval Miracles* (Basingstoke, 1997).

Flandrin, J.L., *Families in Former Times: Kinship, Household and Sexuality* (1976; Cambridge, 1979).

Fletcher, A., *Gender, Sex and Subordination in England 1500–1800* (New Haven and London, 1995).

Fletcher, A. and Hussey, S. (eds), *Childhood in Question: Children, Parents and the State* (Manchester, 1999).

Formanek-Brunell, M., *Made to Play House: Dolls and the Commercialization of American Girlhood, 1830–1930* (New Haven, 1993).

Fuchs, R., *Abandoned Children: Foundlings and Child Welfare in Nineteenth Century France* (Albany, 1984).

Gavitt, P., *Charity and Children in Renaissance Florence: The Ospedale degli Innocenti, 1410–1536* (Ann Arbor, 1991).

Gélis, J., *History of Childbirth: Fertility, Pregnancy and Birth in Early Modern Europe* (Cambridge, 1991).

Gijswijt-Hofstra, M. and Marland, H. (eds), *Cultures of Child Health in Britain and the Netherlands in the Twentieth Century* (Amsterdam and New York, 2003).

Gillis, J.R., *A World of Their Own Making: A History of Myth and Ritual in Family Life* (Oxford, 1997).

Gillis, J.R., Tilly, L.A. and Levine, D. (eds), *The European Experience of Declining Fertility, 1850–1970: The Quiet Revolution* (Oxford, 1992).

Golden, M., *Children and Childhood in Classical Athens* (London, 1990).

Goody, J., *The Development of the Family and Marriage in Europe* (Cambridge, 1983).

Gordon, L., *Heroes of Their Own Lives: The Politics and History of Family Violence* (London, 1989).

Graff, H.J., *Conflicting Paths: Growing Up in America* (Cambridge, Mass., 1995).

Graff, H.J. (ed.), *Growing Up in America: Historical Experiences* (Detroit, 1987).

Greven, P., *The Protestant Temperament: Patterns of Child-Rearing, Religious Experience, and the Self in Early America* (New York, 1977).

Grew, R. and Harrigan, P.J., *School, State and Society: The Growth of Elementary Schooling in Nineteenth-Century France: A Quantitative Analysis* (Ann Arbor, 1991).

Haas, L., *The Renaissance Man and His Children: Childbirth and Early Childhood in Florence 1300–1600* (Basingstoke, 1998).

Halpern, S.A., *American Pediatrics: The Social Dynamics of Professionalism, 1880–1980* (Berkeley, 1988).

Hanawalt, B.A., *The Ties That Bound: Peasant Families in Medieval England* (New York, 1986).

Hanawalt, B.A., *Growing Up in Medieval London: The Experience of Childhood in History* (Oxford, 1993).

Hardyment, C., *Dream Babies: Child Care from Locke to Spock* (London, 1983).

Hareven, T.K., *Family Time and Industrial Time: The Relationship between the Family and Work in a New England Industrial Community* (Cambridge, 1982).

Harris, B., *The Health of the Schoolchild: A History of the School Medical Service in England and Wales* (Buckingham and Philadelphia, 1995).

Hawes, J.M., *Children Between the Wars: American Childhood 1920–1940* (New York, 1997).

Hawes, J.M. and Hiner, N.R. (eds), *American Childhood: A Research Guide and Historical Handbook* (London, 1985).

Heathorn, S., *For Home, Country, and Race: Constructing Gender, Class, and Englishness in the Elementary Schools of Victorian England, 1880–1914* (Buffalo and London, 2000).

Henderson, J. and Wall, R. (eds), *Poor Women and Children in the European Past* (London, 1994).

Hendrick, H., *Children, Childhood and English Society, 1880–1990* (Cambridge, 1997).

Hendrick, H., *Child Welfare: Historical Dimensions, Contemporary Debate* (Bristol, 2003).

Herlihy, D., *Medieval Households* (London, 1985).

Heywood, C., *Childhood in Nineteenth-Century France: Work, Health and Education Among the 'Classes Populaires'* (Cambridge, 1988).

Heywood, C., *A History of Childhood: Children and Childhood in the West from Medieval to Modern Times* (Cambridge, 2001).

Higonnet, A., *Pictures of Innocence: The History and Crisis of Ideal Childhood* (London, 1998).

Hindman, H.D., *Child Labor: An American History* (Armonk, New York and London, 2002).

Hoffer, P.C. and Hull, N.E.H., *Murdering Mothers: Infanticide in England and New England, 1558–1803* (New York, 1981).

Hopkins, E., *Childhood Transformed: Working-Class Children in Nineteenth-Century England* (Manchester, 1994).

Horn, M., *Before It's Too Late: The Child Guidance Movement in the United States, 1922–1945* (Philadelphia, 1989).

Houlbrooke, R.A., *The English Family 1450–1700* (London, 1984).

Houston, R.A., *Literacy in Early Modern Europe: Culture and Education, 1500–1800* (London, 1988).

Hsia, R.P., *Social Discipline in the Reformation: Central Europe 1550–1750* (London, 1992).

Hufton, O.H., *The Poor of Eighteenth-Century France, 1750–1789* (Oxford, 1974).

Hunt, D., *Parents and Children in History: The Psychology of Family Life in Early Modern France* (New York, 1970).

Hunt, L., *The Family Romance of the French Revolution* (Berkeley, 1992).

Hurt, J.S., *Elementary Schooling and the Working Classes 1860–1918* (London, 1979).

Jackson, L.A., *Child Sexual Abuse in Victorian England* (London, 2000).

Jackson, M., *New-Born Child Murder: Women, Illegitimacy and the Courts in Eighteenth-Century England* (Manchester, 1996).

Jackson, M. (ed.), *Infanticide: Historical Perspectives on Child Murder and Concealment, 1550–2000* (Aldershot, 2002).

James, A. and Prout, A. (eds), *Constructing and Reconstructing Childhood*, 2nd edn (London, 1997).

James, A., Jenks, C. and Prout A., *Theorizing Childhood* (Cambridge, 1998).

Jenks, C., *Childhood* (London and New York, 1996).

Kertzer, D., *Sacrificed for Honor: Italian Infant Abandonment and the Politics of Reproductive Control* (Boston, 1993).

Kertzer, D.I. and Saller, R.P. (eds), *The Family in Italy from Antiquity to the Present* (New Haven, 1991).

Kincaid, J.R., *Child-Loving: The Erotic Child and Victorian Culture* (New York and London, 1992).

Kirby, P., *Child Labour in Britain, 1750–1870* (Basingstoke, 2003).

Klapisch-Zuber, C., *Women, Family and Ritual in Renaissance Italy* (London, 1985).

Klaus, A., *Every Child a Lion: The Origins of Maternal and Infant Health Policy in the United States and France, 1890–1920* (Ithaca, 1993).

Kline, S., *Out of the Garden: Toys and Children's Culture in the Age of TV Marketing* (London, 1993).

Koven, S. and Michel, S., *Mothers of a New World: Maternalist Politics and the Origins of Welfare States* (London, 1993)

Ladurie, E. Le Roy, *Montaillou: Cathars and Catholics in a French Village 1294–1324* (Harmondsworth, 1980).

Lasch, C., *Haven in a Heartless World: The Family Besieged* (New York, 1977).

Laslett, P., *Family Life and Illicit Love in Earlier Generations* (Cambridge, 1977).

Laslett, P. (ed.), *Household and Family in Past Time* (Cambridge, 1972).

Laslett, P., Oosterveen, K. and Smith, R.M. (eds), *Bastardy and its Comparative History* (London, 1980).

Lavalette, M. (ed.), *A Thing of the Past? Child Labour in Britain in the Nineteenth and Twentieth Centuries* (Liverpool, 1999).

Lawrence, J. and Starkey, P. (eds), *Child Welfare and Social Action in the Nineteenth and Twentieth Centuries: International Perspectives* (Liverpool, 2001).

Leith, J.A. (ed.), *Facets of Education in the Eighteenth Century, Studies on Voltaire and the Eighteenth Century*, CLXVII (1977).

Levine, D., *Reproducing Families: The Political Economy of English Population History* (Cambridge, 1987).

Lindenmeyer, K., *'A Right to Childhood': The U.S. Children's Bureau and Child Welfare, 1912–46* (Urbana and Chicago, 1997).

Lis, C., *Social Change and the Labouring Poor: Antwerp, 1770–1860* (London, 1986).

McCants, A.E.C., *Civic Charity in a Golden Age: Orphan Care in Early Modern Amsterdam* (Urbana and Chicago, 1997).

McClure, R.K., *Coram's Children: The London Foundling Hospital in the Eighteenth Century* (London, 1981).

Macfarlane, A., *Marriage and Love in England: Modes of Reproduction 1300–1840* (Oxford, 1986).

McGavran, J.H. (ed.), *Romanticism and Children's Literature in Nineteenth-Century England* (Atlanta, 1991).

Macleod, D.I., *The Age of the Child: Children in America, 1890–1920* (New York, 1998).

Macnicol, J., *The Movement for Family Allowances, 1918–45: A Study in Social Policy Development* (London, 1980).

Mahood, L., *Policing Gender, Class and Family: Britain 1850–1940* (London, 1995).

Matthews Grieco, S.F. and Corsini, C.A., *Historical Perspectives on Breastfeeding* (Florence, 1991).

Maynes, M.J., *Schooling for the People: Comparative Local Studies of Schooling History in France and Germany, 1750–1850* (New York, 1985).

Maynes, M.J., *Schooling in Western Europe: A Social History* (Albany, 1985).

Meckel, R.A., *Save the Babies: American Public Health Reform and the Prevention of Infant Mortality, 1850–1929* (Baltimore, 1990).

Medick, H. and Sabean, D.W. (eds), *Interest and Emotion: Essays on the Study of Family and Kinship* (Cambridge, 1984).

Melton, J. van H., *Absolutism and the Eighteenth-Century Origins of Compulsory Schooling in Prussia and Austria* (Cambridge, 1988).

Meyer, P., *The Child and the State: The Intervention of the State in Family Life* (1977; Cambridge, 1983).

Mitterauer, M., *A History of Youth* (Oxford, 1992).

Mitterauer, M. and Seider, R., *The European Family: Patriarchy to Partnership from the Middle Ages to the Present* (Oxford, 1982).

Morgan, J., *Godly Learning: Puritan Attitudes Towards Reason, Learning, and Education, 1560–1640* (Cambridge, 1986).

Mount, F., *The Subversive Family* (London, 1982).

Nardinelli, C., *Child Labor and the Industrial Revolution* (Bloomington and Indianapolis, 1990).

Opie, I. and P., *The Lore and Language of Schoolchildren* (1959; St Albans, 1977).

Orme, N., *Medieval Children* (New Haven and London, 2001).

Ozment, S., *When Fathers Ruled: Family Life in Reformation Europe* (London, 1983).

Panter-Brick, C. and Smith M.T. (eds), *Abandoned Children* (Cambridge, 2000).

Parr, J., *Labouring Children: British Immigrant Apprentices to Canada, 1869–1924* (London, 1980).

Parr, J. (ed.), *Childhood and Family in Canadian History* (Toronto, 1982).

Peter, K., *Beloved Children: History of Aristocratic Childhood in Hungary in the Early Modern Age* (Budapest, 2001).

Phythian-Adams, C., *Desolation of a City: Coventry and the Urban Crisis of the Late Middle Ages* (Cambridge, 1979).

Pickering, S.F., Jr., *John Locke and Children's Books in Eighteenth-Century England* (Knoxville, 1981).

Pinchbeck, I. and Hewitt, M., *Children in English Society*, 2 vols (London, 1969–73).

Platt, A.M., *The Child Savers: The Invention of Delinquency* (1969; London, 1977).

Pointon, M., *Hanging the Head: Portraiture and Social Formation in Eighteenth-Century England* (New Haven and London, 1993).

Pollock, L.A., *Forgotten Children: Parent–Child Relations from 1500 to 1900* (Cambridge, 1983).

Postman, N., *The Disappearance of Childhood* (1982; London, 1983).

Preston, S.H. and Haines, M.R., *Fatal Years: Child Mortality in Late Nineteenth-Century America* (Princeton, 1990).

Pullan, B., *Rich and Poor in Renaissance Venice: The Social Institutions of a Catholic State, to 1620* (Oxford, 1971).

Pullan, B., *Orphans and Foundlings in Early Modern Europe* (Reading, 1989).

Ransel, D.L., *Mothers of Misery: Child Abandonment in Russia* (Princeton, 1988).

Rawson, B., *Children and Childhood in Roman Italy* (Oxford, 2003).

Rawson, B. (ed.), *The Family in Ancient Rome: New Perspectives* (London, 1986).

Rawson, B. (ed.), *Marriage, Divorce, and Children in Ancient Rome* (Canberra and Oxford, 1991).

Riley, D., *War in the Nursery: Theories of the Child and Mother* (London, 1983).

Robins, J.A., *The Lost Children: A Study of Charity Children in Ireland, 1700–1900* (Dublin, 1980).

Rose, L., *The Erosion of Childhood: Child Oppression in Britain 1860–1918* (London, 1991).

Rose, N., *Governing the Soul: The Shaping of the Private Self* (London and New York, 1990).

Rosenblum, R., *The Romantic Child from Runge to Sendak* (London, 1988).

Rothman, D.J., *The Discovery of the Asylum: Social Order and Disorder in the New Republic* (Boston, 1971).

Schafer, S., *Children in Moral Danger and the Problem of Government in Third Republic France* (Princeton, 1997).

Schama, S., *The Embarrassment of Riches: An Interpretation of Dutch Culture in the Golden Age* (London, 1987).

Schlossman, S.L., *Love and the American Delinquent: The Theory and Practice of Progressive Juvenile Justice, 1825–1920* (Chicago, 1977).

Schultz, J.A., *The Knowledge of Childhood in the German Middle Ages, 1100–1350* (Philadelphia, 1995).

Scott, H.M. (ed.), *Enlightened Absolutism: Reform and Reformers in Later Eighteenth-Century Europe* (London, 1990).

Seabrook, J., *Working-Class Childhood: An Oral History* (London, 1982).

Shahar, S., *Childhood in the Middle Ages* (London, 1992).

Sherwood, J., *Poverty in Eighteenth-Century Spain: The Women and Children of the Inclusa* (Toronto, 1988).

Shore, H., *Artful Dodgers: Youth and Crime in Early Nineteenth-Century London* (Woodbridge, Suffolk, 1999).

Shorter, E., *The Making of the Modern Family* (London, 1976).

Skocpol, T., *Protecting Soldiers and Mothers: The Political Origins of Social Policy in the United States* (London, 1992).

Smith, R.M. (ed.), *Land, Kinship and Life-Cycle* (Cambridge, 1984).

Sommerville, J., *The Rise and Fall of Childhood* (London, 1982).

Steedman, C., *The Tidy House: Little Girls Writing* (London, 1982).

Steedman, C., *Childhood, Culture and Class in Britain: Margaret McMillan, 1860–1931* (London, 1990).

Steedman, C., *Strange Dislocations: Childhood and the Idea of Human Interiority, 1780–1930* (London, 1995).

Steward, J.C., *The New Child: British Art and the Origins of Modern Childhood 1730–1830* (Berkeley, 1995).

Stone, L., *The Family, Sex and Marriage in England 1500–1800* (London, 1977).

Strauss, G., *Luther's House of Learning: Indoctrination of the Young in the German Reformation* (London, 1978).

Sussman, G.D., *Selling Mother's Milk: The Wet-Nursing Business in France, 1715–1914* (Urbana, 1982).

Sutherland, N., *Children in English Canadian Society: Framing the Twentieth-Century Consensus* (Toronto, 1976).

Sutherland, N., *Growing Up: Childhood in English Canada from the Great War to the Age of Television* (Toronto, 1997).

Thomas, K., *Rule and Misrule in the Schools of Early Modern England* (Reading, 1976).

Tiffin, S., *In Whose Best Interest? Child Welfare Reform in the Progressive Era* (London, 1982).

Tilly, L.A. and Scott, J.W., *Women, Work, and Family* (New York, 1978).

Todd, M., *Christian Humanism and the Puritan Social Order* (Cambridge, 1987).

Tosh, J., *A Man's Place: Masculinity and the Middle-Class Home in Victorian England* (New Haven and London, 1999).

Trattner, W.I., *Crusade for the Children: A History of the National Child Labor Committee and Child Labor Reform in America* (Chicago, 1970).

Trumbach, R., *The Rise of the Egalitarian Family: Aristocratic Kinship and Domestic Relations in Eighteenth-Century England* (London, 1978).

Tuttle, C., *Hard at Work in Factories and Mines: The Economics of Child Labor During the British Industrial Revolution* (Boulder, 1999).

Weber, E., *Peasants into Frenchmen: The Modernization of Rural France 1870–1914* (London, 1977).

Weissbach, L.S., *Child Labor Reform in Nineteenth-Century France* (London, 1989).

Wiedemann, T., *Adults and Children in the Roman Empire* (London, 1989).

Wishy, B., *The Child and the Republic: The Dawn of Modern American Child Nurture* (Philadelphia, 1968).

Wood, D. (ed.), *The Church and Childhood* (Oxford, 1994).

Zeldin, T., *France 1848–1945*, Vol. I (Oxford, 1973).

Zelizer, V.A., *Pricing the Priceless Child: The Changing Social Value of Children* (New York, 1985).

Zucchi, J.E., *The Little Slaves of the Harp: Italian Child Street Musicians in Nineteenth-Century Paris, London, and New York* (Montreal, 1992).

2. Articles and chapters in books

Alter, G., 'Work and income in the family economy: Belgium, 1853 and 1891', *Journal of Interdisciplinary History*, XV (1984), 255–76.

Beales, R.W., 'In search of the historical child: miniature adulthood and youth in colonial New England', *American Quarterly*, XXVII (1975), 379–98.

Bellingham, B., 'The history of childhood since the "invention of childhood": some issues in the eighties', *Journal of Family History*, 13 (1988), 347–58.

Berlanstein, L., 'Vagrants, beggars, and thieves: delinquent boys in mid-nineteenth century Paris', *Journal of Social History*, XII (1979), 531–52.

Bottigheimer, R.B., 'Bible Reading, "Bibles" and the Bible for children in early modern Germany', *Past and Present*, 139 (1993), 66–89.

Boylan, A.M., 'Sunday schools and changing evangelical views of children in the 1820s', *Church History*, 48 (1979), 320–33.

Brewer, J., 'The genesis of the modern toy', *History Today*, 30 (Dec. 1980), 32–9.

Calvert, K., 'Children in American family portraiture, 1670 to 1810', *William and Mary Quarterly*, XXXIX (1982), 87–113.

Coleman, E.R., 'L'infanticide dans le Haut Moyen Age', *Annales ESC*, 29 (1974), 315–35.

Continuity and Change, 7, No. 3 (1992) on siblings.

Courtwright, D.T., 'The neglect of female children and childhood sex ratios in 19th century America: a review of the evidence', *Journal of Family History*, 15 (1990), 313–23.

Crown, P., 'Portraits and fancy pictures by Gainsborough and Reynolds: contrasting images of childhood', *British Journal for Eighteenth-Century Studies*, 7 (1984), 159–67.

Cunningham, H., 'The employment and unemployment of children in England, 1680–c.1851', *Past and Present*, 126 (1990), 115–50.

Cunningham, H., 'The decline of child labour: labour markets and family economies in Europe and North America since 1830', *Economic History Review*, LIII (2000), 409–28.

De Coninck-Smith, N., 'Copenhagen children's lives and the impact of institutions, c. 1840–1920', *History Workshop*, 33 (1992), 57–72.

Dekker, J.J.H., 'Rituals and reeducation in the nineteenth century: ritual and moral education in a Dutch children's home', *Continuity and Change*, 9 (1994), 121–44.

Dekker, J.J.H., 'Family on the beach: representations of romantic and bourgeois family values by realistic genre painting of nineteenth-century Scheveningen beach', *Journal of Family History*, 28 (2003), 277–96.

Delasselle, C., 'Abandoned children in eighteenth-century Paris', in R. Forster and O. Ranum (eds), *Deviants and the Abandoned in French Society* (London, 1978), pp. 47–82.

Dingwall, R., Eekelaar, J.M. and Murray, T., 'Childhood as a social problem: a survey of the history of legal regulation', *Journal of Law and Society*, 11 (1984), 207–32.

Dupont-Bouchat, M-S., 'Du tourisme pénitentiaire à "l'internationale des philanthropes". La création d'un réseau pour la protection de l'enfance à travers les congrès internationaux (1840–1914)', *Paedogogica Historica*, XXXVIII (2002), 533–63.

Dye, N.S. and Smith, D.B., 'Mother love and infant death, 1750–1920', *Journal of American History*, 73 (1986–7), 329–53.

Ezell, M.J.M., 'John Locke's images of childhood: early eighteenth century response to *Some Thoughts concerning Education*', *Eighteenth-Century Studies*, 17 (1983), 139–55.

Fariñas, D.R. and Gimeno, A.S., 'Childhood mortality in Central Spain, 1790–1960: changes in the course of demographic modernization', *Continuity and Change*, 15 (2000), 235–67.

Forsyth, I.H., 'Children in early medieval art: ninth through twelfth centuries', *Journal of Psychohistory*, 4 (1976), 31–70.

Fuchs, R.G., 'Legislation, poverty, and child-abandonment in nineteenth-century Paris', *Journal of Interdisciplinary History*, 18 (1987), 55–80.

Fuller, P., 'Uncovering childhood', in M. Hoyles (ed.), *Changing Childhood* (London, 1979), pp. 71–108.

Garlitz, B., 'The Immortality Ode: its cultural progeny', *Studies in English Literature*, 6 (1966), 639–49.

Gordon, E.C., 'Accidents among medieval children as seen from the miracles of six English saints and martyrs', *Medical History*, 35 (1991), 145–63.

Grendler, P.F., 'The Schools of Christian Doctrine in sixteenth-century Italy', *Church History*, 53 (1984), 319–31.

Habermas, R., 'Parent–child relationships in the nineteenth century', *German History*, 16 (1998), 43–55.

Hammel, E.A., Johansson, S.R. and Ginsberg, C.A., 'The value of children during industrialization: sex ratios in childhood in nineteenth-century America', *Journal of Family History*, 8 (1983), 346–66.

Hanawalt, B.A., 'Childrearing among the lower classes of late medieval England', *Journal of Interdisciplinary History*, VIII (1977–8), 1–22.

Hardy, A., 'Rickets and the rest: child-care, diet and the infectious children's diseases, 1850–1914', *Social History of Medicine*, 5 (1992), 389–412.

Harrington, J.F., 'Bad parents, the state, and the early modern civilizing process', *German History*, 16 (1998), 16–28.

Hedenborg, S., 'To breastfeed another woman's child: wet-nursing in Stockholm, 1777–1937', *Continuity and Change*, 16 (2000), 399–422.

Helmhloz, R.H., 'Infanticide in the province of Canterbury during the fifteenth century', *History of Childhood Quarterly*, II (1974–5), 379–90.

Herlihy, D., 'Family', *American Historical Review*, 96 (1991), 1–16.

Heywood, C., 'On learning gender roles during childhood in nineteenth-century France', *French History*, 5 (1991), 451–66.

Horrell, S. and Humphries, J., ' "The exploitation of little children": child labor and the family economy in the industrial revolution', *Explorations in Economic History*, 32 (1995), 485–516.

Hunecke, V., 'Les enfants trouvés: contexte européen et cas Milanais (XIIIe–XXe siècles)', *Revue d'histoire moderne et contemporaine*, 32 (1985), 3–29.

Johansson, S.R., 'Centuries of childhood/centuries of parenting: Philippe Ariès and the modernization of privileged infancy', *Journal of Family History*, 12 (1987), 343–65.

Jordanova, L., 'New worlds for children in the eighteenth century: problems of historical interpretation', *History of the Human Sciences*, Vol. 3 (1990), 69–83.

Kern, S., 'Freud and the discovery of child sexuality', *History of Childhood Quarterly*, I (1973), 117–41.

Kertzer, D.I., 'Gender ideology and infant abandonment in 19th century Italy', *Journal of Interdisciplinary History*, XXII (1991), 1–26.

Kroll, J., 'The concept of childhood in the middle ages', *Journal of the History of the Behavioral Sciences*, 13 (1977), 384–93.

Kuefler, M.S., ' "A wryed existence": attitudes toward children in Anglo-Saxon England', *Journal of Social History*, 24 (1991), 823–34.

Larquié, C., 'La mise en nourrice des enfants madrilènes au XVIIe siècle', *Revue d'histoire moderne et contemporaine*, 32 (1985), 125–44.

Levene, A., 'The origins of the children of the London Foundling Hospital, 1741–1760: a reconsideration', *Continuity and Change*, 18 (2003), 201–36.

McLoughlin, W.G., 'Evangelical child-rearing in the age of Jackson: Francis Wayland's view on when and how to subdue the willfulness of children', *Journal of Social History*, 9 (1975), 21–43.

Marshall, D., 'The construction of children as an object of international relations: the Declaration of Children's Rights and the Child Welfare Committee of League of Nations, 1900–1924', *The International Journal of Children's Rights*, 7 (1999), 103–47.

Matt, S.J., 'Children's envy and the emergence of the modern consumer ethic, 1890–1930', *Journal of Social History*, 36 (2002–3), 283–302.

Mechling, J., 'Advice to historians on advice to mothers', *Journal of Social History*, 9 (1975–6), 44–64.

Medick, H., 'The proto-industrial family economy: the structural function of household and family during the transition from peasant society to industrial capitalism', *Social History*, No. 3 (1976), 291–315.

Mentzer, R.A., 'Organizational endeavour and charitable impulse in 16th century France: the case of Protestant Nîmes', *French History*, 5 (1991), 1–29.

Newson, J. and E., 'Cultural aspects of childrearing in the English-speaking world', in M. Richards (ed.), *The Integration of a Child into a Social World* (Cambridge, 1974), pp. 53–82.

Nilan, C., 'Hapless innocence and precocious perversity in the courtroom melodrama: representations of the child criminal in a Paris legal journal, 1830–1848', *Journal of Family History*, 22 (1997), 251–85.

Ogilvie, S.C. (ed.), 'Proto-industrialization in Europe', *Continuity and Change*, 8, No. 2 (1993), 151–355.

Pelling, M., 'Child health as a social value in early modern England', *Social History of Medicine*, I (1988), 135–64.

Peyronnet, J-C., 'Les enfants abandonnées et leurs nourrices à Limoges au xviii siècle', *Revue d'histoire moderne et contemporaine*, XXIII (1976), 418–41.

Pfister, U., 'Work roles and family structure in proto-industrial Zurich', *Journal of Interdisciplinary History*, XX (1989), 83–105.

Plumb, J.H., 'The new world of children in eighteenth-century England', *Past and Present*, 67 (1975), 64–93.

Rapson, R.L., 'The American child as seen by British travellers, 1845–1935', *American Quarterly*, XVII (1965), 520–34.

Rooke, P.T. and Schnell, R.L., 'Childhood and charity in nineteenth-century British North America', *Histoire Sociale/Social History*, XV (1982), 157–79.

Rooke, P.T. and Schnell, R.L., ' "Uncramping child life": international children's organisations, 1914–1939', in P. Weindling (ed.), *International Health Organisations and Movements, 1918–1939* (Cambridge, 1995), pp. 176–202.

Rose, C., 'Evangelical philanthropy and Anglican revival: the Charity Schools of Augustan London, 1698–1740', *London Journal*, 16 (1991), 35–65.

Rose, C., ' "Seminarys of Faction and Rebellion": Jacobites, Whigs and the London Charity Schools, 1716–1724', *Historical Journal*, 34 (1991), 831–55.

Rose, J., 'Willingly to school: the working-class response to elementary education in Britain, 1875–1918', *Journal of British Studies*, 32 (1993), 114–38.

Rudolph, R.L., 'The European peasant family and economy: central themes and issues', *Journal of Family History*, 17 (1992), 119–38.

Sá, I. d. G., 'Child abandonment in Portugal: legislation and institutional care', *Continuity and Change*, 9 (1994), 69–90.

Saller, R., '*Patria potestas* and the stereotype of the Roman family', *Continuity and Change*, I (1986–7), 7–22.

Sandin, B., 'Education, popular culture and the surveillance of the population in Stockholm between 1600 and the 1840s', *Continuity and Change*, 3 (1988), 357–90.

Schlossman, S.L., 'Before home start: notes toward a history of parent education in America, 1897–1929', *Harvard Educational Review*, 46 (1976), 436–67.

Schlumbohm, J., 'Constructing individuality: childhood memories in late eighteenth-century "empirical psychology" and autobiography', *German History*, 16 (1998), 29–42.

Sieder, R., ' "Vata, derf i aufstehn?" Childhood experiences in Viennese working-class families around 1900', *Continuity and Change*, I (1986), 53–88.

Solingo, H. van, Walhout, E. and Poppel, F. van, 'Determinants of institutionalization of orphans in a nineteenth-century Dutch town', *Continuity and Change*, 15 (2000), 139–66.

Spree, R., 'Shaping the child's personality: medical advice on child-rearing from the late eighteenth to the early twentieth century in Germany', *Social History of Medicine*, 5 (1992), 317–35.

Stargardt, N., 'Children's Art of the Holocaust', *Past and Present*, 161 (1998), 191–235.

Stearns, P.N., 'Girls, boys, and emotions: redefinitions and historical change', *Journal of American History*, 80 (1993), 36–74.

Stearns, P.N. and Haggerty, T., 'The role of fear: transitions in American emotional standards for children, 1850–1950', *American Historical Review*, 96 (1991), 63–94.

Strickland, C., 'A transcendentalist father: the child-rearing practices of Bronson Alcott', *History of Childhood Quarterly*, I (1973), 4–51.

Swanson, J., 'Childhood and childrearing in *ad status* sermons by later 13th century friars', *Journal of Medieval History*, 16 (1990), 309–31.

Thomas, K., 'Children in Early Modern England', in G. Avery and J. Briggs (eds), *Children and Their Books* (Oxford, 1989), pp. 45–77.

Thompson, E.P., 'Happy Families', *Radical History Review*, No. 20 (1979), 42–50.

Tilly, L.A. et al., 'Child abandonment in European history: a symposium', *Journal of Family History*, 17 (1992), 1–23.

Trexler, R.C., 'The foundlings of Florence, 1395–1455', *History of Childhood Quarterly*, I (1973–4), 259–84.

Tudor, P., 'Religious instruction for children and adolescents in the early English Reformation', *Journal of Ecclesiastical History*, 35 (1984), 391–413.

Ulbricht, O., 'The debate about Foundling Hospitals in Enlightenment Germany: infanticide, illegitimacy, and infant mortality rates', *Central European History*, XVIII (1985), 211–56.

Vann, R.T., 'The youth of *Centuries of Childhood*', *History and Theory*, XXI (1982), 279–97.

Vassberg, D.E., 'Juveniles in the rural work force of sixteenth-century Castile', *Journal of Peasant Studies*, 11 (1983), 62–75.

Vinovskis, M.A., 'Family and schooling in colonial and nineteenth-century America', *Journal of Family History*, 12 (1987), 19–37.

Walinski-Kiehl, R.S., 'The devil's children: child witch trials in early modern Germany', *Continuity and Change*, 11 (1996), 171–89.

Wall, R., 'The age at leaving home', *Journal of Family History*, 3 (1978), 181–202.

Wall, R., 'Leaving home and the process of household formation in pre-industrial England', *Continuity and Change*, 2 (1987), 77–101.

Weisbrod, B., 'How to become a good foundling in early Victorian London', *Social History*, 10 (1985), 193–209.

Wilson, A., 'The infancy of the history of childhood: an appraisal of Philippe Ariès', *History and Theory*, 18 (1979), 103–26.

Wilson, S., 'The myth of motherhood a myth: the historical view of European child-rearing', *Social History*, 9 (1984), 181–98.

Wilson, S., 'Infanticide, child abandonment, and female honour in nineteenth-century Corsica', *Comparative Studies in Society and History*, 30 (1988), 762–83.

Wright, P., 'The social construction of babyhood: the definition of infant care as a medical problem', in A. Bryman, B. Bytheway, P. Allat and T. Keil (eds), *Rethinking the Life Cycle* (London, 1987), pp. 103–21.

Index